AWAKENED YOUTH

NAVIGATING LIFE'S LABYRINTH

MAHAMMED ZAHID

In the name of GOD, the Most Gracious, the Most Merciful.

To the Almighty — who is the giver of strength, the light in darkness, and the One who guides hearts when all paths seem lost.

"And He found you lost and guided you."
(Qur'an, Surah Ad-Duha, 93:7)

This book is dedicated to Him, for without His will, no word could have been written, and no thought could have reached its conclusion.

And to all seekers of truth — may you find in these pages not just a story, but a reflection of the hidden labyrinths within us all.

Contents

Preface

Every mind holds a labyrinth. Some are carved by memory, others by fear, and a few by secrets too heavy to speak aloud. This book is an exploration of one such labyrinth — where the boundaries of reality, perception, and obsession blur into one another, and where a single choice can ripple into consequences beyond imagination.

"Bogston is a place that swallows those who reach too close, and the forest beyond is not what it seems."

These words might feel like the opening of a legend or a whispered warning, but within these pages, they are alive. You will follow Damian — a boy drawn into a world where maps are not just tools but keys, and where courage is measured not by battle but by the quiet persistence to survive, remember, and act. As he navigates the metal labyrinth, the sentinels of the forest, and the dark experiments hidden beneath the surface, you will question what is real, what is manipulated, and what lies in the spaces between.

This book is not just a story of fear and survival; it is a journey into the human mind under pressure, the will to keep promises, and the fragile threads that connect people, even when everything else seems lost.

The ending will challenge you. It will twist the path you thought you were following and force you to see the labyrinth differently — perhaps even reflecting some hidden corners of your own mind.

Read carefully. Trust your instincts. And remember: not all who wander are lost, but some who follow the ledger may find themselves changed forever.

— Mahammed Zahid

Acknowledgements

This book was born from fragments — fragments of thought, silence, memory, and questions that never left me. Writing it was both a challenge and a reckoning, and I could not have carried it to the end without those who stood with me in ways both seen and unseen.

I owe deep gratitude to my papa and mama, family, for their patience and quiet strength, for letting me disappear into hours of writing and still reminding me of the world outside the page.

To my friends and readers who believed in this story even when it was only a shadow in my mind — your encouragement gave me courage to chase it to its darkest corners.

To the books and voices that shaped me, especially the ones that dared to explore the fragile and unspoken spaces of the human psyche — you lit the path when it seemed too dark.

And finally, to you, the reader: this story belongs to you now. May it haunt you, may it unsettle you, and may it stay with you long after the last page is turned.

Prologue

The night was too still.

Damian had learned, even as a boy, that silence was never empty — it was a warning. Somewhere beyond the trees, the air throbbed with a faint hum, almost mechanical, almost alive. It was the kind of sound one might dismiss as imagination, until it pressed so sharply against the bones of the ear that the body knew: something unseen was listening.

He stood at the forest's edge, eyes fixed on the shifting dark. Branches leaned like watchers, the earth smelled faintly of iron, and every instinct urged him back. Yet he stepped forward, because some part of him — reckless, relentless — believed his father had crossed here once. If truth had a hiding place, it was buried beneath this silence.

The first path was not a path at all but a pattern, carved in the dirt like a spiral that led inward rather than onward. His fingers trembled as he traced it. The soil was damp, almost warm, as though the ground itself remembered something it wished to forget.

And then the sound came — sudden, brutal, alive.

A surge of high voltage, not seen but heard, split the air like lightning without light. It struck his body through the ears, the nose, the marrow. Damian staggered, hands to his head, as the forest tilted and bled into a single, merciless frequency. Warm blood trickled down his lip, down his neck. His last sight before the world folded into black was of the spiral burning faintly on the earth, as if it had been waiting for him all along.

The silence returned. But this time, it did not feel like absence. It felt like a door closing.

ONE

OBSIDIAN TERMINAL 1946

The great iron ribs of Obsidian Terminal arched above Damian like the belly of some colossal beast. The station was alive—steam hissing from the engines, the metallic clang of boots on rails, the low hum of passengers whispering their goodbyes or rushing with anxious urgency. For Damian, the place smelled of rust, rain-soaked stone, and the faintest trace of coal smoke. A scent of departure.

He adjusted the strap of his worn leather satchel, scanning the crowd. His pulse was steady, though there was a fire beneath it. Today was not an ordinary journey—it was the first step toward Shie, the city he had dreamed about since boyhood.

"Here," came a familiar voice.

Choe appeared from the side, slightly out of breath, thrusting a slip of paper into Damian's hand. The tickets, folded neatly but slightly crumpled, bore the seal of the station authority.

Damian raised an eyebrow, his lips curving with a hint of sarcasm.

"At last, you got one," he said, flicking the corner of the ticket as though doubting it was real.

Choe's grin widened, sheepish but proud. "Don't thank me. It was Miska—her aunt's a station guard. You know how strict they are with last-minute permits. Without her, we'd still be begging at the counter."

Damian's expression softened at the name. His eyes darted across the throng. "And where is Miska?"

As if summoned, Miska emerged from the crowd, her steps light but certain. She carried a small bouquet of flowers, wrapped hastily in paper that had already begun to crinkle from the damp air. The colors—deep crimson and pale white—looked almost defiant against the gray station.

Damian smirked. "At least Miska thought of me. You see, Choe? She brings flowers while you only bring excuses."

Miska's laughter chimed, warm and teasing. "Don't flatter yourself. These aren't for you." She tilted her head, eyes bright but touched with something softer. "They're for your mother. You're heading into your dream city, Damian, but in all that excitement, did you even think about her? I thought—well—someone had to.

Damian faltered, his smirk dimming for a fleeting second. The truth in her words cut through his bravado, but before the silence could thicken, Choe broke in.

"Speaking of forgetting things," Choe said hastily, his voice a notch louder, "did you hear about Isak? Caught again in that police raid near the lake. Same old spot—where the gamblers and drug-dealers gather. That fool never learns. Always fishing where he shouldn't. Poor lad thinks he's clever, but he's a walking invitation for handcuffs."

Damian's gaze snapped to him, sharp as a blade. He didn't like the diversion. He didn't like being read so easily.

"Choe," he said quietly, dangerously, "you think changing the subject hides the truth?" His words were low, but they carried weight. "If the police had any sense, they'd make Isak their informer. The idiot is always lurking around those dens, annoying everyone with his fishing rod while the bastards play their dirty games. Might as well turn his bad luck into their advantage."

The words hung in the air, heavy with tension.

But Miska was still elsewhere—in thought, in feeling. She watched Damian, her face shifting in an unspoken language: a flicker of anger, a trace of tenderness, a look that lingered too long to be called casual. She said nothing more, but her silence spoke volumes.

And above them, the station clock struck the hour.

The station clock's iron chime rolled through the terminal, deep and resonant, as though the very walls of the place were warning that time would not wait.

Passengers stirred like restless birds, adjusting luggage, tightening shawls, hurrying children along the edge of the platform. The air grew thicker with smoke and steam.

Damian's jaw tightened. His hand brushed the edge of the ticket again, grounding himself.

Miska's voice cut through the din, soft but edged with something heavier.

"You can glare at Choe all you want, Damian. But deep down you know he isn't wrong. You forget things — important things."

Damian exhaled slowly, his eyes fixed on the gray horizon beyond the tracks. "I forget what I choose to forget."

Before either could reply, a shout erupted from the far end of the platform.

"Stop him! Stop the boy!"

The crowd shifted. A boy of no more than ten tore through the throng, weaving between boots and skirts with the agility of a fox. In his small hands, a satchel dangled — clearly too fine to belong to him. Behind him, a guard thundered in pursuit, his truncheon raised.

The boy darted closer, brushing past Damian so sharply that his sleeve tugged Damian's coat. For a split second their eyes met. Wide. Desperate. Defiant.

Damian froze. He could have reached, could have caught him, but he didn't.

The boy vanished into the crowd, swallowed whole by the smoke and shadows. The guard cursed, shoved past a merchant, and disappeared after him.

Choe chuckled under his breath. "Obsidian never changes. Always rats scurrying through its belly. Bet the boy's caught within five minutes."

Damian's lips pressed thin. The boy's eyes lingered in his mind like an echo.

Miska shifted the flowers in her hands, her gaze steady on him. "Don't look like that. He isn't your burden. Not every runaway can be saved."

Damian said nothing. He only adjusted the satchel at his side.

Another whistle pierced the air, long and shrill. The train to Bogston screeched into the platform, its black engine exhaling steam in thick, ghostly clouds. Metal shrieked against metal as it slowed, sending a tremor through the ground.

The three of them turned toward it.

Choe grinned, though there was nervousness behind his smile. "Well, here it is. The beast that swallows boys and spits out men."

Miska didn't smile. Her fingers trembled around the stems of the bouquet.

A station officer strode down the line of carriages, shouting, "Passengers to Bogston! Boarding at coaches five through twelve! Move quickly!"

The flow of bodies surged forward. The air grew frantic.

Damian turned to them both. "This is it." His voice was calm, but there was steel beneath it.

Choe clapped him on the shoulder. "Don't look so grim, brother. You're the lucky one. You get to leave this mess behind." He forced a laugh. "Write me when you've got rich in Bogston. Or don't — I'll just imagine you living in some palace."

Damian allowed the corner of his mouth to twitch upward, but the smile didn't hold.

Then his eyes met Miska's.

She stepped closer, lowering her voice so only he could hear. "Don't let that city eat you alive, Damian. You think you're untouchable, but even fire dies if it burns too fast."

For a moment, he looked as though he might answer — might let his guard slip. Instead, he reached forward and gently pressed the flowers present in her hands.

"Give them to my mother," he said. His voice was steady, but there was a crack somewhere deep inside. "She'll believe they're from me. She'll like them more that way."

Miska's lips parted. Her breath caught as if the weight of unsaid words pressed against her ribs. She wanted to argue, to beg, to say more — but the moment was stolen by movement behind them.

The guard from earlier returned, dragging the thief-boy by the arm. The boy struggled, kicking, cursing. His eyes darted toward Damian once more — pleading, accusing, burning.

Damian's jaw clenched. His hand twitched at his side, but he did not move.

"Come on," Choe urged, sensing the tension. "Forget him. You've got your own path now."

The train doors clanged open. Passengers climbed aboard, their boots thudding against metal steps. The great machine groaned impatiently.

Miska's voice trembled. "Damian…"

He looked at her one last time. Her eyes were storm and sunlight both. He memorized them in a heartbeat, though he'd never admit it.

Then he turned away.

His boots struck the platform with finality as he moved toward the carriage. Each step echoed louder than the last. The station blurred — the crowd, the smoke, the guards, Miska, Choe, the boy — all falling away into the roar of the train.

Damian's boot touched the iron step of the carriage. The air around him thickened with smoke and steam, swallowing the world in gray.

And then it struck.

A piercing sound — sharp, metallic, relentless — rang in his ears. At first, he thought it was the train's whistle, but no… this was inside him. A shrill, pulsing beep, echoing through his skull.

His vision blurred. The platform tilted.

Faces swam before him — strangers, shadows, and then—his mother. Her hands reaching for him, soft and calloused at once, pressing flowers into his small fists when he was no older than the thief-boy. He smelled her cooking, heard her laughter, then saw her tears. Childhood memories came unbidden, rushing in waves, colliding violently with the noise in his head.

Damian staggered back from the step. His ticket slipped from his hand, fluttering like a wounded bird to the ground.

"Damian?" Miska's voice was sharp now, frightened.

The beeping grew louder. His chest tightened. The iron ribs of Obsidian Terminal closed in around him like jaws.

And then—darkness.

He collapsed, his body striking the platform with a hollow thud.

The world narrowed to muffled voices.

"Choe, help me—lift him!" Miska's cry cracked, her arms already cradling Damian's head.

"Saints above, what happened to him?" Choe's words trembled, though he tried to mask it with urgency. He crouched beside them, eyes darting to the crowd gathering. "Back off! Give him air!"

The last thing Damian knew was Miska's hand on his face, warm against the cold stone beneath him.

Then, silence.

An hour later.

When his eyes opened, the station was quieter, emptied of its rush. His head pounded, heavy as iron. He blinked against the lingering haze until shapes returned — Miska, kneeling close, worry etched deep in her face; Choe, sitting cross-legged nearby, muttering curses under his breath.

"You're awake," Miska whispered, relief flooding her words. "Thank God."

Damian tried to sit up, but his body felt leaden. "What... what happened?" His voice rasped.

"You fainted," Choe answered bluntly. "Collapsed like a sack of bricks. Out cold for a full hour. Scared half the station."

Damian's eyes widened. "The train—"

"Gone," Choe said, grim but almost relieved. "The train to Shie City left half an hour ago. Bogston University's not waiting for you tonight."

The words hit harder than the fall. Damian's hand went instinctively to his satchel, clutching it as if it might anchor him to the ground.

Miska still held the bouquet, though the petals had begun to wilt in the damp air. She met his gaze, steady but unreadable. "Maybe," she said softly, "the city wasn't meant to have you. Not yet."

Damian's chest rose and fell, his mind a storm. The echo of that inner beep, the vision of his mother, the thief-boy's eyes — all tangled threads pulling at him from within.

For the first time that day, he had no words.

Only silence.

Damian rubbed his jaw, pretending to think. "So let me understand this. I nearly die, and my closest friends do absolutely nothing but... babysit me on a stone floor."

Choe threw up his hands. "Babysit? I defended you! Half the station thought you were drunk. I had to shout at them—'No, no, he's a scholar! A noble faint, not a cheap one!' You owe me your reputation, Damian."

"That's rich," Damian said, voice still hoarse but dripping with mockery. "A reputation guarded by you—the man who once sold his shoes for a slice of roasted lamb."

Miska burst out laughing, covering her mouth with her hand.

Choe's ears reddened. "That was strategic sacrifice! My feet grew back, didn't they?"

"They grew blisters," Damian shot back, grinning.

Miska shook her head, her laughter softening into warmth. "You two are hopeless." She tucked a stray strand of hair behind her ear and fixed Damian with a look. "Besides, I didn't leave because... well, you scared me. I wasn't sure you'd even open your eyes again."

Damian's smirk faltered for a heartbeat, but he quickly masked it with mock drama. He pressed a hand to his chest. "Ah, so you do care. I knew it. Miska, don't worry—when I'm a great man in Bogston, I'll dedicate my first book to you: 'To the girl who sat and watched me snore on a public floor.'"

Her cheeks flushed, but her retort was sharp. "Don't bother. Choe deserves that honor more—he's the one who shouted at strangers like a lunatic for you."

"Fine, then," Damian said with exaggerated dignity. "Choe gets the book, you get the statue. A grand one, carved in marble, showing you clutching your bouquet like a heroic nurse."

Miska groaned, but she was smiling despite herself.

Choe, puffing out his chest, leaned back smugly. "And mine will say: 'Choe, defender of fallen fools, guardian of platforms, hero of fainting scholars.'"

All three laughed now, the sound echoing lightly in the near-empty terminal. For a moment, the world outside—the missed train, the mysterious collapse, the weight of dreams and memories—felt distant, softened by the comfort of friendship.

Their laughter still lingered in the air when a voice, brisk and edged with authority, cut through it.

"Miska!"

The three turned. A tall woman in a dark shawl pushed through the thinning crowd, her eyes sharp as flint. Miska straightened immediately.

"Aunt Serah," she breathed, half in surprise, half in guilt.

Serah's gaze swept over Damian, pale but sitting upright, and Choe, who looked as though he'd been caught sneaking sweets. "What in God's name happened here? The whole station has been buzzing—people saying some boy collapsed like he'd been shot." Her eyes narrowed at Damian. "So it was you."

Damian, still leaning against the wall, offered a weak half-smile. "Don't worry, madam. I fainted with dignity."

Choe snorted, earning himself a sharp elbow from Miska.

Serah ignored the joke, folding her arms. "If you still intend to reach Shie City tonight, sitting here won't help you. The train you missed will cross the river and stop at Wetherdam Station an hour from now."

Damian's eyes lifted, a spark of hope flickering. "And if I can get there?"

"You can board the same train," Serah said curtly. "But listen well—it takes a full hour to reach Wetherdam by car or truck. If you waste even a breath, you'll arrive too late. And that's assuming you find transport quickly."

Miska glanced at Damian, then at Choe. "So if we leave now—"

"—you might catch it," Serah finished. "If luck runs with you."

Choe rubbed the back of his neck, his grin returning despite the tension. "Well, Damian, looks like you're not rid of us yet. Shall we go gamble with fate?"

Miska clutched her bouquet tighter, eyes searching Damian's face. "It's risky... but it's your only chance."

The station clock tolled again, each clang a reminder that time was already slipping away.

Damian pushed himself to his feet, his body still heavy but his voice steady. "Then we run."

The toll of the station clock was still fading when Damian straightened fully, his body stiff from the collapse yet driven by a surge of will. He met Serah's gaze one last time, gave a small nod, and then motioned to Choe and Miska.

"Come."

They moved fast, weaving through the dim alleys behind the terminal, boots crunching over cobblestones slick with night mist. The city stretched before them in shadow and gaslight, its bones humming with the quiet of laborers gone home and taverns just beginning to stir.

Damian led them unerringly, the path familiar, etched into his memory since boyhood. Miska caught up to him, clutching the bouquet against her chest, whispering between breaths. "Where are we going? No carter will take us this late—"

Damian cut her short with a single glance, his eyes burning with a determination she had rarely seen in him. "We don't need one."

At last, they reached a squat stone house tucked in a row of forgotten dwellings. Its shutters sagged, its garden overrun. Damian's home. Or what remained of it. He pushed the gate open—the rusted iron shrieked—and strode to the side shed.

The smell hit first: dust, oil gone rancid, iron left too long without care. He pulled open the warped wooden doors, and there it was—an old, forgotten relic beneath a blanket of canvas and time. His father's car.

Miska and Choe exchanged a glance as Damian's hands gripped the cloth and ripped it free. Dust exploded into the night air, swirling like phantoms in the lamplight. Beneath, the machine crouched like a beast long asleep—its once-proud paint dulled to rust, its wheels crusted in grime, its brass lamps cracked but unbroken.

"Saints preserve us," Choe muttered, stepping back. "That thing belongs in a graveyard."

Damian ignored him. He slid into the driver's seat, fingers brushing over the cracked leather of the wheel as though reacquainting himself with an old ghost. For a heartbeat, silence hung heavy—then he twisted the ignition.

The car coughed. Wheezed. Shuddered violently as if in protest.

Choe crossed his arms, shaking his head. "See? Even the machine knows it's suicide."

But Damian's jaw tightened. He slammed his palm against the dashboard, muttered something under his breath, and twisted again. This time the engine roared to life, spitting black smoke from its exhaust like a wounded dragon, the whole frame rattling on its axles.

The sound filled the night, half promise, half warning.

Damian looked up at them, shadows cutting across his face. "Get in."

Choe groaned dramatically but obeyed, tumbling into the back seat. Miska hesitated, clutching her flowers, before she slid in beside

Damian, her hands trembling.

The car jerked forward as Damian slammed the clutch, lurching into the cobbled street with a snarl of tires. Windows along the row lit up, voices called out in irritation, but the old machine tore through the night all the same.

At first there was exhilaration—wind whipping their faces, the streets rushing past in a blur of lamplight and shadow. Choe leaned out, whooping like a madman. "We'll make it! By God, we'll beat that train!"

But then—Damian turned left.

Choe frowned, then leaned forward over the seat. "Wait—no, no, the bridge is right! Why are you turning here?"

Damian didn't answer. His hands gripped the wheel, knuckles white.

The car rattled down narrower streets, away from the city's lifeblood and toward its quieter edges. Miska looked at him sharply, her voice unsteady. "Damian—you're going the wrong way. The river's behind us."

Still, no answer. Only the growl of the engine and the hollow echo of the cobbles under the wheels.

Choe thumped the back of Damian's seat. "Hey! Are you deaf? You'll miss the train for good! What are you doing?"

Damian's jaw clenched, eyes fixed ahead. His silence was louder than any words.

The streets grew emptier, houses sparser. The lamps thinned, giving way to moonlight. Grass sprouted between the stones as the old road sloped gently upward. Miska's breath hitched, realization dawning before Choe's. Her fingers closed tightly around the stems of the wilting bouquet.

"No..." she whispered.

The car climbed a final rise and slowed, its rattling engine protesting the incline. At the top, under the silver gaze of the moon, rose the churchyard. The small stone chapel stood still, its spire black against the sky. Beyond its wrought-iron gates lay rows of graves, marked by crooked stones and weathered crosses.

The car rolled to a halt.

For the first time since leaving the terminal, Damian let out a long, shuddering breath. He cut the engine. Silence descended, broken only by the ticking of the machine's cooling pipes.

Choe sat forward, confused, half-angry. "Damian... what the hell?"

But Miska already knew. She whispered it, her voice trembling as she looked at him. "Your mother."

Damian finally turned his head. His eyes, though steady, carried the weight of years. "If I was going to run to the ends of the world, I couldn't do it without seeing her first."

The bouquet in Miska's hands shook, petals falling softly to the floor of the car.

The churchyard gates creaked as Damian pushed them open. His steps were slow, deliberate, carrying him toward the stone that bore his mother's name. The night air smelled of damp grass and old earth. The moonlight gleamed pale across the carved letters.

He stood there for a long moment, silent. His hand brushed the top of the grave marker, fingers tracing the weathered grooves as though trying to memorize them anew.

Behind him, Miska and Choe stood in silence, their earlier urgency melting into something softer, more reverent.

At last, Damian spoke—his voice quiet, almost to himself. "She should've been the one I brought flowers to."

Miska stepped forward, gently pressing the bouquet into his hands. "Then do it now."

Damian knelt, laying the flowers at the foot of the grave. His breath trembled, but his face remained set, unbroken. The silence stretched, heavy and holy, until even Choe found no words to break it.

And above them, the moon watched, as though keeping its own vigil.

Damian slid back into the driver's seat, the bouquet now resting on the grave behind him. He turned the key, and the car grumbled awake once more. This time he didn't wait—he pressed hard on the clutch, and the machine rolled forward, rattling back down the slope toward the city.

The streets were thicker now with movement. Even at this late hour, wagons creaked under loads of grain, horses stamped their hooves, and the occasional motor-car coughed black smoke into the air. The lamps burned dim in their glass cages, and the mist along the cobbles blurred everything into restless shapes.

Damian kept his jaw tight, eyes fixed ahead. His hands, though steady, gripped the wheel hard. The car jolted over stones, rattling so fiercely that Miska had to clutch the side handle to steady herself.

They reached a busier stretch where the main road bent toward the river. A line of carts clogged the center, moving too slow for their need. Damian pressed the horn—an ugly, brassy bark—but no one moved quickly enough. He leaned his whole weight into the wheel and swerved left, the car brushing so close to the wagons that one driver shouted a curse after them.

"Easy, Damian!" Miska gasped, holding tighter.

But he didn't slow. The machine roared on, wobbling slightly as its wheels gripped uneven stones. Smoke trailed behind them, leaving a bitter taste in the air.

The closer they drew to the heart of the city, the more crowded the roads became. Groups of workers spilled out of taverns, laughing, stumbling across the street without care. Damian had to brake sharply once, the whole car lurching as a drunkard staggered in front of them. The man shouted, waving his fist, but Damian only pressed forward again, teeth clenched.

The river came into view at last, black and glinting under moonlight. The bridge stretched across it, crowded with slow-moving carts and pedestrians. Damian growled under his breath, searching for a gap.

"Damian—we'll never squeeze through," Choe muttered from the back, his voice tense.

But Damian saw it—a narrow lane along the side, barely wide enough for the car. Without warning, he steered into it, the tires scraping against the stone curb. The car rattled violently, the engine coughing in protest, but it held. They shot across the bridge, the water rushing dark beneath them.

On the far side, the streets widened again, and the glow of the station's high lamps rose above the rooftops. The distant toll of the clock drifted across the air—deep, final, calling time.

Damian pressed harder on the clutch, the machine groaning but obeying. The road blurred, the night wind biting their faces, and for the first time Miska dared to hope.

The station was close.

They reached the station in less than an hour — an impossible, breathless dash that felt more like luck than skill. The old engine of the car wheezed and spat as Damian killed the ignition. For a second he simply sat there, chest heaving, palms still clamped to the wheel. The city's lamps blinked around them like tired stars. He laughed once, a short, raw sound.

"This is my mother's blessing," he said, more to himself than to the others. The words were small and steady, and for a moment the ache in his ribs eased.

Miska laid a hand on his arm, fingers warm and trembling. "Then let it ride with you," she said softly.

They ran the last stretch — three figures kicking up dust and smoke — and tumbled onto the platform with the rest of the breathless crowd. The train to Shie hissed and snorted at the rails, steam billowing like a gray curtain. Damian didn't wait to think. He clutched his satchel, shoved through the swinging doors, and found a narrow compartment toward the middle of the coach.

Inside, the carriage was a smaller world: varnished wood with scuffed varnish, fabric seats puckered and worn, gas lamps guttering at intervals, the smell of coal and stale wool and boiled dinner. Passengers sat in small clumps — a tired woman with a child, two men arguing softly over a map, a pair of merchants dozing with their hats over their eyes. The train shuddered with a low, continuous rhythm: click—clack, click—clack. It sounded like a heartbeat. Damian let his shoulders drop against the seat and closed his eyes for a breath that felt like a prayer.

Relief came slow and physical. He checked his things as if the act itself could make all right: fingers through pockets, the ticket creased and filthy but still his; a small piece of bread crumpled in the corner of the satchel; a faded photograph tucked into the flap — his mother's face smiling up at him, the edges worn thin. He touched the photo with the pad of a finger and then tucked it back in, cradling the satchel to his chest. The exhaustion slid over him like a heavy blanket. For a long minute he simply let his head fall back and watched the blur of the platform through the window.

An old man shuffled down the aisle, his back stooped and his eyes quick as if they'd been looking too long at the sun. He stopped at the seat opposite Damian and, before any of the small talk around them could bloom, asked in a cracked voice, "Young man, where are you headed?"

"To Shie," Damian answered without thinking — the name so used to his mouth it was almost automatic.

The old man's laugh came out like a cough. It was short, incredulous. "Shie?" he repeated, as if the word didn't belong in the world tonight. "Ha. You're on the wrong train."

Those four words landed like a stone. Damian's chest tightened. Heat rose along his neck — anger, panic, the sharp sting of every lost minute. "Wrong train?" he snapped. "What—"

The train gave a soft lurch, gathering speed. Outside, the platform receded, lantern light streaking into ribbons.

Damian's hand slid down toward the emergency chain out of reflex more than reason. The little metal ring dangled above the door — a blunt promise of stops and storms. If he pulled it, the world would have to halt and he would have to know, one way or another, if this was finally his passage to Bogston or just another failing.

He stood, shoulders squared, fingers just touching the ring.

A voice, young and firm, cut across the narrow space before he could act. "Father — you're on the wrong train." The speaker was a student in a neat coat, thin and bright-eyed, who had been seated a row up. He addressed the old man as though bound by kinship; the old man turned to him, startled.

"Oh Lord," the old man breathed. His face went white in an absurd quickness, as if an invisible wind had swept through him. He began to shiver uncontrollably, shoulders bobbing under his threadbare coat. "Who would go to Shie?" he muttered, each word a small, fearful thing. "A cursed desert... who would go there?" His voice dropped to a trembling whisper. Around them other passengers glanced up, curiosity and irritation flickering across faces.

Damian's hand froze on the chain. The blast of anger that had been building — the fury at every obstacle, every delay — thinned into confusion. He looked from the old man's ashen face to the student, who was now bent low, murmuring comfort, his hand on the old man's knobby fist.

The old man's fear did not deepen into fury or action. Instead, in a strange, almost childlike collapse, he let his head loll to the side and closed his eyes. Within moments he was breathing slow and even, asleep as if the revelation had pulled all his strength away. The student kept his hand there, watching him with something like apology in his eyes.

Around them, life found its rhythm again. Somebody coughed. A baby in the next compartment began to whimper; a woman smoothed her skirt and went back to reading. The carriage rocked steady on the rails, and the countryside beyond the window melted into long streaks of shadow and lamp light.

Damian eased back into his seat, feeling both ridiculous and raw — a man pulled to the edge by his own temper and stopped by someone else's superstition and a loose hand. He exhaled, slow and deliberate, and the edge of anger dulled into a hard, tired resignation.

Outside, the train kept its speed; inside, the soft clack of the track was the only sound that mattered. Damian stared out at the passing dark, thinking of bridges and blessings, of missed departures and second chances, and let the steady motion try to rock some semblance of sleep into him. The weariness won, finally — his head tilted, his eyelids drooped, and sometime between stations he drifted toward it, the day's chaos folding into the dull, inevitable hush of the journey.

Damian's head lolled against the seat for a while, the click-clack of the train half dragging him into sleep. But something about the silence across from him — the old man's stillness, the student's watchful posture — kept him awake enough to stir. He leaned forward, eyes on the boy whose neat coat still held the faint smell of ink and paper.

"What's your name?" Damian asked, his voice low, roughened by fatigue.

The boy straightened, as though it mattered to answer properly. "Reed," he said, then with a small nod added, "Jonas Reed."

Damian let the name turn over in his mind. It fit him somehow, clipped and careful. "And where are you headed, Jonas Reed?"

"To Bogston," the boy replied at once. His eyes brightened as he spoke, a light that only students carried when their future was still a map unrolled. "I've been admitted as a psychology student there. This will be the beginning."

Damian whistled softly. "Psychology. So you'll spend your days untangling the knots inside men's heads." A faint smile touched his mouth. "That's fine work. Bogston will sharpen you for it."

Reed dipped his chin, modest but pleased.

Damian glanced at the old man slumped beside him, his mouth open, breath rattling faintly. "And him? He's with you?"

Reed's expression shifted — a touch of sadness, a flicker of pride. "Yes. He was once a great priest. A father in our church. People used to travel miles just to hear his sermons." He paused, voice quieter. "But when his wife passed, something in him broke. His mind wandered. He... behaves like this now."

Damian tilted his head, studying the sleeping figure. The priest's hands, though knotted and trembling, still bore the old dignity of years in service. His collar was worn thin, but clean. "And you're saying," Damian asked slowly, "that this old priest is bound for Bogston too?"

Reed nodded. "He is not in the wrong train. He is with me. The church in Bogston needs a new priest. They'll take him in, care for him, maybe let him serve in his own way. He deserves at least that."

Damian let out a quiet breath, his fingers drumming the edge of his satchel. "But he's mad now, isn't he?"

Reed didn't flinch. Instead he looked Damian squarely in the eye, his voice steady as stone. "Madmen only speak truth."

The words hung in the rattling air of the carriage, sharper than the hiss of steam outside. Damian leaned back, turning them over in his mind as the train sped on into the dark.

The train ate the night in long, steady strokes, and by dawn the land outside had changed its face. Hills unrolled like ancient backs under the pale sky, mist clung to their shoulders, and rivers flared silver where the sun touched them. The air through the cracked window grew cooler, carrying the scent of pine and damp earth.

Damian sat awake, his head tipped against the glass, watching it all pass as if it belonged to someone else's dream. He should have felt wonder — the landscapes were vast and untamed — yet the farther the train carried him, the sharper the hollow in his chest grew. Every turn of the wheel pulled him away from Choe's laughter, from Miska's stubborn warmth, from the familiar clamor of home.

Jonas Reed, who had been scribbling notes in a small leather book, noticed the quiet in him. "You look as though the hills weigh heavier on you than the city did," he said, closing the book gently.

Damian huffed out a breath that might have been a laugh. "I should feel alive, shouldn't I? This is my first real journey. But it feels—empty. Like I've left pieces of myself back at the station."

Reed studied him with the calm curiosity of someone already half a psychologist. "You left friends. That kind of emptiness doesn't fill quickly."

Damian turned, half-smiling despite himself. "You sound like you're practicing already. Taking me for one of your first patients?"

Reed chuckled softly. "Perhaps. Though I've found that strangers speak their truest when they don't realize they're being studied." His gaze flicked out the window. "But you're no stranger now."

The train roared into a narrow pass between cliffs, shadows swallowing the carriage before light spilled back in. Damian let the moment stretch, his thoughts pacing between memory and the horizon.

"Do you never feel it?" he asked at last. "That ache. Like you're walking away from the only people who've held you together."

Reed's expression tightened. He glanced at the old priest, still dozing in fragile peace. "Every day," he admitted. "I'm leaving behind a whole parish, people who trusted him, who trusted me to care for him. But Bogston is where the work waits. And sometimes duty is the only thing that keeps the ache from swallowing you."

Damian let that settle. The rhythm of the train filled the silence — click-clack, click-clack — like the sound of a heartbeat steadying them both. He thought of Miska's flowers, of Choe's nervous grin, of his mother's blessing whispered in the rush of the night.

He drew in a slow breath. "Maybe you're right. Maybe duty is all we have, until the emptiness learns to quiet itself."

Reed nodded, and for a while neither spoke. The hills rolled by, rivers glimmered like veins of light, and the day stretched long. Somewhere inside that rhythm, a fragile companionship took root — not loud like Choe's chatter, not warm like Miska's scolding, but steady. The kind a traveler could lean on for the span of a journey. Damian got a good sleep after busy day .

Morning broke soft and strange. The sun was a pale disc behind a veil of fog, and when the passengers stirred awake, they found the train gliding through a wilderness unlike any they had seen before.

Tall trees rose like pillars to the sky, their canopies so thick that only fractured light spilled through, painting the air in greenish haze. Vines hung low, heavy as serpents, and the undergrowth glowed with strange, damp life — mushrooms the size of fists, flowers opening and closing as though they breathed with the passing wind. The air carried a sweetness edged with rot, a forest that seemed older than men, older than memory itself.

Damian leaned forward, eyes tracing the endless woods. "This is Viel," he said, almost in reverence. "A forest no man dares cross. Its heart belongs to Medmica, the forest goddess. They say she walks these trees still — and none who wander in return."

Reed turned his head, studying him with skeptical curiosity. "Then how are we here? If it's so sacred, how did they cut through for the rails?"

Before Damian could speak, the old priest stirred. His eyes fluttered open, cloudy but alive, and his lips curled into a fragile smile as though the question had roused something long buried.

"It was no man's work," he rasped. His voice carried a weight, like the echo of a sermon once spoken from high pulpits. "Medmica would not allow it. For days the men tried — axes broke, rails bent, workers vanished into the thickets. The forest swallowed them whole."

The priest's hands trembled in his lap, but his voice grew steadier. "Then came a holy one... a servant of the gods. He spoke with Medmica, and she demanded blood — eleven young men, their lives bound as an offering. They gave themselves, and the goddess relented. Within eleven days the tracks rose, straight and unbroken, as if laid by unseen hands. A miracle bought with sacrifice."

The train rattled on, its wheels clattering like faint applause beneath his words. A hush seemed to fall over the carriage; even the child in the corner stopped fussing, as though the forest itself pressed its weight into the story.

Damian's eyes gleamed with the gravity of it. "They say their souls still guard the line. That's why no flood, no storm, no beast has ever touched these rails."

Reed only shifted in his seat, unimpressed. His brow furrowed with quiet disapproval. "Old tales to keep fear alive," he murmured. "Sacrifice, miracles, goddesses — stories men use to explain what they don't understand."

The priest fixed him with a look, and though his gaze was faded, there was fire in it still. "Madmen speak truth," he whispered again, as if those words alone carried proof enough.

Reed's jaw tightened. He looked away, opening his little book as though ink could shield him from myths.

Damian sat between them, caught in the space where belief and disbelief clashed, the train carrying them deeper into the shadowed cathedral of trees.

The train crawled out of Viel like a creature slipping from shadow into light. For hours, it had whispered through the forest's throat, hemmed in by towering green walls, every passenger half-afraid to breathe too loud. But as afternoon waned, the trees broke apart, giving way to slopes of stone and sparse fields, the world suddenly wider.

At last, the whistle shrieked — long, final — and the train slowed, its wheels grinding against the rails until it sighed into stillness. The station boards read Shie, their paint weathered, the letters faint but steady.

Damian pressed a hand to the glass. For the first time since leaving home, relief flickered warm in his chest. "We made it," he said, voice hushed as though the forest might still be listening.

The passengers began to stir — bags lifted, coats tugged on, children herded close. Reed closed his book, slipped it into his satchel, and helped the priest to his feet. The old man leaned on his arm, frail but stubborn, eyes darting about as though still searching for ghosts between the timbers.

They stepped down onto the platform together, swallowed at once by the chaos: porters calling, whistles echoing, the smell of coal and sweat thick in the air. Shie was not grand like Bogston was said to be, but it was alive — a crossroads of laborers, scholars, and wanderers, with the hills crouching watchful behind.

And there, waiting at the far end of the platform, stood a figure that caught Damian's eye before any other. A man of lean height, draped in a dark coat that brushed his boots, silver hair tied neatly back. His posture was straight, his eyes bright — the sort that could measure a soul in a glance.

"Professor Kael," Reed murmured with a small smile of recognition. He nudged Damian gently. "That's the one who promised to meet us."

The professor's gaze swept the crowd, then fixed upon them as if he had known where they would step from the first moment. He approached without hesitation, his boots striking the boards in steady rhythm. When he reached them, his expression softened into something almost warm.

"Jonas Reed," Kael greeted, his voice deep, carrying authority and ease together. "And... your companion." His eyes shifted to Damian, studying him as though fitting him into some unspoken equation. Then to the priest, who swayed faintly under Reed's support. For a brief second Kael's face tightened — recognition, perhaps sorrow — before it smoothed again.

"Welcome to Shie," he said. "The edge of the known and the beginning of all questions worth asking."

Damian felt the words settle into him like a stone dropped into water, sending ripples he could not yet name.

TWO

IN THE SHADOWS

Damian quickened his steps to keep pace with Kael. The professor's stride was long and purposeful, his coat sweeping behind him like a banner. Ahead, the streets of Shie thinned toward the road that led into Bogston — the town of spires, bells, and a thousand restless minds.

But a voice called him back.

"Damian—wait!"

Reed's tone was strained. Damian turned to see him struggling with Father Athelston, who had stopped dead at the edge of the square. The priest's cane pressed stubbornly into the cobblestones, his face pale, lips moving as though in prayer or warning.

"He won't step further," Reed said, his arm firm around the old man's elbow. "It's as if... he's afraid of crossing."

Athelston's eyes darted wildly, not at the road ahead but at the air itself — as if he saw shapes in the dust that no one else could. His mouth formed fragments of sentences. "The walls... too loud... bells that never stop... not meant for—no, not meant..."

Damian exchanged a look with Reed, unease rippling through him. Kael had paused too, watching, his expression unreadable but his jaw set tight.

"Father," Damian said gently, stepping closer. "It's only Bogston. The university awaits us. You'll be safe."

But the priest jerked his head sharply. His voice rose suddenly, carrying over the hum of the square.

"No! Not safe. They listen there — the stones, the bells, the glass! Even your thoughts are measured. Do not—do not make me—"

A group of passersby slowed to stare. Reed flushed with embarrassment, but held the man firmer. Kael, however, moved in a single decisive step, his hand gripping the priest's shoulder.

"Enough." His voice was calm but immovable, like iron wrapped in velvet. "You will come. Whatever shadows you carry, you will not drop them here."

Athelston stiffened under the professor's touch. For a heartbeat, Damian thought he might strike out, or collapse. Instead, the old man's resistance faltered. His cane trembled, then lifted, and he allowed Reed to guide him forward — though his muttering did not cease.

And so the four of them walked. The road bent, and with it the world changed.

Bogston rose in the distance like a fortress of knowledge. Spires caught the sunlight, bells tolled in slow, deliberate rhythm, and smoke from countless chimneys curled into the sky. Bridges arched over canals that glimmered bronze in the afternoon light. And beyond all, looming proud, stood the University — a labyrinth of towers and halls, windows glittering, banners snapping in the wind.

Damian felt his breath catch. Here was no simple town. Here was a kingdom of thought, a city that studied the very fabric of the human soul.

They were massive things of wrought iron, blackened by age, their arch crowned with a crest Damian did not yet recognize — a serpent coiled through a circle of stars. On either side, stone sentinels stood, carved in the likeness of faceless men holding scrolls close to their chests.

And here, for the first time since leaving Shie, the world grew still.

The bells in the distance hushed. The chatter of carts and vendors dimmed as though the city itself had swallowed its voice.

Even the wind, which had carried coal-smoke and laughter only streets before, seemed to die at the threshold. Damian drew breath to speak, but found his voice reluctant, as though some unseen hand pressed it back into his chest.

Reed shifted uneasily, glancing to Kael for reassurance. Athelston clutched his cane tighter, muttering under his breath again. Only Kael seemed untouched. He pressed the gates, and with a deep groan, they opened.

Inside lay the university grounds.

The courtyard stretched vast and quiet, cobbled paths winding between looming stone blocks, each draped in ivy. Windows glimmered with pale reflections of the late sun, but behind them, no faces stirred. Damian had expected bustle — students hurrying, scholars deep in debate — but there was none. Only the echo of their own footsteps followed them deeper in.

Kael led them straight toward the North Block, a long rectangular building crowned with a clock that ticked in slow, deliberate measure. Its doors opened without protest, and the air inside was cooler, heavy with chalk dust and old parchment.

As they stepped into the hall, Damian's eye caught movement to the side.

A girl sat on the floor, hunched over a great sheet of paper. She couldn't have been more than fifteen, her ink-stained fingers racing across the parchment. What she was drawing made Damian pause.

It was not a picture, not of faces or fields. It was a labyrinth — a spiraling maze of walls upon walls, doors folding into doors, paths that bent back upon themselves until the eye grew dizzy. The lines were flawless, sharp as if carved with intention, not whim.

Damian found himself leaning closer. He almost asked her what it meant — but then she looked up.

Her eyes darted past Damian, past Reed, even past the priest. They locked on Kael.

In an instant, the ink pen froze in her hand. The scratching ceased. She swallowed hard, her body stiff as if caught in wrongdoing. The unfinished maze lay between them, its spirals halting abruptly where her hand had stopped.

Kael's gaze lingered on her only for a breath, cool and unreadable. Then, without a word, he turned back to lead Damian and the others down the corridor.

But the girl's eyes followed them, wide and unblinking, until they vanished around the bend.

Damian felt her stare like a weight between his shoulder blades. When the corner swallowed the girl from view, Damian finally spoke.

"Who was she?" His voice came low, careful not to echo against the cold walls.

Kael didn't slow. "A student."

"That didn't feel like a student's stare," Damian muttered. "She stopped the moment she saw you. Like she was—afraid."

Reed glanced back, his brows drawn. "Or guilty. Maybe she wasn't supposed to be there."

"She was drawing a maze," Damian said. "A strange one. Lines so sharp it looked... deliberate. Do students here normally sketch labyrinths on the floor?"

Kael's reply came without pause, each word clipped and final. "In Bogston, every mind leaves its trace. Some in books, some in equations, some in nonsense on the floor. Do not read too much into it."

The answer should have closed the matter, yet Damian caught the flicker of tension at Kael's jaw. The professor's pace grew brisker, forcing them to match him.

Father Athelston suddenly laughed — dry, cracking laughter that startled the silence of the hall. He jabbed his cane against the stones. "Labyrinths! You see? She knows. She draws what binds this place. But you—" he pointed weakly toward Kael, "you walk its heart."

Reed's grip tightened on the priest's arm, hushing him. "Father, not now."

Kael halted at a tall oak door. His hand rested on the handle, but his gaze turned, sharp as a blade, to Athelston.

"You will keep him quiet, Jonas. This is not a parish street where mutterings vanish in air. Here, words stay."

Reed swallowed hard, nodding. "Yes, Professor."

Kael pushed the door open. Inside stretched a chamber lined with shelves, tables stacked with papers, and a blackboard scrawled over with chalk equations Damian couldn't begin to follow. The air smelled of ink, chalk, and something metallic he couldn't place.

"This is the faculty chamber," Kael said, his voice settling into formality again. "You, Damian, will have your quarters in the West Block. Reed, the dormitories for students are close by. Father Athelston will be given a place in the chapel annex."

Damian hesitated, watching Kael as he moved to the head of the room. "And what of that girl?" he asked again, unable to let it go.

Kael met his eyes this time. A faint smile, unreadable, touched his lips.
"Curiosity is good, Professor Damian. But remember — in Bogston, some questions are best left unasked."

Damian held Kael's gaze a moment longer, trying to measure whether the words were warning, wisdom, or simply dismissal. The professor gave him nothing more. With a rustle of coat and papers, Kael turned away, already gathering a stack of documents from the desk.

Reed cleared his throat gently, eager to break the silence. "Shall I take Father to the chapel annex now?"

Kael nodded without looking up. "There is a porter outside who will show you. Return after. The student registrar will be expecting you."

Reed guided the priest toward the door, murmuring soft reassurances. Athelston muttered back, his voice ragged and strange. Damian caught a few words as they passed — "walls listening," "iron teeth," "the girl knows." Then their footsteps faded down the hall.

The chamber was suddenly too quiet. Damian crossed to one of the tall windows, its glass dim with dust, and looked out. From here, the view opened across the central courtyard: blocks of stone, ivy crawling like veins, and high towers that cast their shadows over everything. No students wandered the green, though it should have been the hour for study or debate.

"Strange, isn't it?" Kael's voice came from behind, smooth but carrying weight. "You expected a city of noise and activity. Instead, you find silence. Do not mistake it for emptiness. Bogston's strength lies beneath the surface, in work done behind doors, in thoughts never spoken aloud."

Damian turned. "And the silence itself?"

Kael's lips curved faintly, almost amused. "Even silence can teach, if you listen."

The clock somewhere in the building tolled once, the sound deep, carrying through the floorboards. Kael set down his papers and straightened.

"Come. I'll take you to your quarters. Tomorrow you begin your lectures, but tonight—rest. Bogston tests men most when they are weary."

They left the faculty chamber together, Kael leading him through corridors that seemed to double back on themselves, their turns dizzying. At last they reached a stairwell of worn stone that spiraled up to a long hall. Doors lined it, each marked with a brass plate. Kael stopped at one.

"West Block. Your room." He pressed a key into Damian's hand. "You'll find books, papers, and quiet enough for a mind that does not like to rest. Meals are served in the common hall at fixed hours. Do not be late."

Damian slid the key into the lock. The door groaned open, revealing a modest chamber — a narrow bed, a desk piled with unused parchment, shelves already lined with heavy tomes. A single window overlooked the courtyard below.

Before Damian could thank him, Kael spoke again, softer now. "Professor Damian, you've come far, guided by blessings perhaps greater than you know. But tread carefully. In Bogston, curiosity can be both a gift and a snare."

With that, he turned and left, his footsteps fading into the corridor.

Damian stood alone in the room, the key still warm in his hand, the silence pressing close around him. He set down his satchel, sat on the bed, and for the first time since leaving home, allowed himself to breathe.

Yet his mind did not rest. It circled back — to the girl's ink-stained hands, to the maze that seemed to breathe on the page, and to her eyes, wide with something between fear and recognition.

A knock at the door broke Damian's thoughts. He opened it to find Reed, looking a little winded from walking the halls.

"Meal time," Reed said. "Kael told me to bring you down. Apparently, being late to supper is worse than skipping a lecture."

Damian smiled faintly and followed him.

The corridors were livelier now. Lamps had been lit, their glow catching on polished brass rails and faded portraits. Students moved in clusters, carrying books under their arms, talking quickly about lessons, experiments, or gossip. Damian caught fragments of arguments about equations, someone laughing over a prank in the dormitories, a heated debate about whether the library was haunted or simply drafty.

The common hall opened wide before them — a high-ceilinged space, plain but filled with the clatter of cutlery and the hum of voices. Long tables stretched across the room. Professors sat nearer the dais, students at the benches below. The air smelled of broth and warm bread.

Reed led him to a space midway down the table. As they settled, a boy across leaned forward.

"You're the new professor, aren't you?" His tone was friendly, though curious. "Name's Larkin. Mathematics."

"Damian," he replied. "Philosophy and the sciences of mind."

"Ah," another student chimed in, a girl with quick eyes and a sharper voice. "That means you'll be under Professor Kael's department. Be careful — he eats his assistants alive." She grinned, and a few laughed.

Damian raised an eyebrow. "I'll keep that in mind."

The food was passed along: bowls of thick stew, loaves torn apart and shared, mugs of a tart drink. Conversation ebbed and flowed. Reed kept glancing around, as if noting every face. Damian joined in lightly, asking students what they studied, where they came from. Some answered eagerly, others only nodded, guarded.

Halfway through the meal, Kael appeared briefly at the dais, exchanging a few words with the head steward before slipping out again. The hall didn't pause for him; chatter rolled on.

Damian noticed movement near the far end of the hall. The girl from earlier sat with a cluster of students, eating quietly. Her hair was tied back this time, no chalk in her hands, no strange sketches on the floor — just another student among many. When her eyes lifted and met his across the hall, she didn't flinch. She gave a polite nod, then returned to her meal.

Normal. Almost too normal.

When the supper ended, benches scraped back and groups spilled into the corridors. Some students lingered, finishing conversations. Others rushed toward the library or the dormitories.

"Do you walk in the evenings?" Reed asked as they stepped outside into the cool air.

"Always helps me settle my mind," Damian said.

The courtyard was lit by lamps on tall iron posts, their glow forming little pools along the paths. Reed spoke of classes he hoped to take, how he'd dreamt of Bogston since boyhood. Students passed them, some greeting Reed with nods, others too caught up in their own talk to notice.

They circled toward the chapel annex. Through its open door, Damian glimpsed Father Athelston kneeling in prayer, his lips moving quickly, hands gripping the rail as though it anchored him. Reed slowed, concern flickering across his face, but Damian touched his arm. "Let him be. Prayer is what he knows."

As they turned back, laughter drifted from the dormitory windows. A pair of boys chased each other across the courtyard, one wielding a rolled-up parchment like a sword. From another corner came the sound of a violin, hesitant but sweet.

Damian breathed in. For a moment, it felt like any other university — full of life, noise, ambition.

And yet, somewhere beneath, he could not shake the sense that Bogston always held a second layer.

When Damian finally parted ways with Reed, the young man excused himself with a yawn and a grin.

"Big day tomorrow," Reed said. "I should probably get some sleep before Kael has me memorizing half the library."

"Go, then," Damian answered with a small smile. "I'll take the long way back."

Reed gave a wave and disappeared into the dormitory hall. Damian lingered in the courtyard, walking slow circles around the lamplight until the students' voices thinned and the night grew gentler.

By the time he reached his chamber, the corridors were quieter. He lit the lamp on his desk and sat, but found himself restless. His eyes wandered to the empty parchment stacked neatly in a pile, waiting to be used. Almost without thinking, he pulled one sheet free and dipped the pen.

He didn't write notes for lectures. Instead, he wrote two names. Choe. Miska.

A smile tugged at his mouth, unbidden. Choe would have been teasing him already: "Professor Damian, off to become grand and serious. Do the scholars in Bogston even allow laughter?" And Miska — her steadier voice, calmer, would remind him to eat and sleep before burying himself in papers.

He leaned back, remembering their last evening together in Viel. Choe had insisted on walking him to the station, carrying nothing but jokes and a loaf of bread he claimed Damian would "need more than books." Miska had stayed a little longer, speaking softly, pressing a small copper charm into his hand — a token she said had belonged to her father. Damian still carried it, tucked safely in his satchel.

He set the pen down, fingers brushing his temple. Already, the distance weighed heavier than the train ride itself. He wondered if they thought of him now, whether letters would cross the miles between their city and Bogston, or whether the pace of this place would swallow even time for that.

At last, he folded the page carefully — blank but for their names — and slipped it into the drawer.

The clock's chime startled him. Ten. Dinner. He had nearly missed it.

Damian rose, straightened his coat, and left the room. The corridors were quieter than before, most of the younger students gone to bed, but light still spilled from the professors' dining chamber at the end of the hall.

Inside, the room was smaller than the students' hall, lined with tall shelves of books and cabinets of oddities — seashells, pressed plants, glass vials with clouded liquids. A long polished table stretched the length of the chamber, set with platters of roast, bowls of greens, and wine decanters catching the lamplight.

A few professors were already gathered, their voices carrying across the table in an easy ebb. Damian entered quietly, but Kael, seated near the center, noticed him.

"Ah, our new mind among us," Kael said, lifting his glass faintly. "Damian, come."

The others glanced up, some with mild curiosity, others with that guarded look he was beginning to recognize in Bogston. He took a seat two chairs down from Kael.

Professor Halberg, a man with an untamed beard and ink stains even on his cuffs, leaned forward.

"You're the philosophy man, aren't you? Tell me, do you intend to teach our students how to think themselves out of work?"

A ripple of laughter followed, though not unkind.

Damian allowed himself a smile. "On the contrary. I hope to teach them how not to become trapped in their own minds."

"Mm," Halberg muttered, cutting into his roast. "A pity most of them rather enjoy the trap."

From further down, a thin woman with sharp spectacles spoke. Professor Thane — he remembered Reed mentioning her name.

"Tell me, Damian. Do you believe philosophy belongs in Bogston at all? This is a school of sciences. Hard work, proof, the measurable. Not... musings."

Kael intervened, his tone smooth. "Don't prod the man on his first night, Thane. Even musings, in the right hands, can cut sharper than equations."

The table settled into a different current after that — talk of experiments in metallurgy, a lecture on mechanical flight postponed for lack of funding, the endless debates about which sciences deserved the most attention. Damian listened, contributing sparingly. He noted the rivalries hidden under polite phrases, the way some spoke over others, how Kael only needed to raise a hand for silence.

Dinner stretched long, the food almost an afterthought compared to the talk. When the wine had been poured a second time, Kael pushed his chair back and fixed Damian with a look. "Come," he said simply.

The others barely glanced up as Damian followed him out.

They moved through quieter corridors, past heavy oak doors and staircases that creaked under their weight. Finally, Kael stopped before a tall set of double doors at the far end of a wing. He rapped once, then opened without waiting for an answer.

The chamber inside was dim, lit only by a fire and a pair of lamps. The air smelled of pipe smoke, leather, and old wood. Behind a desk carved from dark oak sat a figure Damian had seen only in portraits: Dr. Heckrog.

His hair was silver, thinning but long, and his back slightly bent, though his eyes — sharp, almost burning — betrayed no softness. He looked up slowly from the papers in front of him.

"Kael," he said, voice like gravel smoothed with age. "And this must be our new recruit."

"Damian," Kael supplied. "Philosophy and sciences of mind."

Heckrog gestured to the chairs opposite. "Sit. Both of you."

On the table, a decanter of deep red wine gleamed beside two crystal glasses, and a box of cigars lay open. Heckrog poured the wine himself, unhurried, then slid a glass toward Damian.

"Young blood," he said, leaning back with a cigar in hand. "I've seen it arrive here for sixty years. Some burn bright, some sputter out, some... cause trouble." His eyes held Damian's. "Which are you, I wonder?"

Damian lifted the glass but didn't drink yet. "I've never thought of myself as fire, sir. More as the one who studies its light."

Heckrog's mouth curved slightly, not quite a smile. He struck a match, lit his cigar, and let the smoke coil into the lamplight.
"A watcher, then. Watchers are dangerous in their own way. They see too much. Sometimes more than they're meant to."

Kael sipped his wine, silent. His expression gave away nothing.

The old man went on, voice lowering. "Bogston has rules, Damian. Written and unwritten. You may find the written ones in your books, but the unwritten — those are kept here." He tapped his chest, then the desk. "They are what keep this place standing. Do you understand?"

Damian inclined his head. "I think I will, in time."

Heckrog finally drank from his own glass, eyes never leaving him. "Good. Time is the one resource Bogston consumes fastest. Remember that."

The fire snapped in the grate, and for a moment, all Damian could hear was the crackle of wood and the steady drag of Heckrog's cigar.
Damian let the warmth of the wine pool in his chest, though he did not drink. He studied Heckrog as he leaned back, the smoke curling in languid spirals, framing his sharp, knowing eyes. There was an intensity in the man that commanded not just attention, but a careful measurement of one's own thoughts. It was as if he weighed Damian with every flicker of the amber light.

"You will find, Damian," Heckrog continued, voice low but steady, "that Bogston is a place that grows along with you, or consumes you entirely. There is no middle ground. One misstep, one lapse in judgment... and your mind, your reputation, even your life here, can unravel without the slightest whisper."

Kael remained seated, glass poised, silent — the quiet sentinel beside this force of sixty years. Damian sensed it: this was a ritual, a test of observation before even a single lecture.

Heckrog leaned forward, cigar smoke coiling between his fingers. "Tell me, when you first arrived, what did you see in the girl?"

Damian blinked. "The one drawing in the hall?"

Heckrog's eyes narrowed, and for a heartbeat, Damian thought he had spoken out of turn. Then the old man chuckled, soft, almost a growl. "Yes. Not the maze — the girl herself. Most newcomers fixate on patterns or curiosities. Few notice the thread beneath."

Damian hesitated. "I... noticed her looking at Kael."

"And what did you make of it?" Heckrog's voice sharpened, demanding.

"That she... recognized something. Perhaps respect. Or fear. I cannot say."

"Good," Heckrog said, reclining, puffing lightly. "Do not try to quantify what you do not understand. Your mind will trip on its own curiosity if you do. Bogston tolerates knowledge, yes. But it despises assumptions."

Kael finally spoke, voice low, smooth. "He will learn, Heckrog. Give him his first week before unraveling him with shadows of conjecture."

"Ah, Kael," Heckrog said, smoke curling over his lips. "Always the protector. Yet one day, even you must stand aside. All of Bogston must eventually face its own mirrors."

The words struck Damian more sharply than he anticipated. Mirrors. Reflections. Were they literal, symbolic, or something else entirely?

Heckrog gestured toward the decanter. "Wine, Damian. Taste it. Let the fruit and the years tell you something beyond the textbooks. Consider it your first lesson: history is drunk as much as it is written. The past will speak — if you listen."

Damian lifted the glass this time, inhaled the sharp scent, and sipped cautiously. Heat spread through him, unfamiliar but grounding. He met Heckrog's gaze and, for the first time in hours, felt neither fear nor uncertainty, only the weight of expectation pressing against his shoulders.

The old man studied him, nodding slowly, then shifted in his chair. "Tomorrow, you begin your lectures. Tonight, think of Bogston as a room you must enter carefully. Every voice, every gesture, even the silence, has a story. Remember that you are never merely a guest here. You are, in time, part of the machinery — whether you like it or not."

Kael stood, signaling the end of the meeting. "I suggest we leave him now, Heckrog. He has walked a long day. Let him digest more than wine."

Heckrog waved a hand, dismissive but not unkind. "Do as you will, Kael. But remember, the boy has eyes. Keep them sharp, or Bogston will sharpen them for him."

Damian rose, feeling both dwarfed and strangely invigorated. The old man's words echoed in his mind like the distant chime of the university's clock — relentless, precise, and yet full of secrets he was only beginning to sense.

As Kael led him back through the quiet corridors toward the West Block, Damian could feel the city's pulse beneath the stones, under the walls, threading into the very air. Somewhere far above, a window glimmered in the darkness, and for a fraction of a second, he thought he glimpsed the girl's eyes, calm now, but unblinking.

And in that glance, Damian understood something he could not yet name: Bogston did not simply observe its students. It remembered them. It waited. It tested. And he, new as he was, had just taken his first step into its true heart.

The first light of dawn seeped through Damian's window, pale and hesitant, brushing the edges of the West Block corridors. He rose, feeling the stiffness of a night half spent in restless thought, and dressed quickly. A glance at the clock reminded him: the first lecture would begin shortly, and Professor Kael expected punctuality.

By the time he reached the faculty hall, the morning air had grown brisk, carrying faint scents of wood smoke and dew from the courtyard. A few students moved toward the classrooms, hoods drawn over their heads, murmuring greetings to one another. Damian noted their quick glances, the subtle nods, as though each one measured him already.

Kael was waiting, leaning against the doorway to the lecture hall. "You are late if you linger in thought. Remember that here, Damian — time marks more than the hour."

Damian inclined his head. "I will not linger."

The lecture hall was vast, rows of high-backed chairs arranged in a semi-circle, all facing a raised platform. Chalkboards lined the walls, some filled with equations, others with diagrams Damian could not immediately parse. A cluster of students had gathered, shuffling papers and whispering. A few faces he had glimpsed during supper nodded at him, others were new.

Kael gestured to the platform. "Begin. Introduce yourself, state your intent. Keep it short. Bogston rewards clarity, not embellishment."

Damian stepped forward, settling on the podium. He cleared his throat. "I am Damian. Philosophy and the sciences of mind. My lectures will explore reasoning, perception, and the methods by which thought shapes understanding. I expect questions, and I expect challenge. We are here to think, not to be silent observers."

A low murmur ran through the hall. One student, seated near the front, raised an eyebrow. "You speak boldly for a newcomer."

"I speak plainly," Damian replied. "If you learn to measure that, you will know more than many who have studied here for years."

Kael's hand lifted subtly — a signal, Damian realized, to move forward. He cleared a space on the desk, spreading sheets of notes, diagrams, and a few small, curious instruments he had brought. Students leaned forward, some scribbling, others observing quietly.

"Consider perception," Damian began. "Not the mere act of seeing, but of knowing that what you see is filtered — by memory, expectation, and preconception. I want each of you to look at these objects," he indicated a small, oddly faceted crystal, "and describe exactly what you observe. No assumptions. Only observation."

A hesitant hand rose. "It appears… blue, with a shimmer?"

"Good," Damian said. "But do not stop there. What does shimmer mean? How do you measure it? And can you separate the shimmer from what you expect to see?"

Murmurs of discussion spread through the hall. Students turned to one another, debating quietly, leaning over desks. Some questioned, others tested, and a few scribbled furiously.

Midway through the lecture, a familiar figure appeared in the doorway — the girl from the hallways, her hair tied neatly, notebook in hand. She stepped quietly inside, scanning the room, then took a seat near the back, unremarkable except for the intensity in her eyes. Damian noticed her but did not pause; the students' attention was his.

As the morning progressed, questions became sharper. Some challenged his assertions, others sought clarification, a few simply tested him with hypothetical scenarios. Damian welcomed each, letting the exchange sharpen his own reasoning.

Kael observed silently from the side, arms folded, expression unreadable. Occasionally, he would jot notes on a slip of paper, glance at a student, then return his gaze to Damian. The silent assessment weighed upon Damian — not a threat, but an invisible standard he knew he could not ignore.

When the hour finally ended, Damian stepped back, letting the murmurs of discussion continue among the students. Kael approached him, silent until the hall had emptied.

"Well," Kael said finally, voice low, "you survived the first test without faltering. That is… acceptable."

Damian allowed himself a small nod. "The students are sharp. Faster than I anticipated."

"They must be," Kael replied. "And you must be sharper. Bogston does not tolerate hesitation, only precision. Remember that as the days stretch ahead."

Damian left the hall, his mind already turning over the questions, the students' expressions, and the quiet, observant presence of the girl who had appeared so deliberately yet so unassumingly.

That night, Damian lay in his chamber, the lamp casting a dim circle of light over the desk. His mind, still spinning from the day's lectures, refused to quiet itself. He stared at the empty parchment, the crystal instruments resting untouched, and finally closed his eyes, hoping for rest.

But sleep did not come easily. Almost without warning, the familiar darkness of the dream he had been haunted by for a decade crept in — heavier this time, more insistent.

He found himself in the same twisting corridors he had known in nightmares since boyhood, a labyrinth whose walls seemed to grow taller with each step. Shadows pooled in corners where light should have been. And there, in the center of the maze, was his father. Trapped, rigid, eyes pleading.

"Damian..." the voice was both familiar and terrible, echoing off walls that seemed alive. "Find me... get me out..."

Damian's chest tightened. Panic clawed at him, familiar yet visceral, as he ran toward the voice. Corridors twisted unnaturally; doors led to dead ends, floors dropped away into darkness. He called out, "Father! I'm here! I'll get you!"

The air thickened, time stretching unreasonably. Each step was met with another obstacle — a wall appearing where it hadn't been, a passageway folding back upon itself. But he pressed on, heart hammering, the voice guiding him in fits and starts.

Finally, after what felt like hours, Damian reached a room, a small square chamber at the heart of the maze. His father stood there, silent now, expression fixed in a quiet desperation. Damian reached for him — and then, as if touching air, his hands met nothing.

"Damian..." the voice came one last time, distant, fading. "Remember..."

And the walls dissolved. The labyrinth vanished into the gray haze of pre-dawn, leaving Damian lying on his bed, damp with sweat, his breath coming in short, sharp bursts.

He sat upright, shaking, hands clutching the edges of the blanket. His chest heaved, but slowly, as the reality of his room — West Block, the lamp, the faint murmur of the courtyard below — anchored him.

The dream had left its mark, lingering on his skin like an echo. But sleep, exhausted though he was, eventually claimed him. This time, it was unbroken.

When he awoke, the sun had not yet risen, and the corridors were quiet. Damian rose, straightened himself, and prepared for the day, carrying the weight of the vision like a reminder — that even here, in the structured, exacting halls of Bogston, shadows from the past had a way of following, testing, shaping him.

The morning unfolded quietly. Light seeped through the tall, arched windows of West Block, spilling onto the polished stone floors. Damian moved through the corridors with the measured rhythm he had begun to adopt, nodding to the few students he passed. They were still cautious around him, whispering in hushed tones, as though even a glance in his direction carried weight.

The day's lectures proceeded in their usual cadence. He began with philosophy, carefully tracing lines of argument across the blackboards, pausing to ask questions that prompted thought rather than memorization. Students leaned in, occasionally debating with one another before turning their attention back to him. The girl — sat quietly at the back, pen moving steadily across her notebook.

Later, during the mid-morning break, Damian found himself wandering the East Wing. Its corridors were narrower, the walls lined with faded paintings of past rectors, their eyes oddly lifelike in the half-light. A few students passed, laughing softly at a private joke, and he noticed the delicate clatter of cups from the faculty café tucked into a corner.

He stopped by the small fountain in the courtyard, water whispering over stone, and was approached by a younger professor he had not met before.

"Professor Damian?" the man said, voice polite but curious. "I'm Halver, chemistry. I've heard a bit about your lectures. Thought I'd see them firsthand."

"Halver," Damian said, inclining his head. "It's always good to meet a new colleague. I hope the lecture wasn't too unorthodox."

Halver smiled, eyes flicking toward the fountain. "Unorthodox? Perhaps. But it makes them think. And that's what Bogston is for, isn't it?"

Damian allowed himself a small nod. "Indeed."

By noon, he was led to the dining hall, a sunlit space with long wooden tables and high windows. Conversations hummed across benches, students comparing notes, arguing quietly, or sharing morsels of food. He ate alongside Reed, who had returned to his usual energy, albeit still curious about the previous night's excursion.

"Did you notice the new library annex?" Reed asked between bites. "It's on the north wing. They've got rare manuscripts in there. Half of them are from before the city even had a proper record office."

"I saw it," Damian replied. "Perhaps we'll explore it later. Quietly."

After lunch, the day continued with practical sessions. Damian accompanied students through the experimental halls: small laboratories where basic mechanical and chemical experiments were conducted under watchful eyes, halls of mathematics where equations sprawled across chalkboards in sprawling complexity. He introduced techniques for observation, asking them to document not just the results but the reasoning, the assumptions, and the uncertainties.

During one such session, a student approached him hesitantly. "Professor... do you think Bogston will ever allow open debates like in the universities of the south?"

Damian considered. "Open debate is... risky," he said carefully. "Not because ideas are dangerous, but because people are. But yes, there is room for discussion here, if one measures words carefully and chooses moments with attention."

The afternoon waned into quiet hours of study. Damian took a slow walk through the smaller, lesser-used corridors of West Block. He noticed the intricate woodwork on the staircases, the subtle carvings of animals and symbols almost forgotten, worn smooth by generations. A few students were stationed in small study rooms, their heads bent over parchment, pens scratching as the fading light fell across their shoulders.

By evening, he returned to his chamber. The lamp cast its dim circle once more, and the day's ordinary rhythm had left him with a sense of controlled, almost comforting, monotony. He wrote brief notes for the next lecture, organizing observations from the day, and allowed himself a quiet moment to watch the courtyard empty under the soft glow of lamps.

It was a normal day at Bogston: measured, disciplined, almost mundane, yet threaded with an undercurrent of tension that only someone attentive could feel. Outside, the wind whispered along the stone walls; inside, Damian sat quietly, aware that each ordinary day was a layer upon which the extraordinary was quietly building. The following days settled into a rhythm, each blending into the next with the quiet insistence of Bogston's routines. Damian moved through them with the careful awareness of someone attuned to patterns, even as the hallways and lectures appeared ordinary on the surface.

Morning lectures ran with a measured precision. Damian taught philosophy and cognition, sometimes pausing mid-lecture to observe how students argued, how they reacted to subtle challenges, how curiosity flickered across their faces. Some questions were straightforward, others veiled, designed to test him as much as he tested them.

During breaks, he wandered the faculty corridors, occasionally meeting professors he had not yet encountered. There was Professor Marrow, whose interest in human anatomy bordered on obsession, though his demeanor was polite; Professor Tyle, who taught advanced mathematics, always carried a notebook of impossibly small scrawls; and Professor Ethelwyn, the soft-spoken botanist, whose experiments with rare plants seemed almost ceremonial. Each had their rhythms, their peculiarities, their way of marking territory within Bogston.

One afternoon, Damian accompanied Reed to the new library annex. The space was hushed, walls lined with books older than the city, some so fragile their pages seemed to whisper when turned. Damian traced the spines, noting marginalia and annotations left by generations of scholars, while Reed poured over manuscripts detailing early mechanical experiments and primitive neurological studies.

"This place," Reed said softly, "it's like a city under the city. Layers of knowledge, and people who guard it like treasure."

Damian inclined his head. "Yes. And knowledge is power, Reed. Always remember that here, even ordinary curiosity can attract attention."

The dining hall was the center of daily gossip and conversation. Conversations ranged from mundane arguments over the best chemical reactions to more personal remarks about the professors' peculiar habits. Damian listened more than he spoke, taking in the subtle hierarchies: which students deferred to which professors, who held influence in quiet ways, the small gestures that revealed allegiance or fear. Reed occasionally tried to engage him in louder, more excited chatter, but Damian remained reserved, watching, cataloging.

Evenings were for study, small meetings, or brief strolls through the courtyards. Damian discovered the hidden alcoves — small gardens enclosed within the walls, fountains long-unused, and shadowed corners where the wind moved in odd patterns through stone. Each place felt like a secret, and each secret seemed almost deliberate, as if the university itself was guiding attention, observing how students interacted with its spaces.

One night, Reed approached him quietly, notebook in hand. "Professor, did you see that? In the chemistry hall — a vial, glowing faintly, left on the counter. I swear it wasn't there before class."

Damian studied the description carefully. "Perhaps an experiment left unfinished. Or perhaps... someone testing observation. Take note, Reed. Even the smallest anomaly can reveal intention."

By the end of the week, Damian had mapped not only classrooms, professors, and routines, but also the subtle undercurrents of Bogston — the guarded whispers, the careful glances, the student alliances, and the professors' unspoken hierarchies. He had observed enough to know that even when everything appeared ordinary, there was always a structure beneath the surface, a pulse guiding the actions of the university and its inhabitants.

And yet, despite the ordinary, there was an edge to the days. Each lecture, each corridor, each quiet conversation was a reminder that Bogston was both a school and a stage — one where knowledge, observation, and subtle power played out under layers of routine, waiting for those perceptive enough to see the patterns beneath the order.

Damian returned to his chamber each night, the lamp casting its familiar circle of light. He would write notes, trace diagrams, and catalog observations, aware that even normalcy carried lessons, and that within routine, secrets waited — patient, silent, and precise.
Nights, however, brought Damian back to the labyrinth he had long known in dreams. Though the days were quiet, the visions were persistent. That night, as he closed his eyes, the familiar gray corridors unfurled again.

The labyrinth was quieter this time, less chaotic, yet its walls still seemed alive, bending and stretching as he moved. At the center, his father stood, trapped as always, eyes fixed on him with the same silent plea.

"Damian..." the voice echoed faintly, carrying the weight of unspoken things. "Help me..."

Damian ran through the familiar paths, turning corners and threading through narrow passages. Each time he reached toward his father, the walls shifted, closing just enough to prevent contact.

Yet tonight, there was no panic, only methodical effort. He traced the patterns of the maze, memorizing the turns, noting which corridors repeated and which were false.

Finally, he arrived at the small chamber where his father always waited. Damian reached out again, hands meeting the same empty space, but he felt a strange steadiness, a focus born from repeated practice.

"Remember…" the voice whispered, fading once more as the walls dissolved, leaving Damian lying on his bed, calm now, sweat drying on his skin. He sat for a moment, letting the memory settle, the dream less menacing but no less real.

The next day at Bogston returned to normal. Lectures, student discussions, and hallway observations filled the hours. Damian moved among the routines with the quiet precision he had developed — noting subtle changes in student behavior, the unspoken influence of certain professors, and the rhythms of the university that seemed ordinary on the surface but were layered with intent.

During a midday break, he and Reed explored a quiet courtyard he had not noticed before, small fountains murmuring over mossy stones, the afternoon light catching on weathered statues. "Another layer of Bogston," Damian said, almost to himself. "Even in the ordinary, the university shows itself to those who look."

Reed glanced at him, notebook open, scribbling observations. "Do you think the labyrinth will come again tonight?"

Damian nodded, standing by the fountain, fingers brushing the smooth stone. "It will. And each time, it teaches something new — not just about my father, but about perception, patterns, patience. The labyrinth is a part of me now, as much as Bogston is."

Evenings continued with study and careful observation. Damian cataloged, traced patterns, and allowed the ordinary flow of the university to carry him while the undercurrent of unseen structures whispered hints of larger truths. Though nothing extraordinary happened during the day, the shadow of the labyrinth at night, the rhythm of Bogston, and the quiet vigilance he maintained kept him alert.

He had learned that normalcy here was only a surface, and within that surface, every corridor, every conversation, every lesson contained its own quiet weight — waiting for attention, waiting for understanding.

The weekend brought a rare reprieve from lectures, and Damian decided to take Reed with him to the old church at the edge of Bogston's grounds—a place he had noticed only in passing, its spire rising like a silent sentinel over the campus. The stone walls were worn, ivy crawling along their edges, and the wooden doors, heavy and ancient, creaked softly as they pushed them open.

Inside, the air smelled of polished wood and old incense, a faint chill rolling over the stone floors. Sunlight streamed through stained-glass windows, casting muted colors on the pews and altar. Damian led Reed forward, careful to move quietly. The place felt empty, almost sacred in its stillness, yet he knew its significance—this was where Father Athelston performed services, counseled students, and maintained a quiet presence over the spiritual life of Bogston.

"Quiet, Reed," Damian whispered. "Observe first. Listen. The ordinary here carries its own weight."

They moved toward the front, where Father Athelston usually sat in contemplation or prayer. Today, he was not visible in the main hall, but the room smelled faintly of the incense he burned, a mixture of lavender and something sharper, almost medicinal. Damian's mind cataloged details—the arrangement of candles, the precise folding of prayer books, the subtle signs of wear on the lectern, each revealing how often and how meticulously the space was used.

Reed whispered, "He's not here. Do you think he's in the vestry?"

Damian nodded, leading the way to a side door partially hidden behind a tapestry. Inside, the vestry was smaller, cluttered with robes, ritual items, and shelves of books, many of them annotated in Father Athelston's careful hand. On the desk, a single candle burned, its light steady. Damian crouched slightly, observing without touching anything.

They left the vestry as quietly as they had entered, retracing their steps through the hall, careful not to disturb the lingering scent of incense or the subtle hush of the empty church. Outside, the wind brushed over the courtyard, carrying the faint rustle of leaves and distant voices from students walking to their next lecture.

THREE

FINDINGS

When he awoke the next day , the sun had not yet risen, and the corridors were quiet. Damian rose, straightened himself, and prepared for the day, carrying the weight of the vision like a reminder — that even here, in the structured, exacting halls of Bogston, shadows from the past had a way of following, testing, shaping him.

After the morning lecture, Damian lingered in the hall, watching students file out, their murmurs fading into the corridors. The girl from the previous days stood near the doorway, her notebook clutched to her chest. Damian hesitated, unsure whether to call her, but before he could speak, she stepped forward herself.

"Professor," she said, her voice calm but steady, "may I come to your chamber? I... I have something I wish to say."

He gestured for her to follow, heart quickening with curiosity and a strange apprehension. Once inside his room, she set her notebook carefully on the desk, her eyes scanning the shelves of instruments and papers as if taking everything in before speaking.

"I am Anesthesia Guss," she began, almost rehearsed, "student here. I see... hope in you, Professor." Her gaze met his directly, unflinching. "I want to say something I have seen until now but haven't said, haven't expressed. This—Bogston—is not what it seems."

Damian froze, trying to gauge whether this was some elaborate student jest. "What... what are you saying?" His voice was low, incredulous. "How can you say such things? How do you know?"

She drew a steady breath, as if preparing herself. "I wish I could say everything. But I'll tell you this much. This university... it is a research center for minds. Patients of different disorders, high IQs, even normal people are brought here. Brain surgeries, experimental treatments—they are performed and... sold. Theories and techniques for mind control are developed. A secret society funds much of this. All the lectures, the professors, the university itself—they are a banner, a front."

Damian blinked, the words striking like a sudden gust. "How... how do you know this? Are you... exaggerating?"

She shook her head. "I wish it were exaggeration. I've seen things... observed things... things that cannot be spoken aloud. I have watched patterns, experiments. People disappear, records are sanitized. Bogston is not merely an academy—it's... a hub for control."

He swallowed hard, feeling a mix of disbelief, horror, and fascination. "And... the labyrinth on the first day? The drawings I saw?" His voice was measured but tense.

Anesthesia's expression flickered, a hint of confusion. "What are you saying? I wasn't drawing anything. I wasn't there at all that day. Professor... are you... okay?"

Damian stepped back, blinking, as if trying to shake off the sudden rush of words. His mind raced, trying to reconcile what she had said with the orderly, disciplined structure of Bogston he had seen. "I—I'm fine," he said finally, though his voice betrayed his uncertainty. "I just... I need to think. You... you really mean all this?"

She nodded, eyes steady. "I do. But there are limits to what I can say, even here. Still... I needed you to know the truth, at least in part. I... I trust you might understand."

Damian stared at her, torn between skepticism and an uneasy realization that Bogston's walls may indeed conceal far more than lectures and experiments. Outside, the hall was quiet, but inside his chamber, the weight of her words pressed heavily.

He finally sank into a chair, rubbing his temples. "Then... we must be careful. And observant. If what you say is true, this place is far more dangerous than I imagined."

Anesthesia gave a faint, approving nod. "Exactly. And sometimes, observation is the only safeguard we have."

For a long moment, neither spoke, the room filled only with the faint scratch of her pen against the notebook as she adjusted her papers. Damian could feel the pulse of Bogston around them, both familiar and ominous, realizing that what she had revealed might change every step he took here.

ᐯᐯᐯ

That night, after the corridors had emptied and the halls of West Block had sunk into silence, Damian waited until the muted tick of the clock gave him a rhythm, then slipped a note under Reed's door. Within moments, the younger man appeared, rubbing his eyes, hooded and uncertain.

"Professor... it's late. Where are you taking me?" Reed whispered, his voice a mixture of curiosity and hesitation.

"Somewhere you haven't been before," Damian replied quietly, glancing down the dim corridor. "Restricted areas. I want to see something... and I need you to follow exactly."

Reed hesitated, brow furrowed. "Restricted? But how do you know your way there? Who told you about them?"

"Just listen to me," Damian said firmly. "Stay close. We can't risk anyone seeing us."

They moved along the shadows, stepping lightly past sleeping dormitories and flickering lanterns. Damian led, keeping to corners, scaling small ledges, slipping through maintenance stairwells that creaked under their weight. Every footfall was measured; every shadow a potential witness.

Reed followed silently, trust and anxiety colliding in his eyes. Damian motioned him down a narrow stone corridor, pressing himself against the wall as the distant murmur of voices echoed faintly from the east wing. They paused at a locked grate, eyes scanning the surrounding walls.

"This way," Damian muttered, spotting a ventilation ladder leading to a small maintenance hatch above the hall. "We climb, quietly. Keep your weight balanced."

Step by step, Damian led the ascent, Reed following, muscles taut, ears straining. The metal groaned faintly under their weight. A single slip could draw attention. But they reached the hatch without incident, and Damian pushed it open, revealing a narrow passage above the floor, the faint scent of antiseptic and something else — iron, copper, fear.

"Stay low," Damian whispered, dropping silently onto the narrow walkway. Shadows stretched like fingers along the walls as they inched forward. From above, a flickering light traced the outline of barred windows. Beyond them, the faint murmurs of patients reached their ears.

Reed swallowed hard. "Professor... these are the people you meant?"

Damian nodded, eyes fixed ahead. "Yes. Watch. Don't speak."

They moved with precision, careful not to disturb the pipes or loose floorboards. Damian spotted a side door, partially ajar. Through it, they could see the rooms where patients were confined — some lying quietly, others moving with restless energy, eyes wide and vacant. The dim light revealed intricate machines and glass vials, devices wired across bodies, monitors tracking responses, subtle experiments in progress.

"See that?" Damian whispered, gesturing slightly. "This is what I talking about. Minds in cages, being tested, manipulated. Everything we take for granted in the university... it's a facade."

Reed's breath was shallow. "I... I can't believe it."

Damian remained quiet, observing — cataloging every detail, every pattern of light and motion, the whispered commands of unseen supervisors. His mind raced, but he kept Reed close, silent, aware of every possible witness.

When they had taken in as much as they could without detection, Damian led Reed back along the same route: crouching through the ventilation, descending the ladder, retracing their careful steps through the empty corridors. The distant hum of the university night was unchanged, oblivious to their intrusion.

Back in the relative safety of West Block, Damian exhaled, finally allowing a fraction of tension to ease from his shoulders. Reed looked at him, wide-eyed and pale.

"You... you knew how to get there?" he whispered.

Damian shook his head, almost a smirk playing on his lips. "Not exactly. I followed patterns. Watch, listen, observe... it tells you more than maps ever could."

Reed swallowed, still processing. "And no one saw us?"

"No one," Damian said firmly. "And if we are careful, no one ever will. But remember this, Reed — what we saw tonight is only the beginning. Bogston has layers... and not all of them are meant to be understood."

Reed nodded slowly, a mixture of awe and unease on his face. Damian allowed him a moment to recover, then turned toward his own chamber, the night quiet but heavy with secrets that would shape everything to come.

Once inside his chamber, Damian closed the door softly, leaving the night's chill behind. He leaned against the door for a moment, letting his mind run through every detail he had seen. Reed, still pale, slumped into a chair, fingers tapping nervously on his knees.

"Professor," Reed said finally, his voice tentative, "what... what do they do with them? Those... patients?"

Damian moved to the desk, picking up the small crystal he had shown in lecture earlier. He turned it in his hands, focusing on its facets to steady his thoughts before answering. "Reed... these aren't just experiments in learning or medicine. They're studying the mind itself — its vulnerabilities, its potential. The patients we saw, they're more than subjects. They're... instruments. Tools to test theories about cognition, obedience, and control."

Reed's eyes widened. "Control? You mean... mind control?"

"Yes," Damian said, his voice low but firm. "Not everyone here knows it, and not every professor is directly involved. But the techniques, the devices, the surgeries — they're all aimed at manipulating thought, behavior, sometimes even memory. The patients are observed, measured, altered. Some leave with no clear trace of what was done, others... never leave at all."

Reed shivered. "But why? Why the secrecy? Why not just research openly?"

"Because," Damian replied, setting the crystal down and leaning forward, "what they're doing is illegal, unethical... even beyond that, it's dangerous. Minds are not meant to be owned or reshaped at will. The secret society Anesthesia mentioned funds it because it wants control. Influence over people, over knowledge, over power itself. Bogston is their shield — the lectures, the university, all of it a perfect cover."

He paused, letting the weight of his words settle. Reed ran a hand through his hair, trying to process it. "And the experiments? They... they actually work?"

Damian's gaze hardened. "Some of them do. Some fail. And the worst part is the uncertainty — even those who succeed may carry consequences they can't predict. Minds are fragile, and the human will... it's not something to bend lightly."

He moved to the window, looking out toward the courtyard now blanketed in moonlight. "Reed... what we saw tonight isn't a single story. It's part of a system — a hierarchy of observation, control, and testing. Every lecture, every lab, every experiment contributes to it. And anyone who notices too much or asks too many questions becomes... a variable."

Reed's voice was barely a whisper. "So... we can't tell anyone."

"No," Damian said, shaking his head. "Not yet. Not until we understand more. But we watch, we listen, and we remember. That is how we survive here. That is how we can even hope to protect those who can't protect themselves."

The room fell silent for a moment. Damian sank into his chair, pressing his forehead to his hands. "This is why I came here, Reed. To teach, yes, but also to see. To understand. Bogston is not just a university — it's a proving ground for the mind. And if we're careful, we might just find a way to turn what it tests against it."

Reed nodded slowly, absorbing the magnitude of what Damian had revealed. Outside, the night remained still, the echoes of the hidden corridors — the restricted wings, the whispered experiments — pressing in through the walls. Inside, the two of them sat in quiet resolve, knowing that the real lessons at Bogston were far beyond any lecture, any textbook, or any crystal.

Reed speaks ,his voice hesitant but insistent. "So... what the priest said," he murmured, fingers gripping the edge of his chair, "about... control, the experiments, the patients... that was true?"
Damian replies "may be .."

The next day, after the morning lecture, Damian asked Anesthesia to follow him to his chamber. Her expression was unreadable as she entered, but the moment her eyes fell on Reed already seated there, she stiffened, clutching her notebook tighter.

She turned to Damian at once, voice low but sharp. "Did you tell him?"

Damian met her gaze evenly. "Yes."

Her composure cracked; fury flared in her eyes. "How could you? You don't understand! You can't trust anyone here. What if he speaks? What if he's followed? Do you have any idea what happens when suspicions are raised?"

Damian lifted a hand calmly, though his voice carried weight. "Don't worry. He's one of us now. We both saw it, Anesthesia—the patients, the rooms, the machines. There's no denying it anymore."

Reed, caught between them, straightened in his chair, his face pale but resolute. "I swear I'll say nothing," he said quickly. "Professor showed me everything. I saw it with my own eyes. I know what's happening here isn't right."

Anesthesia's jaw tightened. She paced once, notebook still clutched, before turning back to Damian, her voice colder now. "You risked everything. You don't know how deep this runs, how closely they watch. Trust is the most dangerous currency in Bogston."

Damian's tone was steady, measured. "And yet without trust, we have nothing. Alone, we're just observers. Together, we stand a chance to understand, perhaps even resist. Reed has proven himself already—he followed, he kept silent, he listened. He knows."

Reed added, more firmly this time, "You may not trust me yet, but I trust Professor Damian. And if he believes I belong in this, then I'll stand with you both. Whatever Bogston is hiding, I want to uncover it."

Anesthesia looked at him hard, searching his face for cracks, for doubt. Her eyes lingered, measuring him against the weight of her own caution. At last, she exhaled sharply, though her anger did not fade entirely.

"Then both of you need to understand," she said, voice tight, "that from this moment on, every step matters. Every word, every look. They notice. They record. And they never forgive."

She turned back to Damian, her tone softening only slightly. "You've brought him into this, Professor. Now the risk is doubled. Pray you're right about him."

The chamber fell into silence. The faint scratching of the courtyard wind against the window was the only sound. Damian held her gaze, unwavering, while Reed sat tense, shoulders squared but hands restless on his knees.

At last, Damian spoke quietly. "Then we move forward. Carefully, together. There's no turning back now."
At last, Damian spoke quietly. "Then we move forward. Carefully, together. There's no turning back now."

He leaned back slightly, his eyes shifting from Anesthesia to Reed. "We'll meet again tomorrow. Here, in this room. Same time. No one else can know."

Anesthesia's fingers tightened around her notebook, but she gave a short nod. Reed, still tense, murmured, "I'll be here."

Damian rose, signaling the conversation's end. "Then it's settled. Until tomorrow, we act as though nothing has changed."

No more words were needed. Anesthesia slipped out first, her steps sharp and deliberate.

Reed lingered a moment longer, still gripping the back of the chair as if steadying himself. He opened his mouth to speak, but Damian cut in quietly.

"We both will meet again today," Damian said, his tone firm but low. "Evening. Four o'clock. Same place."

Reed nodded quickly, the tension in his shoulders easing just slightly. "I'll be here, Professor."

"Good," Damian replied, his eyes fixed on him. "Now go. And remember—nothing unusual until then."

Reed gave a faint, understanding nod before slipping out into the corridor, leaving Damian alone with the silence of the chamber and the steady tick of the clock.

The evening light filtered dimly through the tall windows of Bogston, painting the stone corridors in long shadows that crept like watchful sentinels. At precisely four o'clock, the silence was broken by the faint creak of a door—Damian's chamber opening. Reed slipped inside, his steps hesitant but measured, his expression taut with curiosity and unease.

Damian was already there, standing near the window, his hands clasped behind his back. He did not turn immediately, only spoke in a tone that was steady, deliberate.

"You came."

Reed's reply was soft, almost defensive. "You asked me to."

Finally, Damian turned, his sharp eyes locking on Reed. For a moment, neither spoke, as if the weight of unspoken truths hung between them. Then Damian moved to the desk, drawing a folded piece of parchment from the stack of papers. He did not hand it to Reed—he only kept it, resting it beneath his fingers.

"Tonight," Damian said, his voice low, "we're not staying within these walls. There's something you need to see. Something that has been buried too long."

Reed blinked, his brow furrowing. "Where?"

A faint smile flickered across Damian's lips, though it did not reach his eyes. "Patience. You'll know soon enough. For now, trust that what lies ahead is necessary. Dangerous, yes—but necessary."

Reed's grip tightened against the back of the chair he had instinctively reached for, his voice betraying both eagerness and dread. "Dangerous how?"

Damian leaned forward slightly, lowering his tone until it was almost a whisper. "Because the truth is never found in daylight, Reed. It hides in the dark places... the places no one dares to look."

For several moments, silence reigned again, broken only by the muted ticking of the clock on the mantel. Reed searched Damian's expression, but the professor gave nothing away—only a controlled calm that seemed more unsettling than anger or fear would have been.

Finally, Reed gave a slow nod. "I'll go with you."

Damian's gaze sharpened, approval flickering there for just an instant. "Good. Then prepare yourself. We leave after midnight."

The hours that followed passed in restless anticipation. Reed could not concentrate on his work; every sound in the corridor made him tense. His mind ran in circles, imagining a dozen possibilities: a hidden archive, a forbidden chamber, perhaps even patients chained in the dark like the whispers claimed.

By the time the great clock struck twelve, Reed found himself standing once more outside Damian's chamber door. The corridor was silent, the torches casting faint pools of light that trembled against the stone. The air seemed heavier at night, as if Bogston itself breathed differently when the rest of the school slept.

Damian opened the door before Reed could knock. He wore a dark coat, plain and inconspicuous, and carried a lantern, its glow shuttered so that only the barest sliver of light escaped.

"Come," Damian said softly. "And tread carefully."

They moved swiftly through the back passages, their footsteps muffled by years of dust and neglect. The lantern's glow brushed against walls lined with old iron hooks, abandoned tools, scraps of cobweb. Neither spoke; only the sound of breathing and the occasional creak of wood filled the air.

At last, Damian stopped before a narrow door, half hidden behind a sagging shelf. He set down the lantern and pushed the shelf aside with deliberate force, revealing a rusted lock. From his coat pocket, he drew a small key, its surface dull with age.

Reed's pulse quickened as the lock gave way with a groan. Damian pushed the door open, revealing a stairway descending into blackness. A breath of stale, cold air drifted upward, carrying with it a faint, metallic tang.

Reed hesitated at the threshold, peering into the dark. "What is this place?"

Damian's voice was quiet, but certain. "A bunker. Built long before you or I arrived here. They say it was meant for protection during the old wars. But over time, it was... repurposed."

Reed's throat tightened. "Repurposed? For what?"

"Come," Damian said again, stepping into the stairwell. "You'll see."

The descent was long and suffocating, each step creaking beneath their weight. The stone walls pressed close, damp with moisture, while the lantern's glow carved small islands of light in an ocean of dark.

Reed's imagination tormented him—he pictured iron cages, twisted instruments, whispers of the forgotten. He clutched the stair rail tighter, the cold biting into his palm.

When they reached the bottom, the corridor stretched ahead, narrow and low-ceilinged. The smell was stronger here: a mingling of dust, mold, and something sharper, something that carried the faintest echo of rot.

Damian raised the lantern higher, and the light revealed alcoves cut into the walls. Within them, shapes rested—shapes that made Reed's breath catch.

Not patients. Not living bodies.

Skeletons.

Row after row of them, seated against the stone as though they had once waited, silently, for release that never came. Some still bore scraps of fabric clinging to their frames, others showed rusted shackles around their wrists or ankles. Empty sockets stared out at the two intruders, silent witnesses to a story long buried.

Reed staggered back a step, his hand flying to his mouth. "Dear God…"

Damian's expression was unreadable, but his eyes lingered on the remains with something like grim recognition. He spoke quietly, each word deliberate.

"This… is what they never told you. Not experiments in progress, no patients hidden away. Only the aftermath. The evidence of what was done here—of those who were left to die, forgotten in the dark."

The lantern's glow trembled, flickering across skulls and bone, casting shadows that seemed almost to move, as if the dead themselves shifted in the corners. Reed felt the air grow heavier, his heartbeat loud in his ears.

And Damian stood still, his gaze fixed on the silent hall of skeletons, as if he had expected this all along.

Reed pressed himself back against the damp wall, his chest heaving as though the air itself had turned poisonous. His eyes darted from skull to skull, sockets black and endless, jaws frozen mid-scream or slack as if in surrender. The lantern's light flickered, and in that trembling glow, the skeletons seemed to shift—lean closer—mock his trembling disbelief.

He whispered, though even his whisper cracked.

"Why… why are they here? Who left them like this?"

Damian stepped forward, calm where Reed shook. He tilted the lantern slightly, letting its glow sweep across the alcoves. The bones gleamed pale against the black stone, arranged not in chaos but in dreadful order. Each body seated, as though once instructed to wait—an audience of the forgotten, forced into silence.

His voice was low, measured, but there was steel beneath it.
"This is not accident. This was design. Men do not sit so neatly before death unless placed, or commanded."

Reed's mouth went dry. His voice rasped.
"You mean... someone put them here? Alive?"

Damian did not answer at once. He crouched before one of the alcoves, setting the lantern on the ground. The shadows leapt upward across the skull, across the tattered remnants of a sleeve that clung stubbornly to bone. His fingers hovered inches above the rusted shackle still clasped at the ankle, as though touching it might burn.

When he finally spoke, his tone carried the weight of knowing—knowing more than he revealed.
"They were prisoners of something greater than iron. Not merely confined... but erased."

The words seemed to hang in the stagnant air, heavier than the silence.

Reed swallowed hard, his gaze locked on the hollow eye sockets. He could not help imagining them filled—faces once alive, voices that once cried out. His chest ached with the ghost of their breath, the echo of despair now swallowed by stone.

He muttered, almost to himself, "It's like they're still watching us..."

Damian lifted the lantern again, casting long, skeletal shadows across the walls. The light flared against the skulls, making them appear as pale lanterns themselves, grinning in death. His eyes narrowed, though his face remained steady.

"They are," he said simply.

Reed froze, his blood running cold.

Damian turned to him fully then, his expression sharp but unreadable, as though testing the younger man's courage.
"Every bone here is a witness. Every silence a warning. What you feel—the weight pressing on you—that is not your imagination. It is memory. Memory that refuses to sleep."

The words settled like ash.

Reed ran a trembling hand through his hair, his voice breaking. "Professor... how can you stand so calm in this place? How can you look at this and not—" He faltered, gesturing helplessly at the rows of dead. "Not lose your mind?"

Damian regarded him for a long moment. The lantern light carved hard shadows across his face, making his features seem older, sterner. When he finally spoke, his tone was quiet, almost weary.

"Because, Reed, I lost my mind to these halls long ago."

The silence that followed was more dreadful than the words themselves. Somewhere in the darkness, water dripped—a hollow, steady beat that marked time in a place where time had long since stopped.

Reed forced himself to breathe, shallow and quick. His eyes swept over the alcoves again, trying to count, but the bones blurred into a sea of white and shadow, endless.

He whispered, barely audible, "How many?"

Damian's eyes lingered on the skeleton nearest, then on the row beyond. "Enough to be forgotten. More than enough to be erased."

Reed felt his knees weaken, his stomach twist. He wanted to run back up those stairs, back into the world of torches and voices, where the living still walked. Yet some part of him—small but unyielding—held him there, tethered by both fear and fascination.

He turned toward Damian again, his voice a raw whisper. "What now?"

Damian raised the lantern higher, its light spilling further down the corridor, revealing yet more alcoves stretching into the dark. His gaze was fixed ahead, steady, as though he had expected all of this.

"Now," he said softly, "we go deeper. The truth never ends at the surface."

The sound came sudden—soft, metallic, and out of place.

Both men froze.

It was faint at first, like the scrape of something heavy against stone, followed by the dull thud of a sack hitting the ground. Reed's head whipped toward the sound, his breath catching in his throat. Damian lowered the lantern instantly, dimming the glow to a faint circle of trembling light.

The corridor beyond them was black, stretching into a silence broken only by that sound.

Another scrape. Another thud.

Reed leaned closer, whispering so low it was almost breath: "Someone's here..."

Damian's reply was equally quiet, though steady. "Hide."

Without another word, he gestured sharply, then melted into the shadows along the wall. Reed, his pulse racing, stumbled toward an alcove, pressing himself back beside one of the skeletal figures. The cold bones brushed his shoulder, sending a jolt of dread through him, but he forced himself still.

They waited.

A faint shuffle of footsteps echoed, slow and deliberate, as though whoever walked these halls knew them well. Then came the sound again—the rustle of something being dragged, followed by the dull weight of it being tossed aside.

Reed dared to peer, just barely. He caught a shape at the far end of the corridor—a figure stooped, carrying a sack dark and shapeless. The man, or whatever he was, paused, adjusted the load, and hurled it into an alcove with casual force. The bag landed with a muted thump. Something inside shifted, soft but heavy, like discarded refuse.

Reed bit his lip hard to stop a gasp.

The figure lingered, muttering under his breath—words too low, too distant to catch. Then, slowly, he turned and vanished into another corridor, his footsteps fading, swallowed by the stone.

Silence returned.

Only then did Reed release the breath he had been holding. His chest ached with it. He turned, expecting Damian beside him, but the professor was gone.

"Professor?" Reed whispered hoarsely.

No answer.

Panic prickled his skin. He slipped out of the alcove, the lantern's faint glow still flickering a little further down, where Damian must have gone. He hurried toward it—but in his haste, he took a wrong turn. The corridor split into two, and he chose without thinking.

Stone pressed around him. The air was thicker here, close, and the smell of damp rot clung to him. He stumbled over loose stones, his breath echoing louder than he wished.

"Professor?" he whispered again, this time shakier. The darkness swallowed his words.

Somewhere behind him, he thought he heard a faint shuffle. He spun, lantern trembling in his hand, casting wild shadows across the walls. The skeletons seemed to lean forward in their alcoves, hollow eyes glinting in the flicker.

Nothing moved.

His heart thudded painfully, but he pressed forward.

—

Elsewhere, Damian moved with quieter steps, his lantern raised just enough to guide him. He knew Reed had slipped another way, but he did not call out. Not here. Not where every echo could betray them. He trusted that the boy would find him—or that he would find the boy.

What caught his attention instead was the sack the stranger had dropped. He crouched near it, lifting the edge gingerly. The stench hit him first—sour, chemical, and unmistakably human. Inside was waste: torn garments, rags stained dark, and something else beneath, something bone-like. He let the fabric fall quickly, face tightening.

"This place," he muttered under his breath, "still feeds its silence."

—

Reed, meanwhile, had come upon a collapsed passage. Stones littered the ground, and water dripped steadily from cracks above. He tried to retrace his steps, but the corridors twisted and doubled back, identical walls leading nowhere. The lantern sputtered, shadows clawing at the edges.

He swore softly, running a hand down his face. The stillness pressed too hard. Every alcove looked the same, every skull seemed to grin wider as though amused by his fear. He could almost hear them whisper, though the sound was nothing but his mind straining.

Finally, faintly, he saw light ahead—not his, but Damian's. Relief surged through him, and he stumbled forward.

The professor was waiting at a junction, his lantern steady. He gave Reed a sharp look.

"You wandered."

"I—I lost the way," Reed stammered. His voice cracked, but steadied. "I thought something was behind me."

Damian's gaze lingered on him, unreadable, before he turned away.

"Then remember the paths. This place is a maze by design. It keeps the careless."

Reed swallowed his shame and followed closely this time.

—

Their return through the corridors was slower, cautious. Twice more, they heard faint sounds—water shifting, stone creaking as though settling, perhaps footsteps in the distance. Each time, they froze, held their breath, then moved again.

Once, Reed brushed past another sack half-hidden in shadow. He glanced down but turned quickly away, unwilling to see more.

Damian said nothing, but Reed noticed the way the professor's jaw tightened, his silence heavier than words.

Finally, the staircase appeared again, stone worn smooth by ages of feet, leading upward. Reed nearly rushed toward it, but Damian's hand caught his arm.

"Slow," Damian whispered. "Always leave as you entered. No sound. No trace."

Together, they climbed.

At last, the weight of stone lifted. The air changed. They emerged into the night, the lantern dim against the vastness above. Stars spread wide across the sky, sharp and clear, a cruel contrast to the suffocating dark below.

Reed breathed deep, the fresh air cutting his lungs. He glanced at Damian, who stood still, lantern lowered, his face unreadable in the starlight.

Neither spoke.

The silence of the bunker clung to them still.

They lingered for a moment under the starlit sky, letting the cold night air fill their lungs, as though drawing in some of the world's living pulse to replace what the bunker had stolen. Damian finally broke the silence.

"Come on," he said quietly, his voice low but firm. "We've seen enough for tonight."

Reed nodded, still pale, and they moved through the quiet halls of Bogston. The corridors were empty, the usual hum of the university replaced by an almost sacred stillness. Footsteps echoed softly on the stone floor, measured, careful, as they returned to their respective quarters.

Damian reached his chamber first. The familiar surroundings offered little comfort; the weight of the underground silence still clung to him. He placed the lantern on the desk, its dim glow reflecting off scattered instruments and papers. For a moment, he simply stared at the floor, letting the images of skeletal alcoves and discarded sacks settle in the quiet recesses of his mind.

Up the hall, Reed slipped into his room. The bed felt impossibly distant, and sleep seemed like a stranger. He sat on the edge for a long moment, running a hand over his face, replaying every detail—the bones, the arrangement, the strange presence of someone else in the bunker. The air in his small room felt lighter, but the darkness inside his head refused to fade.

By 3:30 in the morning, Damian, restless and unsettled, stirred from sleep. He had been dozing lightly, the memories of the night beneath the stone corridors still fresh, but now the dream returned—the labyrinth, always the labyrinth.

The vision was vivid: walls twisting impossibly, corridors folding in on themselves, shadows of his father stretching long and accusing, eyes fixed on him with a mixture of disappointment and warning. Damian's chest tightened, and he could hear his father's voice, not loud, but carrying across the impossible halls.

"Do you understand yet, Damian?"

He woke with a start, cold sweat clinging to his temples. The room was silent, the faint tick of the clock the only sound, but the memory of the labyrinth lingered like a shadow at the corner of his vision.

He sat on the edge of his bed, letting the lantern's dim light from the desk illuminate the room. Thoughts tumbled over each other: the underground skeletons, the stranger in the bunker, Reed's reactions, Anesthesia's warnings. Everything pressed against him, as though the night itself was whispering secrets meant only for him.

Damian leaned back, rubbing his eyes. The dream had left a hollow ache in his chest, a sense of urgency he could not shake. The labyrinth was not just a dream—it was a warning, a reminder of patterns, of consequences, of paths yet untaken.

Outside, the first hints of pre-dawn light had begun to stain the sky pale gray, but Damian remained seated, thinking. Reed would be awake soon, or at least attempting to sleep, haunted by his own version of the night's horrors. And tomorrow, they would meet again, carrying not only the weight of what they had seen but the burden of what was still hidden.

The next morning, after the morning lectures had ended and the hallways had begun to hum faintly with the shuffle of students and professors, Damian's chamber once again became a quiet refuge—a place removed from the steady rhythm of the university.

Anesthesia arrived first, notebook clutched tightly against her chest, her steps brisk but controlled. She cast a wary glance at the door as Reed entered, the tension from last night still etched across his features. Damian, seated behind his desk, gave a subtle nod in acknowledgment.

"Sit," he said quietly, motioning toward the chairs. "We need to discuss last night—and what comes next."

Anesthesia's eyes narrowed, and she didn't bother hiding her frustration. "Last night?" she said, voice low but sharp. "You went to the bunker without me. After everything I've told you about caution—after all my warnings—you went alone and brought Reed?"

Damian's expression remained calm, measured. "I went to confirm what I suspected. The bunker... the alcoves, the arrangements... it was real. And Reed needed to see it, to understand the weight of what lies beneath. It's not about secrecy for its own sake—it's about survival, and preparation."

Reed shifted in his seat, still pale, his hands gripping his knees. "I—I didn't expect to see what we saw," he said quietly, voice trembling slightly. "The skeletons... the way everything was... it's... it's more than I imagined."

Anesthesia's eyes flashed with anger and concern. "And yet, you didn't even think to involve me? After everything I've shared about this place? Do you think I would have stood idle while you walked into its depths?"

Damian leaned back slightly, his gaze steady on her. "Your story is known to me, Anesthesia. I understand your reasons. But sometimes, we must act first, even when it risks angering others, to ensure we are prepared for the dangers that wait. This is one of those times."

The room fell silent for a moment, the weight of the underground horrors still pressing against their thoughts. Damian's voice broke the quiet, calm but carrying authority.

"Now, let's speak frankly," he said. "You, Anesthesia—why are you here? Why this obsession with the bunker, with Bogston's hidden chambers?"

Anesthesia's hands tightened around her notebook, her gaze dropping for a fraction before meeting his eyes again. "My father came here long ago," she said, voice low but firm. "He never returned. The people in this place... they cover their tracks, hide their experiments, erase the traces of what they do. I am here to expose it, to make the world see what has been hidden for generations. Nothing should remain buried, nothing forgotten."

Damian studied her, absorbing the weight of her words. "And Reed," he said, turning slightly, "you've seen what lies beneath. You've felt its presence. Do you understand what it means to step into this world? To step into a place that does not forgive curiosity or fear?"

Reed swallowed hard, voice steadying despite the lingering dread. "I—I do. I want to understand. I want to uncover the truth, even if it's... terrifying. Even if it changes me."

Anesthesia nodded slowly, a faint acknowledgment of his courage. "Then we are aligned, in purpose if not in method," she said. "But remember—the consequences are real. This place is patient. And Bogston is always watching."

Damian leaned forward, placing his hands lightly on the desk, the lantern between them casting long shadows across the room. "Then we prepare," he said softly but firmly. "We plan carefully, we act cautiously, and we move together. The truth beneath Bogston is not something we stumble upon lightly. It demands patience, precision, and an unflinching resolve."

The three of them sat in silence for a long moment, the weight of the previous night and the promise of what lay ahead pressing heavily against them. Outside, the distant hum of the university

continued, oblivious to the trio who had glimpsed the hidden darkness, and were now bound by its memory and its secrets.

Finally, Damian's voice cut through the quiet, soft but deliberate: "Tonight, we go back. Not recklessly—but deliberately. We follow the paths, we watch, and we learn. The bunker still holds more than skeletons. And if we are to uncover it, we must do so with every step calculated."

Reed nodded, determination flickering through the fear in his eyes. Anesthesia's gaze hardened, the fire in her eyes undimmed. And Damian, as ever, remained steady, the calm center of the storm, preparing them for the night that would bring them deeper into Bogston's shadows.

As Reed and Anesthesia stepped out of Damian's chamber, the dim corridors of Bogston stretched before them, silent and unyielding But the shadows themselves seemed to harbor more than the memory of the past. Behind a set of reinforced concrete bars, hidden in a recessed alcove that Reed and Anesthesia hadn't noticed, a figure lingered. The dim glow of the corridor cast the silhouette in sharp relief, angular and menacing.

Kael. The master brain of the underground operations. He had been watching, silent, assessing, waiting watching .

The evening arrived with a quiet weight, the last lectures of the day fading into the distant corridors of Bogston. Damian's chamber felt different now, heavier, anticipating the descent into the depths once again. Reed and Anesthesia gathered quietly, their eyes betraying fatigue but also resolve.

Damian leaned over the desk, tracing faint lines on a worn map of the underground corridors he had begun sketching. "We go deeper tonight," he said softly, almost to himself. "The first bunkers revealed only what I expected: the skeletons, the evidence of past prisoners. But the source... the true experiments... that is elsewhere. We need to map the passages more carefully. Observe the traffic, the hidden entrances, the traps that may remain."

Reed nodded, eyes scanning the map. "We follow the same paths as last night?" he asked.

"Partly," Damian replied. "But we expand. We need to understand the patterns. These halls have rhythm, even if it is hidden. Every footstep, every scrape of stone—it tells us something. If we move recklessly, we miss it."

Anesthesia's voice broke the quiet. "And if someone else is down there? Someone who doesn't want us wandering?" Her tone was sharp but not accusatory. There was caution beneath the anger.

Damian's gaze met hers. "We expect it. That is why we move together, slowly. Last night was a test of patience. Tonight, we add observation."

They left the chamber under the cover of early evening shadow, their lanterns casting long, wavering beams on the cold stone floors. Each step was measured, deliberate. Reed's hand hovered near the wall, feeling the rough texture of stone, using it as a guide in the darkness. The air smelled of damp and decay, but also of the history embedded in these walls, of secrets long whispered.

As they entered the familiar staircase leading to the lower levels, Damian paused. "Remember," he whispered, "do not speak above a whisper. Every echo carries further than you think."

The first level of the bunker was eerily quiet. The skeletons remained, seated and arranged as before. Reed swallowed hard, the memory of their hollow sockets pressing against him again.

"This is... the same," he murmured.

"Yes," Damian said. "But tonight, we move beyond. We follow the corridors that branch from this place."

Anesthesia adjusted her notebook in her grip. "I hate this feeling. Like someone is always just beyond the wall."

Damian did not answer immediately. He had learned to listen first. And then, as a faint sound reached them—a shuffle, the dragging of heavy boots—they froze.

"Someone is moving," Damian whispered, dropping the lantern slightly to cast longer shadows. "We watch."

The sound drew closer, a professor, unlikely and unexpected, emerged from one of the adjoining passages. His face twisted in confusion as he saw them.

"Professor...?" Reed's voice barely rose above a whisper.

The man's eyes widened. "What are you—?"

Damian stepped forward, quiet and controlled. "We are... checking the lower passages. There are reports of structural issues. Nothing more."

The professor frowned but seemed uncertain, glancing between them. "These areas... are off-limits," he muttered. "You shouldn't—"

Damian's gaze sharpened slightly. "Then you will see why we must." He gestured subtly toward the shadows, the lantern's light flickering. "Please, step aside, quietly. No one else must know."

The professor hesitated, then, sensing the authority and calm in Damian's tone, gave a reluctant nod and retreated. Reed exhaled slowly.

"That was too close," he whispered.

Damian did not respond immediately. He waited until the echoes of the professor's retreat had faded. "Every step is a test," he said finally. "Bogston watches even those who claim authority. Even professors are constrained here."

They continued deeper, the corridors twisting and doubling back, faint drafts brushing past them, carrying whispers of history—drips of water, rustling of fabric, something distant and unidentifiable. They found alcoves of rubble, old storage rooms, and broken machinery—but no living subjects. Nothing suggested ongoing experiments.

Hours seemed to stretch. Reed stumbled once over a loose stone; the lantern wobbled, and shadows danced wildly against the walls. Damian caught it with a steady hand. "Focus on the path, not the fear," he said quietly.

Anesthesia, moving beside him, muttered, "It feels like we are chasing ghosts."

"Maybe we are," Damian replied softly. "But ghosts leave traces. That is what we are looking for."

They explored passage after passage, noting small details—doors that had been welded shut, rusted chains, the smell of decay, faint scorch marks on stone—but all signs pointed away from their initial expectation. No fresh traces of experiments. Nothing alive.

Finally, after what felt like endless corridors, Damian stopped. He crouched, running a finger along the cold stone floor. "We are... not in the right place," he said slowly. "This is history. Old horrors, yes, but not the active center. The experiments... the ones Anesthesia seeks to expose... they are elsewhere. We need to reconsider, plan our approach differently."

Reed sank to his knees, exhausted. "All this... for nothing?"

Damian shook his head, though his eyes did not leave the walls. "Not nothing. We know more now. We understand the patterns, the traps, the risks. Knowledge is never wasted. This bunker... it is a warning, a perimeter, not the source. And that is invaluable."

Anesthesia, notebook pressed to her chest, looked at him sharply. "Then we move forward. Somewhere else. But we do not falter."

The three of them sat in silence for a moment, absorbing the weight of their slow, cautious exploration. The bunker had revealed nothing live, but the shadows, the skeletons, the echoes of movement—they had taught them patience, the art of careful observation, and the certainty that the real source of the experiments lay somewhere deeper, hidden, and more dangerous.

Finally, Damian stood, lantern in hand. "We return, carefully. Map what we have, remember every step. The truth is not here—but it exists. And we will find it."

The corridors of Bogston were silent as they separated for the night. Reed went to his room, moving slowly, still carrying the fatigue of the underground passages in his legs and the echo of hollow eye sockets in his mind. Anesthesia retreated to her quarters, clutching her notebook, flipping through sketches of corridors and alcoves, trying to find patterns in the chaos of stone and shadow.

Damian lingered for a moment in the empty hallway outside his chamber, the lantern's faint glow swinging gently. His fingers traced the railing along the wall, and he closed his eyes, taking in the silence. Each echo of his boots on stone seemed to carry memory, whispers of past horrors that no longer walked the living halls—but still lingered in his mind.

By the time he entered his chamber, the familiar surroundings offered little comfort. He placed the lantern on the desk, its light flickering across scattered papers, maps, and the faint stains of ink from his endless notes. He sank into his chair, resting his head against the cool back, but exhaustion brought no relief. The bunker's dark, endless passages seemed to have followed him, curling around his thoughts like smoke.

Sleep came slowly, reluctantly. Damian's mind churned through the day's observations: the skeletons, the sealed doors, the strange movements, the professor who nearly caught them. His notes were precise, meticulous—but they only highlighted the frustration of the night. No experiments. No live evidence. The real site remained hidden, somewhere beyond the twisted labyrinth of passages he had mapped.

And then, as if drawn by the weight of memory, the dream returned.

It began in familiar darkness—a corridor folding impossibly upon itself, walls stretching and bending in impossible angles. Damian moved cautiously, lantern in hand, but the light flickered as if uncertain whether it should illuminate or conceal. He heard a voice before he saw the figure—a voice he had not expected to hear again.

"Damian... help me..."

He froze. The voice was unmistakable. His father. But how? He had not spoken to him in decades, had not heard his tone since childhood, yet there it was, echoing through the impossible geometry of the dream.

The corridors shifted. One moment, the walls were stone and mortar; the next, they were flesh and shadow, pulsating, alive. Damian ran his hands along the walls, tracing the uneven surfaces, feeling them twist beneath his fingers.

"Father?!" he called, voice trembling. "Where are you? I'll find you!"

"Here... trapped... Damian... save me..." The voice was both near and impossibly distant, echoing as though coming from every corner of the labyrinth at once.

The ground beneath his feet seemed to collapse in places, gaps opening into dark, bottomless chasms. He jumped, landing hard, and the shadows stretched long, wrapping around him like fingers. His chest tightened; his lantern flickered violently, then stabilized, revealing a long hall lined with doors. Each door rattled, squealing on its rusted hinges. Behind them, he swore he could hear scratching, breathing, cries of someone—or something—waiting.

"Father! I'm coming!" Damian shouted, running. Each step felt heavier, the labyrinth resisting his progress. The voice grew louder, more urgent.

"Damian... you must... save me... before it's too late!"

The walls pressed closer, narrowing the passage. He reached out to grab the door handles, trying to force them open, but they would not budge. Shadows seeped from the cracks, whispering, moaning—each syllable indistinct yet filled with dread. Panic rose, unbidden, curling tight around his chest.

He woke with a start, gasping, sweat clinging to his temples. The chamber was silent, the lantern's light dim but steady. Outside, the first faint pre-dawn glow filtered through the curtains, pale and fragile. His heart pounded, his breaths coming in shallow bursts.

Damian sat at the edge of his bed, hands gripping the sides, trying to shake the remnants of the dream. His father's voice lingered in his mind, echoing through the stone corridors of both dream and memory. He could still hear the plea: "Save me... save me..."

The dream left a hollow ache in his chest, a weight that felt older than sleep, older than the bunker itself. It was not just warning or memory—it was a call, a puzzle, a thread linking the past and the present, pulling him toward something deeper.

Damian leaned back, closing his eyes briefly, trying to steady himself. He thought of Reed and Anesthesia, their cautious steps through the maze, the skeletons, the false trails, the professor who had almost revealed them. The labyrinth in his dream and the tunnels beneath Bogston were somehow connected—layers of the same mystery.

And somewhere in that connection, Damian knew, lay the truth. The real experiments, the source of horror and secrecy... it awaited.

He exhaled slowly, letting the faint light from the desk lantern fall across his notes. He could not sleep again—not now. Not with the labyrinth calling him, and his father's voice still echoing in the dark.

Labyrith

FOUR

THE CITY OF BEGINNING 1917

The city where Damian was born was not vast, nor was it poor—it existed in the in-between, a place where the clamor of trade mixed with the quiet traditions of old streets. Narrow lanes twisted into wide boulevards, and the rhythm of life was steady, almost predictable. To a child, however, even its smallest corners felt enormous.

Damian's earliest memory of the place was not of streets or markets, but of his father's voice. It came often in the evenings, after supper, when the city's bustle had softened into the murmur of neighbors and the distant chime of the clock tower. His father, Alaric, would sit by the worn wooden desk near the window, books spread open, spectacles low on his nose. The light from the lamp carved his face into deep lines, shadows making him look older, sterner than he appeared by day.

Damian, no more than six, would sit cross-legged on the floor, watching his father trace words across the page. Sometimes, Alaric would pause, look down, and ask in his measured, thoughtful voice:

"Do you know what the mind fears the most, Damian?"

The boy would shake his head.

"Not darkness. Not pain. It fears being misunderstood. That is why we study it, why we must listen."

He spoke of psychiatry not as science alone but as something near sacred, a duty to unravel the human mind where others saw only chaos. His words were heavy, and at that age, Damian did not understand them fully. But he remembered the way his father's eyes glinted, how he leaned closer to emphasize, "Every labyrinth has a key. The mind is no different."

Sometimes, these conversations would turn strange. Once, Damian awoke late in the night to hear murmurs from the study. He crept to the door, peeking through the gap, and found his father speaking not to anyone visible but to himself—or perhaps to the shadows. His tone was urgent, low, like a doctor taking notes from an unseen patient. Damian stood frozen, torn between fear and curiosity, until Alaric noticed him.

"Couldn't sleep?" his father asked, his voice soft again. The boy nodded, hesitant. Alaric smiled faintly, though there was a tightness in his jaw. "Then sit, and I'll tell you how thought can become a prison if we do not watch it carefully."

That night, Damian listened to stories not of fairy kings or warriors, but of men trapped in their own illusions, women who mistook whispers of their minds for voices from the divine. His father spoke with compassion but also fascination. To Damian, the stories felt haunting. He went to bed restless, the images curling into dreams.

There were incidents, too, that etched themselves into memory. Once, while walking through the market with his father, Damian watched as a man collapsed in the street, thrashing, frothing at the mouth. The crowd recoiled, muttering of curses. But Alaric pushed forward, kneeling beside the stranger. He placed a firm hand on the man's chest, steadying him, whispering calm words until the seizure passed. Then, turning to the onlookers, Alaric said sharply, "Not demons. Not curses. The mind and body are one, and both can falter. You fear what you do not understand."

Damian never forgot the way the crowd fell silent, the shame in their lowered eyes, nor the way his father walked on afterward as if nothing had happened.

At home, though, things were not always steady. There were nights when Alaric grew restless, pacing the small study, muttering fragments of medical terms, theories, or simply silence stretched too long. Damian's mother, weary but patient, would usher him away, whispering, "Your father carries too much in his mind. Let him be."

But Damian lingered at doors, in shadows, listening. He began to sense that his father was not merely fascinated by psychiatry—he was haunted by it. And in those early years, the labyrinth began to form in Damian's own dreams: corridors without end, shadows that looked too much like his father's figure calling from within.

The house Damian grew up in was not large, but to him it felt like an entire world. Its walls carried the faint smell of old paper and varnished wood, and every creak of the floorboards had a voice of its own. There was the long corridor that led from the entrance to the study, lined with portraits of stern-faced ancestors, and a narrow staircase that curled upward into dim-lit bedrooms. Damian often traced his fingers along the railings, feeling the grooves carved by years of touch.

The courtyard was his favorite place. Paved with uneven stones and shaded by a lone tamarind tree, it was where he spent long afternoons chasing shadows. In the evenings, his mother would sit on the steps with her sewing, while his father, Alaric, paced slowly, speaking half to himself, half to his son.

"Every mind," Alaric would begin, hands clasped behind his back, "is like this courtyard. Open to the sun, yes, but also filled with corners where shadows hide. To understand someone, Damian, you must not just look at the light—they show that easily. You must search the corners."

Damian frowned once, plucking at the tamarind pods that had fallen to the ground. "But what if the shadows frighten them?"

Alaric paused, crouched down, and met his son's eyes. "Then you do not frighten them further. You bring a lamp. Quietly. Patiently.

That is the duty of those who study the mind."

School was another world entirely. Damian attended the old brick schoolhouse at the edge of the market district, where classrooms smelled of chalk and ink, and the echo of boys reciting lessons filled the air. He was not the loudest among his peers—if anything, he spoke little—but he watched everything.

One day, when Damian was about seven, a teacher asked the class to draw what frightened them most. The other children drew snakes, storms, wild dogs, even ghosts. Damian's paper showed something different: a man standing inside a winding maze, the paths stretching endlessly in every direction. The teacher frowned.

"What is this, Damian?"

"The mind," he answered simply.

The classroom erupted with laughter. But when his father came for the monthly meeting and saw the drawing pinned on the wall, Alaric only placed his hand on Damian's shoulder and said quietly, "Good. You're learning to see what others ignore."

There were smaller incidents, the kind that etched themselves into his memory not because they were loud but because they lingered.

Once, walking home from school, Damian noticed a boy crying near the steps of a bakery. His knee was scraped, blood oozing. Most children hurried past, wrinkling their noses. Damian crouched beside him.

"Does it hurt much?" he asked softly.

The boy nodded, hiccupping.

Damian tore a strip from his own handkerchief and tied it carefully around the wound, mimicking what he had seen his father do. Then he added, almost repeating Alaric's tone, "It will heal. The body always remembers how."

When he returned home with a dirt-stained uniform and no handkerchief, his mother sighed, scolding gently. But his father only listened as Damian recounted the story. Later, Alaric bent down and whispered, "Compassion is sharper than knowledge, Damian. Never lose it."

Nights were often the most vivid. The city would fall into silence, but Damian's dreams rarely did. He would find himself wandering through corridors made of stone, their walls dripping with shadows. Sometimes he heard his father's voice calling from within, calm but distant: "Every labyrinth has a key…" Other times, the corridors would twist until they became the study at home, books whispering from their shelves, pages fluttering though no wind touched them.

In the mornings, he would sit quietly at breakfast, pushing his bread around his plate. His mother noticed, asking, "Dreams again?" Damian would nod.

"Your father fills your head with too many thoughts," she muttered, half in jest, though her eyes betrayed concern. "A boy should dream of play, not of endless halls."

But Alaric only looked across the table, serious as always. "Better he learns early, Liora. The world will not wait for him to be ready."

There was a ritual Damian had come to expect in the evenings. After supper, when the house grew hushed and the neighbors' chatter drifted faintly through the thin windows, Alaric would summon him to the study. The room smelled of ink, old leather, and the faint metallic tang of the oil lamp. Books crowded every shelf, and stacks of loose papers lay like small towers around the desk.

Alaric would sit, spectacles perched low, while Damian curled on the floor, knees to his chest. Sometimes his father read aloud—fragments of medical journals, case studies, notes from foreign physicians. Other times, he spoke as if to an unseen audience, and Damian became both student and witness.

"Do you know," Alaric began one night, "why madness frightens men more than death?"

Damian shook his head.

"Because death is certain. It ends the story. Madness..."—his father tapped the desk with two fingers—"madness rewrites the story while you are still inside it. It turns you into a stranger to yourself."

The boy's brow furrowed. "So can you fix it? Can you make them... themselves again?"

Alaric leaned back, eyes narrowing in thought. "Sometimes. But not always. You see, Damian, the mind is not like a broken bone. It doesn't always heal the way we want. But even when we cannot cure, we can listen. And listening, my boy, is sometimes more powerful than all the medicines in the world."

Damian tucked this away silently, though he wasn't sure he understood.

There were nights when his father's words carried a different edge. Once, Alaric sat at the desk with a trembling hand, pen scratching furiously across a page. Damian crept closer, peering at the inked lines—circles, arrows, words that blurred together: labyrinth, voices, perception.

"Father?" Damian whispered.

Alaric flinched, then quickly covered the page with his palm. He forced a smile, though his eyes betrayed fatigue. "Still awake?"

"I heard you talking."

"Talking, yes. Thinking aloud." He hesitated, then drew Damian closer. "Remember this, son. A man must never be afraid to wrestle with his own mind. But he must also know when to rest, or the mind begins to wrestle back."

Damian nodded, though the words sat heavy in him.

The city itself became part of his lessons. On quiet mornings, Alaric would take him walking through the market. Stalls burst with spices and fabrics, their scents thick in the air—cardamom, turmeric, fresh-cut wood. But Alaric rarely lingered at goods. His eyes watched people.

"Look there," he whispered once, nodding to a woman bargaining too fiercely for a sack of grain. "See her hands? Trembling. Her voice, too sharp. That is not greed—it is fear. She has mouths to feed, and coins enough for only one more day."

Damian studied her carefully, realizing for the first time that people's faces hid stories.

Another time, they passed a beggar rocking back and forth, muttering fragments to himself. The crowd avoided him, some tossing coins without looking. Alaric crouched, placing a hand on the man's shoulder. "What do you hear?" he asked gently.

The beggar's eyes darted wildly. "Whispers. Always whispers."

"Not demons," Alaric murmured, standing again, more to Damian than the man. "Not curses. Only a mind turned inward too far."

Damian's small hand tightened around his father's coat. "Can he be helped?"

Alaric looked down, expression unreadable. "Perhaps. But not by those who choose to look away."

At home, his mother often watched these lessons with unease. One evening, when Damian sat copying letters by candlelight, Liora bent close and whispered, "You do not have to carry all your father's burdens, Damian. You are a child. You may run, laugh, be foolish."

He looked at her earnestly. "But Father says the world will not wait for me to be ready."

Her hands stilled over the sewing in her lap. She glanced toward the study, where Alaric's voice drifted faintly. "Your father is right... but sometimes he forgets that childhood is also a gift." She kissed the top of his head softly. "Do not lose yours too quickly."

Damian pressed the words into his memory, though part of him already felt that childhood was slipping—traded piece by piece for the weight of shadows, books, and labyrinths.

The days in Damian's house moved with a rhythm, but beneath it ran a quiet strain—like a note too low for most ears.

Some evenings, Alaric's voice filled the study with calm instruction, but other nights the tone shifted. He would pace, muttering under his breath, scribbling diagrams of circles, arrows, and winding shapes. Damian would sit still, watching, the oil lamp throwing long shadows against the wall.

Once, Alaric stopped suddenly in front of him. His eyes were sharp, almost fevered. "Do you know why men build labyrinths, Damian?"

The boy hesitated. "To... get lost?"

A faint smile crossed his father's face. "No. To hide something. A labyrinth is never built for wandering—it is built for guarding. Remember that."

The words carved themselves into Damian's thoughts. That night, he dreamed again of endless corridors, but this time there was a door at the center, locked, and someone calling from the other side.

The courtyard, once a place of play, slowly became another place of lessons. Alaric would stand under the tamarind tree with his son, speaking in the same calm, deliberate voice.

"One day, Damian, you will see that people wear masks. They smile, they laugh, they even embrace you—but behind it, there are shadows they will never show. To see those shadows is both a gift and a curse."

Damian frowned. "Then why see them at all?"

Alaric crouched, resting a hand on his son's shoulder. "Because if you do not, someone else will use them. And the world is crueler than you know."

From the kitchen steps, Liora called softly, "Enough, Alaric. He is only a boy."

But Alaric did not move. His gaze stayed fixed on Damian. "The sooner he learns, the stronger he will stand."

Damian nodded, though part of him wished he could simply chase shadows again, instead of studying them.

School grew heavier as well. Damian noticed how quickly his classmates grew tired of him. He spoke differently, sometimes repeating his father's phrases without realizing it. Once, when a boy mocked him for being quiet, Damian answered calmly:

"You are loud because you are afraid of silence."

The classroom fell silent, the other children staring. The teacher scolded him for insolence, but the boy who had mocked him avoided him after that.

When he told his father, Alaric only nodded approvingly. "Words are weapons, Damian. But wield them carefully—they cut deeper than steel."

His mother, hearing this, grew worried. "He is seven, Alaric," she said that evening, her voice low, strained. "Not a soldier."

Alaric's reply was simple. "He must be ready before the world requires it."

There were tender moments too, though they carried their own weight. On one rainy afternoon, Damian sat at the window, watching water stream down the glass. Alaric joined him, kneeling beside the chair.

"What do you see, son?"

"Just the rain."

"Look closer." His father pointed. "Each drop follows a path, twisting, turning, splitting, but always pulled downward. That is the mind. Always moving, never still, but drawn toward something—toward its center."

Damian whispered, "And if it loses its path?"

Alaric looked at him with an intensity that made the boy shiver. "Then it drowns itself."

The words sank into him like stones, and even years later, Damian would remember the sound of rain as something heavier than comfort.

It was during his eighth year that Damian first noticed the boy who would change the rhythm of his days. His classmates had long since learned to keep their distance from him—whispering that he was odd, that he spoke like an old man in a child's body. He had stopped expecting company, stopped looking for someone to sit beside him when lessons ended.

But then came Choe.

Choe was not the brightest boy in the class, nor the strongest. He was wiry, restless, with a crooked smile that seemed to bloom even when no one else found reason for it. Where others mimicked and mocked, Choe only watched. He did not nod in agreement when Damian spoke in his quiet, measured voice about silence, about fear, about shadows people hid. He would frown, tilt his head, and then shrug as if saying, You're strange, but maybe that's all right.

One afternoon, when the teacher dismissed the class, Damian found himself again alone, stacking his slate and chalk with careful precision. The others had already scattered, their laughter spilling into the courtyard like birds taking flight. But Choe lingered at the doorway.

"You always take so long," he said, not unkindly.

Damian looked up, startled. "I like things in order."

Choe walked back inside, leaning against a desk. "You talk too much like a grown man. Nobody likes that."

Damian felt the familiar pinch in his chest. "I know."

But then Choe grinned. "I didn't say I don't like it. Just that nobody else does."

The boy's candor was disarming. Damian blinked, unsure if it was an insult or a gift.

"Why are you talking to me?" he asked at last.

Choe shrugged, slinging his satchel over one shoulder. "Because you're interesting. Everyone else says the same things, thinks the same things. You... don't. It's like you see something different. I don't understand it, but I don't mind."

For a long moment Damian studied him, trying to measure the weight of those words. No one had ever spoken to him like that—not with pity, not with derision, but with plain honesty.

That evening, when he told his father about the boy, Alaric only listened quietly, tapping his fingers on the desk. "If he does not fear your difference, then he is either very brave... or very foolish."

Damian frowned. "Which one is he?"

His father's lips curved faintly. "Time will tell. But remember, Damian—friendship is also a mirror. It will show you not only who they are, but who you are."

The next day, Choe sat beside Damian at lunch. No one else dared question it. The air around them shifted, faintly, like the first note of a new song.

Damian, for the first time in his short life, did not feel entirely alone.

At first, their friendship was quiet, almost tentative. Choe did not demand much, nor did Damian know how to give much. They would sit side by side, sharing the same bench while the others huddled in their usual groups. Sometimes they spoke; sometimes they didn't.

It was enough.

One afternoon, as the sun slanted golden through the classroom shutters, Choe nudged Damian's arm. "Why do you always write so neatly? Even when it's just sums, you make the numbers look like little soldiers standing in line."

Damian hesitated, glancing down at his slate. "Because if they're not in order, they… bother me."

"Bother you how?"

"They feel wrong. Like they're whispering."

Choe raised a brow, then laughed—not in mockery, but in a way that lifted the heaviness of the words. "Whispering numbers? You're strange, Damian. But it makes you different. I like different."

Damian, unused to such easy acceptance, only gave a small nod. Yet later, when he lay in bed, those words replayed in his mind like a lullaby: I like different.

Their bond deepened in the small corners of the day. In the courtyard, while the others chased each other with sticks, Choe and Damian sat under the neem tree, scratching shapes into the dust. Choe drew crooked houses, clumsy suns, faces with wide grins. Damian drew spirals, winding corridors, doors with locks.

Choe squinted at them. "You always make everything look like a maze. Why?"

Damian answered quietly, "Because there's always something hidden inside."

Choe thought about that, then smirked. "Then one day I'll find the center of your maze."

The words were light, careless—but Damian felt them lodge somewhere deep, as if Choe had unknowingly spoken a promise.

Not everyone welcomed this friendship.

One boy, Maren, who often led the others in mocking Damian, scoffed when he saw them together. "Why sit with him, Choe? He's cursed. Talks like a madman."

Choe's grin vanished. He stepped closer, eyes flashing. "Better cursed than stupid."

The courtyard fell silent. Maren flushed, fists clenched, but he turned away under the weight of Choe's boldness.

Later, Damian asked, "Why did you defend me?"

"Because you're my friend," Choe said simply, as if it were the most obvious thing in the world.

Damian had no reply. But inside, something that had long been hollow stirred, filling with warmth.

At home, Liora noticed the change in her son. She saw how his eyes softened when he spoke of Choe, how his voice—usually so careful and weighted—carried a lighter thread.

One evening, she whispered to Alaric, "Do you see it? He's happier."

Alaric leaned back in his chair, unreadable. "Happiness is fleeting. But the lessons he learns will last."

Liora shook her head gently. "And perhaps the lesson he needs most is that he doesn't always have to walk alone."

Alaric said nothing more, but his fingers tapped restlessly against the desk, as though measuring a rhythm only he could hear.

The weeks that followed carried a subtle shift. Where once Damian had walked home alone, his satchel pressed neatly to his side, now Choe often joined him. Their paths overlapped—Choe's house lay two streets beyond, and though it added steps to his way, he never seemed to mind.

Sometimes they spoke of school, though Choe's words tumbled out quick and careless, skipping from one thought to another. Damian listened, answering only when pressed. Other times, they walked in silence, the sound of their footsteps syncing, the quiet between them not heavy but whole.

One evening as they passed the bakery, Choe suddenly stopped. "Wait here." Before Damian could reply, he darted inside, reemerging with a small paper-wrapped sweet. He thrust it into Damian's hands.

"Why?" Damian asked, startled.

Choe shrugged, grinning. "Because you look like someone who forgets what sugar tastes like."

Damian stood there, the weight of the sweet in his palm stranger than any gift he had known. When he bit into it later, the grainy sweetness lingered long after, as if tying the day to memory.

But with warmth came questions.

One night, as Alaric laid out his papers across the desk, Damian mentioned softly, "Choe walked home with me again."

Alaric did not look up. "And what did you learn from him?"

Damian blinked. "Learn?"

"Every person teaches you something. If not about the world, then about yourself."

Damian hesitated. "He makes me laugh."

At that, Alaric's pen stilled. Slowly, he raised his gaze, studying his son. "Laughter is a fragile teacher. Do not mistake it for wisdom."

From her place near the window, Liora spoke firmly, "But laughter is also life, Alaric. Let him keep it."

The silence that followed was taut, stretched like a string between them. Damian sat still, the sweetness of the bakery treat still lingering on his tongue, and wondered which of them was right.

The friendship grew in fits and bursts. Choe would pull him into mischief—climbing the half-broken wall by the well, sneaking into the old watchtower at the market's edge, daring Damian to race him barefoot across the courtyard stones. Damian resisted at first, uneasy, but Choe's laughter was a tide hard to fight against.

"Come on," Choe called one afternoon, hand outstretched from the top of the wall. "The world won't wait for you to climb."

The words echoed something his father had once said, yet they carried none of the weight—only the sparkle of challenge. For the first time, Damian reached out, fingers catching Choe's wrist, and pulled himself upward.

From the top, the town spread before them—rooftops, smoke curling from chimneys, the distant glint of the river. Choe grinned. "See? Doesn't it feel different from here?"

Damian nodded slowly, his heart pounding with more than fear. "Yes... different."

And though he did not say it aloud, he knew: it felt alive.

It was late in the season when the mornings began to carry a sharper chill, the kind that made breath visible in pale wisps. The schoolyard filled as always with noise—children chasing each other, the scrape of slates on stone steps, the faint clatter of the market drifting in.

It was on such a morning that Damian first noticed her.

She sat alone at the edge of the courtyard wall, a book balanced on her knees. Her hair was tied back hastily, a few strands falling across her face as she read. The other children didn't bother her, but neither did they invite her. She seemed to exist on the margin, quiet but unbothered, as if she had chosen her distance.

Choe spotted her before Damian did. "That's Miska," he whispered one afternoon, leaning against Damian's desk. "She came from the northern quarter last month. Doesn't talk to anyone much."

Damian glanced toward her, curious. Something about the way she turned pages—slow, deliberate—reminded him of evenings in his father's study.

"Should we talk to her?" Choe asked, already grinning as if he knew the answer.

Damian hesitated. The idea of approaching anyone still filled him with unease. But Choe didn't wait for an answer. That afternoon, as the bell rang, he marched up to where Miska sat and tapped the book in her hands.

"What are you reading?" he asked brightly.

She looked up, startled. Her eyes, dark and steady, flicked from Choe to Damian standing a step behind him. "Stories," she said simply.

"Stories about what?"

"About a traveler. He gets lost in a forest."

Choe laughed. "Then Damian will like it. He's always drawing mazes."

Damian flushed, but Miska tilted her head, curious rather than mocking. "Mazes?"

Choe nudged him forward. Damian shifted uncomfortably, then pulled a folded scrap of paper from his satchel. On it was a spiral he had drawn during arithmetic, twisting inward to a locked gate at the center.

Miska studied it in silence, then looked up. "It's not a maze," she said softly. "It's a secret."

The words startled Damian. For the first time, someone had named what he himself had never been able to. He met her gaze, and in that moment, something wordless passed between them—a recognition, fragile but undeniable.

From that day, the three of them began to linger together. It was not immediate; at first, Miska remained reserved, speaking little while Choe carried the noise between them. But slowly, as days stretched into weeks, their silences grew comfortable.

On the playground, Choe would leap across stones, daring them to follow. Damian would calculate the safest path. Miska, quiet but quick, often outpaced them both.

"You're supposed to wait for us," Choe complained once, panting as she landed lightly on the far side of the well.

"I don't wait," she replied matter-of-factly, brushing dust from her hands. Then, turning to Damian, she added, "But you don't need to either."

Choe laughed at her bluntness, but Damian carried the words with him long after, the way he carried all things.

At home, Liora noticed the change again. "Now there are three," she remarked one evening as Damian sat sketching at the table. "Your world grows larger."

Alaric, from behind his papers, merely muttered, "Numbers do not grow clearer by adding more of them. They only grow more complicated."

But Damian was already lost in thought—his sketch that night no longer a solitary labyrinth, but three paths crossing at a single point before spiraling onward.

The days folded into one another, and with them, a rhythm began to form—three shadows always somewhere near each other, overlapping like threads being woven without their knowing.

In the mornings, Miska would sometimes wait by the old stone arch near the market lane, her book tucked under her arm. Choe arrived loud and winded, always late, claiming he had been caught in some adventure that sounded half-made. Damian, steady as the clock tower's toll, would be the one who noticed the smallest things: the way Miska's braid frayed at the edges, the scrape on Choe's knee he never mentioned, the scent of roasted chestnuts drifting faintly from the stalls.

It was Choe who tied them together, noisy and insistent, always dragging them into motion. It was Miska who grounded them, her silences never cold but heavy with thought. And Damian—he was the bridge, watching, listening, carrying what the others left unsaid.

One afternoon, they wandered beyond the schoolyard into the crumbling remains of an old storage shed. Sunlight slipped through broken beams, casting long stripes across the floor. Dust hung in the air, glittering when they stirred it.

Choe leapt onto a barrel and declared, "This is our place now. A fortress."

Miska raised an eyebrow. "A fortress full of mice."

Sure enough, a faint scuttling echoed from the shadows. Damian tensed, but Choe only laughed. "Then they're our soldiers."

Damian knelt, brushing dust off a patch of the wooden floor where the boards warped in strange patterns. He traced the uneven lines with his finger, half to himself. "It looks like... paths."

Miska crouched beside him, her gaze sharp. "No. It looks like it's hiding something."

Choe's eyes brightened. "Then we'll find it!"

Together, they pried at the boards until one came loose. Beneath it lay nothing but earth—hard-packed, unremarkable. Choe sighed dramatically. "Every secret ends in dirt."

But Miska didn't look disappointed. She pressed her palm against the cool earth, almost as if listening. "Not every secret shows itself at once."

Her words settled into Damian like a seed. He said nothing, only placed the board back carefully, aligning it with a precision neither of the others bothered with.

Evenings at home, Alaric began to notice the change in his son's sketches. The mazes that once wound solitary now had figures—two small shapes alongside the central one.

"You've let others into your design," Alaric remarked one night, his voice unreadable.

Damian didn't answer at first, shading carefully around a path. Then, without looking up, he asked, "Does that make it weaker?"

Alaric set his pen down, considering. "Not weaker. More dangerous. Every bond is another path to guard."

From the hearth, Liora's voice carried, warm but firm. "Or another path that guards him."

Alaric said nothing further, but Damian felt the tension between their words, like the walls of a maze pressing closer.

The fortress of the shed became their refuge. They brought scraps of chalk to mark the boards, old jars to trap fireflies, half-stale bread to share.

Once, Choe dared them to sneak out after dark. Damian resisted—he always did—but Miska's calm eyes rested on him, steady, as if asking without words whether he trusted her. He went.

The three of them sat on the shed roof that night, the stars spilling wider than any labyrinth could hold. Choe pointed out constellations, most of them made-up. Miska listened, but her gaze stayed fixed, searching deeper, as though she could read truths written between the stars.

Damian sat silent, his heart restless. He didn't say it aloud, but for the first time he wondered if the world outside his father's maps and diagrams was larger than he had ever believed—and if these two, noisy and quiet, were part of what would show him how to walk it.

Days passed, and with them came the subtle push and pull that marks every friendship, even among children. For the first time, Damian experienced not only the comfort of companionship but also the friction that accompanies it.

One crisp afternoon, the three of them were back in the fortress-shed, sketching maps in the dust. Choe, impatient as ever, had grown restless and started drawing haphazard lines over Damian's carefully measured paths.

"Stop that!" Damian snapped, his voice sharper than he intended.

Choe laughed, waving a hand. "Relax! I'm making it more interesting. Your lines are too... serious."

Miska frowned, setting her book aside. "You're ruining it, Choe. Look at him—he's precise. It matters to him."

Choe turned to her, mock indignation on his face. "And since when do you care about precision, Miska? You always disappear into your books!"

Damian's hands shook slightly, tracing the disrupted maze. "You both... you both just—" He stopped, exhaling. "You don't care."

For a moment, silence fell, heavy and brittle. Choe sat back, the grin gone. Miska's eyes, usually calm, were sharp, almost accusing. Damian felt a strange swell of frustration—anger at them, at himself, at the quiet house waiting for him in the distance.

Finally, Choe's voice softened, almost sheepishly. "I... I didn't mean to ruin it. I just thought—" He hesitated, glancing at Damian. "—that maybe you'd like it messy sometimes."

Miska's hand landed on Damian's shoulder. "He's saying sorry. Are you going to let him off the hook?"

Damian blinked, staring at the two of them. He wanted to stay angry, to retreat into the neat corridors of his mind, but the warmth of the afternoon, the sunlight spilling across the shed floor, reminded him that some things were worth more than stubbornness.

Slowly, he nodded. "Fine. But next time... ask first."

Choe's grin returned, tentative but bright. "Deal. But you have to admit, a little chaos is fun."

Damian gave a small smile, though it carried the weight of lessons learned: that friendship, like the labyrinths he drew, had paths that twisted unexpectedly, and the turns were sometimes as important as the straight lines.

Other fights were smaller but just as sharp. One day, Miska wanted to linger in the library longer than usual, and Choe, growing impatient, dragged Damian out before she was ready. She scowled at them both.

"You never wait!" she exclaimed, snapping her book shut. "Always running off somewhere!"

Choe huffed, throwing his hands up. "We waited five minutes! That's enough for me!"

Damian, standing in the hallway, tried to mediate. "Miska... it's okay. He didn't know—"

She turned on him, eyes blazing, and Damian flinched. "You think this is okay? You always pick sides!"

The tension simmered, and for the first time, Damian felt the suffocating knot of indecision: wanting peace, yet caught between two strong wills. He wandered quietly outside, leaving Choe and Miska to simmer in their frustration.

By evening, however, the quiet worked its magic. Choe approached Damian first, crouching near the old tamarind tree. "Hey... I didn't mean to—y'know—push you away from her."

Damian nodded slowly. "It's... okay."

Miska came next, settling beside them. She said nothing at first, only touched the small wound on Choe's knee—he had tripped during a game earlier—and smiled faintly. "I still don't like you rushing things," she said softly, her voice gentle now.

Choe laughed quietly. "Fine. I'll try to wait. Not forever. But for now."

Damian felt a strange relief settle over him, a warmth that came not from victory but from the fragile, quiet reconciliation that only the three of them understood.

From then on, their small arguments became part of the rhythm of their friendship. Fights flared, tempers snapped, silence stretched—but each time, they found a way back. Choe's exuberance would soften, Miska's sternness would bend, and Damian's careful mind learned when to yield, when to speak, and when to simply observe.

They were learning, in those slow, winding days, that friendship was itself a labyrinth—full of twists, dead-ends, missteps—but that sometimes, the path through chaos was the one that revealed the most.

The changes in Damian did not escape Alaric's notice. He watched from his study window one evening as Damian, Choe, and Miska raced across the courtyard, laughter spilling like spilled ink. He set down his papers and stepped outside, the shadows of the tamarind tree stretching long across the ground.

"Damian," he called, voice low but carrying weight, and the boy froze mid-step, the other two halting as well.

"Yes, Father?" Damian said, trying to sound composed, though his chest thumped.

Alaric's eyes, sharp as always, softened only slightly. "I see you spend more time chasing shadows in the sun than attending to the truths that lie in the darkness."

Choe, ever bold, opened his mouth, but Damian raised a hand, silencing him.

Alaric's gaze sharpened further. "Friendship is a fine thing, if it teaches you to grow. But I fear your attentions wander too freely. You are beginning to mimic others, losing the discipline required to see what is hidden beneath the world's surface. And that... that will cost you."

Damian swallowed hard, feeling the old familiar tension coil in his chest. "I—I'm not losing anything. I'm learning... too."

"Learning?" Alaric's voice rose, controlled but firm. "Learning is not laughter, not frivolity, not the foolish companionship of those who cannot see beyond their own noses. Discipline is the mind's architecture. You cannot build mazes in dust and call it wisdom."

Miska shifted beside Damian, her dark eyes cautious, while Choe's lips pressed together, sensing the unspoken tension. Damian opened his mouth but Alaric held up a hand.

"You have time enough to learn about others later. Now, your task is the truth. Nothing else."

That evening, the house felt heavier than usual. Damian lingered in the kitchen while Liora prepared the supper. She noticed the tight line of his shoulders, the way he traced the edge of the table with his fingers.

"Your father was harsh today," she said softly, placing a hand on his shoulder. "He worries... but not in the way you think."

Damian looked up, frustration flashing in his gaze. "He thinks having friends distracts me. He doesn't understand that they make me... feel more."

Liora knelt beside him. "He wants you to see the world in one way. That's all he knows. But seeing the world differently doesn't make you weak, Damian. You can carry both—the truth he teaches and the warmth they bring."

"But he..." Damian faltered. "He said... laughter and companionship are frivolous. That they will cost me the lessons I need."

His mother's eyes were gentle but firm. "No, Damian. They do not cost you. They teach in ways he cannot measure. You have to learn to balance, to listen to both voices."

The next evening, Alaric approached the topic again, standing over Damian's desk where he sketched spirals and lines. Damian flinched as his father's shadow fell across the page.

"Why is your work interrupted?" Alaric asked, voice steady. "Your drawings now include them—the other children. You are... distracted."

Damian drew the line thicker, holding the pencil tight. "They help me understand paths, Father. They show me angles and turns I could not see alone."

Alaric's jaw tightened. "Do you think you are different from all men simply because you carry companions at your side? Wisdom is solitary. Insight is lonely. Friendship... is a distraction."

Damian's pen faltered, hovering over the page. "But sometimes," he said slowly, "even the darkest labyrinth needs a hand to guide you, or someone to walk beside you."

Alaric's eyes narrowed, as if measuring the boy for weakness, for folly. "Then you risk losing yourself in what is not real. In what is... merely comforting."

Damian's chest tightened. "Then what if comfort... makes me stronger?"

The room fell silent, save for the scratch of the pencil against the page. Alaric did not answer immediately. Finally, he straightened, voice low but carrying its old finality. "You will learn soon enough, Damian. You will see where loyalty, distraction, and truth collide—and you must choose which path endures."

Later, when Liora tucked him into bed, she whispered, "You do not need to choose yet. Let your heart measure, let your mind weigh. The world outside your father's lessons is wide... and you are not alone there, either."

Damian closed his eyes, thinking of Choe's laughter and Miska's steady gaze. The labyrinths on his page seemed to pulse, twisting in on themselves, as if the paths of friendship and the solitary corridors of thought were both winding toward the same hidden center.

One evening, Damian lingered near the window, staring at the darkened courtyard where he had once raced with Choe and Miska. Liora approached quietly, her hand resting on his arm.

"They will wait for you," she whispered. "You are not leaving them behind—you are simply holding onto what you need to hold for yourself right now."

"I can't," Damian said, voice tight. "Father... he says I cannot. He says I am wasting my time. He says..." His words broke, the weight of them catching in his throat.

Liora knelt beside him, her presence steady, a small island of warmth. "He speaks from fear, Damian, not understanding. Fear that you may stray from the path he values. But you are not the path he walks. You are you, and that matters."

The days stretched long, and Damian's defiance grew quiet but firm. He began to avoid the areas of the house where Alaric spent his evenings, retreating to his room or the small study where only his mother's gentle eyes could reach him. Alaric noticed the withdrawal, his face hardening further.

"You are becoming secretive," Alaric said one night, voice low and cold as he stepped into the doorway. "You hide your mind, your work... your thoughts. Do you imagine that you can learn truth while keeping your distractions close?"

Damian met his father's gaze, steady now, his voice calm despite the tension in his chest. "I am learning, Father. Not from you, not alone—but from what I live, what I see, and who I trust."

Alaric's eyes flared briefly, then hardened. "Do not speak to me of trust. It is a luxury the wise cannot afford."

"I will not give up my trust for fear," Damian replied, the words falling with the weight of certainty. "Even if it angers you."

The room went still. Liora, standing in the shadows near the door, felt the delicate balance snap. She stepped forward, her voice firm, unwavering.

"Alaric, enough. Your son is not a shadow to be molded. He is alive, he is learning, and he needs your understanding—your guidance, yes—but not your control."

Alaric's jaw clenched, a slow, deliberate tension that Damian had learned to recognize. "He is my son. I will guide him as I must."

"And I will protect him as I must," Liora said, eyes meeting his with unyielding resolve. "But you will not break him in the name of your lessons."

The words hung in the air, a line drawn between them. Damian felt a mixture of relief and fear ripple through him. For the first time, he sensed that the quiet, unseen support of his mother was more powerful than the rigid authority of his father.

In the following days, the rift widened irreparably. Damian no longer spoke openly with Alaric, his responses clipped, careful, measured to avoid argument. Alaric, for his part, no longer pressed him directly, retreating to his studies with a quiet frustration that the boy could feel but not touch. The house, once filled with a shared rhythm of learning and instruction, now carried two separate beats: one of stern, distant control, and one of quiet, steadfast encouragement from Liora.

Damian's world contracted and expanded at once: the fortress-shed, the courtyard, the paths with Choe and Miska—they became his private corridors, the places where he could breathe, think, and laugh. Alaric's lessons remained, precise and unyielding, but they were no longer the sole paths in his mind. He had chosen, silently, the labyrinth of his own making, and in it, he would walk alone when necessary, yet never without the invisible support of those who truly understood him.

By the time winter settled in, a cold, sharp air filling the town, Damian and Alaric had ceased speaking except for necessities. Words of reprimand and defense were replaced by measured silence, a chasm between father and son that even the warmth of the hearth could not bridge. Liora remained, steady and unwavering, the quiet center Damian returned to when the world outside threatened to unbalance him.

And in that silence, Damian realized something profound: the truth he sought would not be handed to him alone. Strength could be solitary, yes—but wisdom, and the courage to live it, often required a different kind of lesson—one given not from fear or authority, but from trust and choice.

FIVE

THE CITY OF DESTINY

That evening, the house was unusually still. The wind pressed gently against the shutters, carrying with it the brittle scent of winter smoke. Damian sat at his desk, fingers hovering over his old sketches . He could feel the weight of something pressing against his chest—an urge he could no longer keep folded away.

At last, he pushed back his chair and walked, steady but hesitant, to the study. The door stood open, the golden glow of the oil lamp spilling across the hall. Alaric sat at his desk, writing, the sharp scratch of his quill the only sound in the room.

Damian lingered in the doorway, heart hammering. "Father," he said softly.

Alaric did not look up. "What is it?"

Damian stepped forward, his shadow stretching long across the floorboards. "Next week is... my birthday. I will turn thirteen."

The quill paused. Alaric's head tilted slightly, though he still did not raise his eyes. "I am aware."

Damian swallowed. The silence pressed heavy, but he forced the words out. "I want to invite Choe and Miska. To the house. To be here... with me."

Now Alaric did look up, the lamp catching the hard lines of his face. His eyes narrowed, weighing the words as though they were pieces of stone laid before him. "Invite them?" he repeated. His tone was neither anger nor approval, but a quiet, incredulous restraint.

"Yes." Damian tried to steady his voice. "They are my friends. I want them here."

Alaric leaned back in his chair, folding his hands. "And what will they bring into this house? Laughter? Nonsense? More of the distractions you already cling to?"

Damian's chest tightened, but he stood straighter. "They will bring themselves. And that matters to me."

Alaric's jaw shifted slightly, a slow grinding movement. "This house is not a playground, Damian. It is a place for discipline, for study. Do you wish to invite chaos into it?"

Before Damian could speak, another voice broke the tension. Liora stood at the threshold, her hands folded before her apron, her eyes soft but firm. "Perhaps," she said, "a little laughter will not poison the walls."

Alaric's gaze flicked to her, his expression unreadable. "You would encourage this?"

"I would encourage balance," Liora replied, stepping into the room. She placed a hand lightly on Damian's shoulder, grounding him. "Our son is thirteen. Thirteen, Alaric. Childhood does not wait for the weight of truth. It slips by if not held. Let him have this—let him mark his years not only with lessons and silence, but with moments he will remember."

Damian looked at his father, forcing the tremor from his voice. "I'm not asking to abandon your lessons. Only... for them to stand beside me. Just for one day."

The study fell into a long, brittle silence. The lamp hissed faintly, its flame flickering as if even it waited. Alaric's eyes shifted between his son and his wife, the hard edges of his face caught between resistance and something quieter, deeper—an unspoken recognition that he was outnumbered not by argument, but by something harder to break: love.

Finally, he exhaled, slow and measured. "Very well," he said at last, his voice clipped but not cold. "Invite them. But know this,

Damian—this is not permission to turn your path into theirs. You may welcome them into your day, but the truth will remain your burden alone."

Damian felt a flood of relief break in his chest. He bowed his head, not out of submission but gratitude. "Thank you, Father."

Liora's hand squeezed his shoulder gently, her eyes shining with quiet triumph. "It will be a good day," she whispered.

Alaric returned his gaze to the papers on his desk, but his hand lingered, unmoving, over the quill. Though he did not speak, Damian thought—just for a moment—that he saw something flicker across his father's face. Not approval. Not warmth. But perhaps a small, reluctant acceptance that even in a house built of silence, there must be room for a voice other than his own.

The next morning, the air still held the faint bite of winter. The school courtyard was alive with voices—the shuffle of shoes on stone, the clang of the morning bell, the bursts of laughter rising above it all. Damian walked through the gate, his satchel pressing against his hip, but his thoughts were elsewhere. Each step seemed to carry the echo of last night's conversation with his father.

Thirteen.

Permission given.

The words still didn't feel real.

He found Choe first, leaning lazily against the old elm by the wall. A half-eaten apple swung idly in his hand. When he saw Damian, his grin spread wide, careless as always.

"There you are," Choe called, straightening. "I thought you'd forgotten school existed. Your head's been somewhere else lately."

Damian tried for a small smile. "Not forgotten. Just... thinking."

Choe arched a brow, tossing the apple core into the grass. "Thinking? Dangerous habit. What about?"

Before Damian could answer, Miska approached. She moved with that unhurried steadiness that seemed to belong to her alone, her braid swinging lightly against her back. She carried her books cradled to her chest, their corners worn from use.

"Choe's right," she said softly, though her eyes were warm. "You've been quieter than usual. And that's saying something."

Damian's fingers tightened around the strap of his satchel. The words sat heavy in his chest, wanting to be spoken yet stumbling on their way out. "It's... my birthday next week," he managed at last. His voice was low, almost swallowed by the noise of the courtyard.

Choe blinked, then let out a sharp laugh. "Birthday? And you tell us now? How long were you planning to keep that buried?"

Miska tilted her head, studying him. "Thirteen, isn't it?"

Damian nodded.

Choe slung an arm around his shoulder, pulling him close. "Well, look at you, finally catching up to the rest of us mortals. And here I thought you'd stay twelve forever, brooding over your books."

Damian shifted under the weight of his arm but didn't pull away. His throat felt tight, but he forced the words out. "I... asked my father if I could invite you. Both of you. To the house."

For a heartbeat, the noise of the courtyard seemed to blur, the voices fading at the edges. Choe's eyes widened, his grin faltering into something almost disbelieving.

"You mean—actually inside? Your fortress of silence? The place where joy goes to die?" He whistled low. "You're serious?"

Damian nodded again, firmer this time. "Yes. He agreed. Only for the day. But I want you there."

Miska's lips curved into a smile, gentle but steady. "That's... important, Damian. Thank you for asking."

Choe gave him a light shove, laughter bubbling back into his voice. "You hear that, Miska? We're honored guests in the house of shadows. Should we bow now or wait until the actual day?"

Miska rolled her eyes, though amusement softened her expression. "Maybe wait. Save some of your theatrics for the visit."

But Damian's gaze stayed on them, something fragile flickering in his chest. "It matters to me," he said, quieter than before.

And for once, Choe didn't laugh. He just clapped Damian on the back, his grin turning easier, warmer. "Then we'll be there. Both of us. Just don't expect us to behave."

Miska's voice followed, calm and certain. "We'll make it a day worth remembering."

Damian felt the corners of his mouth lift—small, but real. The weight on his chest eased, not gone but shifted, shared. For the first time, his birthday did not feel like a date etched only in silence. It felt like a promise waiting to unfold.

Today ,it was his birthday.They woke before dawn on the day itself, as if the calendar had pulled at them by an unseen string. Damian moved through the house with the practised carefulness of someone trying to turn worry into plain tasks: he swept crumbs from the table edge, folded the spare cloth into a neat square, arranged the three wooden bowls so their chips faced inward. Liora worked beside him, the kitchen bright with steady motions — she rolled dough, set the kettle on the stove, smoothed the small round of sweet bread until it shone with butter. The ordinary things—kneading, boiling, wiping—kept panic at bay.

Choe arrived first, breathless and wild-eyed, clutching a paper-wrapped pastry that had survived a run across the market. He came in by the back gate with the exuberance of a boy who had rehearsed a hundred entrances.

"Damian!" he whooped, nearly tripping over the threshold. "I brought the good kind. Not the dry ones."

Damian laughed, short and thin at first, then more genuine. "You didn't have to run, Choe."

Choe dropped the parcel onto the table and sat on the nearest chair with theatrical solemnity. "Don't tell me I have to behave. I'll try, but I won't promise."

Miska arrived a little after, quieter and composed. She carried a small cloth-wrapped object and the faint smell of the northern quarter's spice-stalls clung to her cloak. She handed Damian the parcel with both hands.

"For the tree," she said. "The carver said it is for keeping watch. For travellers, he said. For those who leave and come back."

Damian peeled back the cloth. Inside was a tiny wooden spiral much like the one he'd shown her months ago in the shed: simple, worn, made by someone who'd worked with small things all day. He felt the weight of it and the weight of their ordinary care.

Liora lit the candle at the center of the table; its small flame made the three faces around it look closer than they usually were. They ate simply: bread, stew, the pastry Choe had saved enough of to present ceremoniously. Conversation moved in small, warm circles—Choe's loud stories about how he'd "rescued" the pastry from a cats' conspiracy, Miska's dry remarks about teachers, Damian's soft thank-yous.

At the end of the meal Damian rose to clear his plate and found himself standing in the doorway of the study, looking at the empty chair still imprinted with his father's scent of ink and coal. Liora followed him with a practiced smile, one that did not quite reach her eyes.

"Shall I call your father?" she asked. "It would be proper for him to come."

Damian nodded and Liora left the room to fetch him in the kind of politeness that treats a man as if he were only in the next room. She opened the study door and spoke through it, calling his name like she would call the laundry in from the line. No rustle answered. She stepped fully into the study, glanced at the desk, and the line of small details—quill set down, the inkwell dry at one side, a scrap of folded paper—told her the first thing she had not wanted to know: Alaric was not there.

At first Liora assumed he had slipped out the back to fetch something from the apothecary or to take a breath of air. She called again. Then she checked the usual places: his coat-peg, the key on the tray he always kept in hand, the back stair that led to the lane. Nothing. A small smear of ink on the doorstep and a slight muddle of footprints in the yard told her only that he had left after last night and not returned.

She told Damian quietly — not to alarm him before she knew — and he felt the room tilt a fraction. Choe, who had just been about to announce a ridiculous game involving three chairs and a pretend crown, fell suddenly silent. Miska closed the study door behind her and peered at the street as if she might read messages in the pale light.

"We'll find him," Choe said, too loud to be convincing.

"Let us not jump," Liora replied, steady-handed. "I will ask the neighbors. Maybe he went to the hospital lane as he often does to consult with that apprentice. These things sometimes take time."

They went out as a small searching party. The town, at its market-edge, smelled of wood smoke and wet straw. People took the news with the slow kindness of small places—questions and offers of help, notes of where they'd last seen him.

At the baker, Old Nari wiped his hands and thought. "I saw him once this morning," he said finally. "Walking near the clinic at dawn. Head down. He passed me by, didn't stop for bread." It was not anything like an answer, but it was a place to go.

They checked the clinic, where an apprentice remembered Alaric's voice in a conversation about a remedy; he had left before the light changed. They walked the river path where Alaric sometimes sat and traced the same line of stones in silence. A fisherman shrugged and said he had seen no one calling their name over the water. With each stop, the net of witnesses tightened and offered small scraps.

Afternoon bled toward evening with nothing to show for hours of calling and knocking. The festival of mundane kindness took shape around them: neighbors brought a thermos and a spare lantern, a cousin from the next lane produced a list of places Alaric liked to visit, and someone else offered to check the far road. Choe ran messages between people like a man trying to outrun a worry he did not know how to hold; Miska moved from shop to shop, her questions exact and businesslike. Damian felt the elasticity in him stretch and fray with every report: seen here, not seen there, maybe he went on, maybe he did not.

Night fell and sharpened their movements into necessity. Lantern light pooled along the stones as groups organized. The town constable, a broad-shouldered man with tired eyes, agreed to sound the watch. They split in pairs where they could. Choe and a neighbor took the market lane; Miska and another neighbor went along the river; Liora, with a small knot of women, combed the back alleys and the old hospital lane; Damian, because he would not be kept away, walked with Choe until the boys' breath steamed in the cold.

They checked the watchtower steps, kicked at the reeds along the bridge, called into doorways and under porches. At each shout someone replied with a name, an apology, an absence. Once, in the dim light beside the river, Choe nearly fell into the mud reaching for what he thought was a coat snagging on a post; for a second both of them laughed, the brief madness of relief, but when there was only the sodden cloth the laughter died as quickly as it had flared.

At the apothecary the apprentice's brow furrowed. "He asked me for a tincture two nights ago," the apprentice said. "Said he had a notion to test a theory. He left in the dusk. Said he was going to the west lane." It was a possibility, but the west lane led out of town and into rough country; with winter, such paths were long and dangerous after dark. The apprentice offered his mare for a quick search, but the animal's owner had already lent it elsewhere.

They asked at the far bridge where the road forks to the hilltops. A lamplighter there said he'd seen a man matching Alaric's coat go by before dusk — alone, walking fast. It was the first account that sounded purposeful rather than incidental. Damian kept walking, listening for reasoning in that detail. Purpose suggested a destination; destination suggested a path they could follow.

The constable rounded up a larger party as night pressed and more people volunteered. Lanterns multiplied like patient stars. Miska organized runners, mapped who would check which segments—bridge, apothecary, the small crossroads, river path, and the lane by the old helmsman's cottage. Damian found himself on the river bank again in the lantern light, calling until his throat hurt, until the sound came out as a raw thing that did not belong in a boy's voice.

At one point they crowded the little square in front of the chapel. The priest moved among them with quiet gestures, hands clasped. He offered what he could: prayers, a place to rest if people needed it, a promise to light a lamp by morning and to send relation to the next towns beyond if anyone saw him leave. His calm was a small steadiness in a list of scattered possibilities.

Hours passed in a rhythm of hope and small defeats. A cloth spotted at the roadside that might have been Alaric's faded into a milkman's shawl. A lamplighter's report of a figure crossing the far hill became a shepherd's rounding of his own flock. Choe slipped at the river bank and came up with mud on his palms and a grin he could not hold.

At the hill's edge, Miska stood looking out over the mist and the black ribbon of the river. "We must not stop," she said, voice even. "We check the roads, we ask the toll, we speak to the inns. He might have gone to clear his head—or to meet someone. Either way, we do not stop until morning."

They kept going until the cold gnawed at their fingers and the lanterns burned low. Then people began to drift back, leaden and quiet. Some promised to return at dawn; others, exhausted, went to rouse those able to ride further. Choe and a neighbor had argued briefly about whether to follow the hill road alone; the neighbor used common sense and convinced him to wait until a horse could be fetched. The town moved in fitful waves of concern and practical decisions.

By the small hours, they gathered again at the house: Liora with her face made of resolute weariness, Miska with mud on her boot, Choe with his sleeve torn and eyes red-rimmed. They had walked every known way into the dark and found only impressions that could be read in more than one way. No Alaric. The study door stood closed, the quill still at its blot, the chair empty.

They made plans with the tired, careful precision of people who will not let worry turn into despair. A list of places to check at first light, names of neighbors who would ride or walk the farther roads, an agreement that someone would return to the house continuously until word came. Liora pinned the little wooden spiral Miska had brought onto a string and put it in Damian's hand.

"Carry this," she said simply. "If he sees it, he will know we have not given up."

Damian held the charm until its grain warmed to his palm. There was a smallness to that gesture, a plain human thing—no grand declarations, only work to be done, lists to make, doors to knock. He felt a careful, new kind of anger: not at Alaric, but at the helplessness that yearned to be covered by action.

They did not sleep that night. Liora sat by the study desk and sorted the papers as if tidying might lead to understanding. Choe dozed on the kitchen bench and woke coughing from the cold. Miska sat with a small notebook, copying names and routes so nothing would be lost. Damian watched them all and tried to make sense of the small patterns of their faces.

At last, as the sky thinned toward pale gray, they paused. No one had found him. No one had even found a trail that promised a direction. They had searched with lanterns and shouts and steadiness until their voices were raw; they had asked the town and the little trade roads; they had roused the watch and the apothecary; and still the study chair was empty.

Liora folded her hands over the blot on the desk and for a moment simply looked at the small splash of ink as if it might offer a clue. She stood slowly and said, "We go again at first light. We will not give up."

Damian nodded. The wooden charm dug into his palm like a tiny compass. He wanted sleep, wanted the kind of shut eye that would vanish into the small, forgetful oblivion of dreams, but something in him remained awake, like a sentry. He felt at the edge of things, the old labyrinth in his mind sharpening: the corridors were no longer only dreams now; one of its doors had opened onto the day, and a person he loved had walked through.

They left the kitchen like a small, worn party moving to separate tasks. The town, as it woke, began again to do what towns do: people carried water, swept their steps, and accepted the way the world insisted on continuing. Yet inside the house, in the quiet the morning had not yet erased, a different pattern had settled—an unanswered question, a list of places waiting to be checked, and the knowledge that they would spend the day looking.

They had searched through the night and come up empty. The absence sat in the house like a shape you could not fill. Damian took one last look at the chair, at the page of notes left like a punctuation, folded the charm into his palm, and stepped out into the thin morning, ready to start looking again.

The days that followed were marked not by hours but by the rhythm of footsteps, doors, and questions. They scoured the town again and again: the apothecary's lane, the west road, the quiet bend of the river. Each time they returned with nothing more than scraps of guesses. Each time the silence in the study grew heavier.

By the end of the first week, the constable drew up the report himself. He sat across from Liora at the kitchen table, the ink drying slowly on the page. His voice was steady, but there was something in the way he tapped his quill that betrayed discomfort.

"Mrs. Liora," he said gently, "we've searched the roads, spoken to inns, and sent riders to the next towns. We've found no sign. For now, the best we can do is file the disappearance. Notices will be sent to neighboring stations. If anyone sees him, you'll be the first to know."

Damian sat at the edge of the bench, fists pressed hard into his knees. "So that's it? We just... wait?"

The constable looked at him, eyes tired but kind. "Waiting isn't nothing, lad. Sometimes people return when you least expect."

Liora's voice cut through softly, almost trembling. "And if they don't?"

The constable folded the paper, avoiding her gaze. "Then the world keeps looking. But answers don't always come quick."

When he left, the kitchen seemed to shrink. The wooden charm Miska had given Damian sat on the windowsill now, its spiral catching the weak light. He found himself staring at it as if it might open into a door.

Months passed. They tried everything—visiting stations, posting notices, sending letters carried by riders. Damian watched his mother become two people: one who still baked bread, lit the lamp, and straightened his collar for school, and another who moved like a shadow through the house, her eyes fixed on doorways as if waiting for Alaric to step through.

At the police station in the next town, a clerk thumbed through ledgers while Damian sat beside his mother. "Name?" the clerk droned.

"Alaric," Liora said, her voice trembling but firm. "Alaric of the south quarter."

The man scribbled, uninterested. "Disappeared? Mmm. We'll send word if we find a match."

As they walked back, Damian tried to speak, but Liora's silence was heavy, like a locked gate. Only when they reached the riverbank did she stop. She touched the railing, her hand white against the iron. "He would not just leave us," she whispered, almost to herself. "Something happened. Something they don't see."

"Mama," Damian said, forcing the words out, "maybe he—maybe he chose to go."

Her eyes flashed with sudden fire, wet with unshed tears. "Don't say that. Don't you dare say that. He was your father. He carried burdens you couldn't yet see."

Damian fell silent, the river's dark current filling the space between them.

Years began to trickle past. Each birthday was marked not with celebration but with absence. Choe still brought him ridiculous little gifts, Miska always remembered with something small and deliberate, but the house no longer rang with laughter.

Damian noticed how his mother's hair grayed faster, how her hands shook sometimes when she poured tea. She would still rise early and leave, visiting the station, the chapel, the neighbors—anyone who might have heard a rumor. Each time she returned, her shoulders sank a little further.

One evening, Damian overheard her speaking in the dark to herself—or perhaps to Alaric.

"You told me truth was a burden," she murmured, rocking slightly by the fire. "But you never told me silence would be worse."

Damian wanted to go to her, to take her hand, but something in her posture held him back: a loneliness so private it was like a wall.

The breaking point came years later. Damian was seventeen when the sickness first took her—an illness of the heart more than the body. She grew frail, her steps slower, her voice softer. She still spoke of Alaric as if he might return any day.

One night, she called Damian to her bedside. Her voice was thin, but her eyes still burned with that same refusal to let go.

"Damian," she whispered, her hand trembling in his, "promise me you will keep looking. Even if the world says it is finished—don't let it be finished. Promise me you'll carry him in your steps."

Damian swallowed hard, the wooden charm heavy around his neck on its string. "I promise, Mama."

Her fingers squeezed his once, weakly, before falling still.

The house that had once been filled with silence now felt cavernous, hollowed by two absences instead of one. His birthday—the day that had begun with laughter and stew and small gifts—had become the hinge on which everything turned. That was the day his father vanished, the day his childhood ended, the day his mother began to fade.

Now, when he stood in the study, the chair seemed more than empty. It was a monument.

And Damian, no longer a boy, felt the truth settle into him like stone: that his life had been split by that one day, and the labyrinth he carried in his mind was no longer a dream, but the shape of his own fate.

She left in the thin light before dawn, like the rest of her leaving had been gradual—small things first, and then the shape of the day itself. Damian had been beside her bed. The room smelled of boiled tea and the lemon-scented soap she used on Sundays; the quilt lay folded at the foot of the bed in the way she had always folded it herself.

"Damian," she said, voice paper-frail but steady. "Listen."

He leaned down, the cot springs creaking under him.

"Keep looking for him," she whispered, as if repeating something she'd promised herself a hundred times. "Don't let the waiting go hollow. And—" she paused, thumb finding the line of his cheek "—look after yourself. Eat. Write. Laugh when you can. Promise me."

He said the promise like a prayer. She smiled once, a bright careful thing, and then the breath that had been weathered for months left her. Her hand relaxed in his.

For a long time he did not move. Outside, a rooster called; in the corridor, a neighbor fetched water. Those ordinary sounds felt like an accusation: life continuing. He closed his mother's eyes with the gentleness she had taught him years ago and, when he rose, found that his knees shook as if he had run a long way.

—

They did not bury her at once. There are practicalities that wait for no grief: the constable to sign papers, the priest to speak in a voice measured and kind, the neighbors who came with jars of broth and soft loaves. Choe arrived first at the house, breathless and too large in his coat, hands shoved deep into his pockets as if he could injure the world by feeling it. Miska came after, quiet, carrying a folded blanket and the steady, practical air she always had.

"It's small," Choe said when he saw Damian by the bed. His bravado broke in the face of the stillness—he looked like a boy trying on a man's sorrow and failing.

Miska only reached out and took Damian's hand. "We'll help," she said, which in her tone was both promise and plan.

The priest was methodical. He sat with them and asked questions that felt like gentle probes: was there a will, next of kin, any account that needed to be closed? He spoke of Liora as a woman of quiet courage, and when that was said, the room felt slightly less crowded by things left unsaid.

Neighbors came in waves. Old Nari from the bakery brought boiled pears; the apothecary's apprentice arrived with warm vinegar compresses for Choe's raw hands. The constable, with the same tired kindness he had shown on the first night, made a small official note and left a promise to post word to the surrounding towns.

At dusk they carried Liora to the chapel. The chapel smelled of wax and straw. A thin coffin, wrapped in plain linen, waited beneath the beams where spiders kept their slow watch. Damian walked at the head. Choe and Miska flanked him like brothers. People from the market stood in a line, faces softened by the kind of sorrow that knows its neighbor's shape.

The priest read; there were prayers and a hymn that sounded too bright in the small room. Words about rest and memory were appropriate to the ears but inadequate to the chest. After the final knot of ritual, when the choir's last note had gone thin, the earth closed on her in a rhythm as old as the town. Damian put the wooden spiral that Miska had given him into the coffin with his own hand. It felt like both a key and a weight.

—

Afterward, the house wanted work. People stayed away from rooms where ghosts might be obvious and, at the same time, they insisted on filling the kitchen with clatter and conversation so no one would sit alone with too much thinking. Choe cleaned the yard until his arms ached and Miska sat with Damian while they sorted papers—Liora's letters, a few lists pinned and folded, recipes. They found the little things she had kept: a ribbon, a child's mitten, the charred corner of a book she had read too often.

There were moments that arrived without warning: a neighbor mentioning a laugh that sounded like Liora's from across the street; Choe dropping a plate and swearing so loudly the room jumped; Miska sitting very still and then finally letting a single tear fall that she did not try to explain. Damian managed the paperwork—letters to the station, signing the forms with the constable, making the arrangements no mother had wished on her son—and through it all he wore the sameness of being who was now the head of that small house.

Once, late, when the neighbors had left and the kitchen was a series of small shadows, Choe cleared his throat and said, "You could come with me when I go to the market tomorrow. Make sure you eat something besides stew." His voice tried to be funny and failed there, falling into something like tenderness.

Miska folded a shawl and handed it to Damian. "I'll come by each morning to help with the chores," she said plainly. "And I'll send you word if I hear from anyone about the roads."

It was neither rhetoric nor prayer; it was work, and Damian clung to it.

—

There were lighter incidents as well—small, human things that kept the hard edges from cutting everything in two. Old Nari insisted on teaching Damian how to make the morning bread just so; the apothecary lent a remedy for sleeplessness that tasted awful but worked enough to let him rest for short, dangerous intervals. A cousin came and, after a long silence, handed Damian a small sealed envelope Liora had asked him to keep should she ever be gone. Inside was a note in her hand—few words, precise, like the rest of her.

"Don't stop looking. If the world tells you to stop, keep asking. Let your hands do the searching when your voice cannot."

He folded the paper into his palm and felt its edges press like a stern, warm promise.

—

Questions about money and home followed in quieter, dull voices. There were debts left from the times Liora had managed the household alone; there were favors owed and quietly repaid. Damian negotiated with the constable, the baker, the apothecary. He signed his name until it felt like an imprint on the world. A small fund was gathered by neighbors so the household could continue—neighbors never meant to be charity, only neighbors keeping the small city from sinking one of its own.

At one point, a distant cousin—an ordinary, practical man—came to measure the house with an eye toward what repairs it might need. He suggested, in a voice without malice, that Damian might consider lodging in the house with relatives until he was able to manage the bills. Miska and Choe both bristled.

"You are not sending him anywhere," Choe said hotly.

"We are all right," Miska answered, eyes narrowed. "He does not leave."

The cousin, surprised by the steadiness of the children, retreated with a shrug. In the weeks after the funeral, the three of them held to the house like hands clasped over a map.

—

At night, when the neighbors had gone and the lamp burned low, Damian found his mother's shawl folded in a drawer. He drew it across his shoulders and sat at the window. Outside, the market emptied. In his head the labyrinth came—different now, sharper—and in it his father's voice seemed to come from a corridor he could not yet reach. He promised the room, the quiet, the small pile of things that had been left to him, that he would keep looking. He said it aloud once, clinging to the sound, and Choe, who had not been able to sleep either, muttered from the bench where he had fallen exhausted, "Good. Don't stop then. We'll help."

Miska, by the door, nodded. "We will hold the map while you find the paths."

They developed a routine: chores in the morning, visiting the station and the constable in the afternoon, checking the roads and asking at inns. They wrote the names of people and places on a list and pinned it above the hearth like a small altar. The list grew sticky with soot and with the touch of fingers mapping hope.

———

The months that followed were not heroic. They were patchwork. There were evenings when Damian wanted to rage or to run and evenings when the weight of ordinary tasks—mending a hole in a sleeve, sweeping the hearth—kept him steady. He learned to pay the bills, to barter where coins were short, to let Choe's jokes get through to him and to let Miska's practical orders carry him through the day. Their companionship became a scaffolding; it steadied the parts of him that might otherwise have cracked.

Sometimes, when the house felt unbearably full of absence, he would light a candle in the study and place the wooden spiral beside it. He would fold the paper Liora had left him and read the thin sentence again. He did not know yet where the search would end. He only knew how to keep going.

And in the quiet that followed the small, ordinary labor of living, the labyrinth returned in dreams. It had not gone. It was not simply a child's fear. It had become a map made of longing and obligation, and in its corridors he kept hearing both his father's voice and his mother's last instruction. He was no longer merely a boy who drew mazes on slates. He was a young man with a promise he had neither chosen nor could choose to unmake.

The house remained theirs: the three friends, the small neighborhood, the rituals of chores and lists. The town kept its steady business; the market kept its sound. Life, in a way that both comforted and hurt, continued.

And Damian, who had lost two of the people who had shaped him most, learned to carry their absence like something alive—an incision that taught him where to press and where to be careful. He kept the spiral on the mantle, a small knot against the empty chair, and he kept looking.

Days passed, each one pulling Damian a little farther from the rawness of loss, though the scar of it lingered in his chest like a silent weight. Miska and Choe stayed close, anchoring him to the present.

"Damian," Miska said one morning as they shelled peas by the kitchen window, "you need to let yourself live. Your mother wouldn't want you to be only a shadow of her absence."

Choe, sprawled in the chair opposite, added gruffly, "Yeah. Don't keep walking around like you're made of glass. Go to the market, laugh when you can. You're not betraying her if you breathe."

Their words sank into him slowly. He tried. He helped in the market, carried wood for the chapel, even smiled when Choe's clumsy jokes earned laughter from neighbors. But when night came, and silence crept into the corners of the house, his thoughts always turned inward.

One evening, alone by the lamp, Damian found himself wondering again about his father. Where could he have gone? The question grew sharp, cutting through the haze of grief. He thought of distant towns, of places on the maps he'd studied in childhood, of libraries where thinkers gathered, of old ruins whispered about in taverns. His father had always carried that restless gleam in his eye, the hunger for ideas. Perhaps he had gone to some hidden place where people thought as he did, where their words spun into riddles and philosophies, a place ordinary folk would call strange but he would call home.

The thought clung to him, almost comforting. It made his father's absence seem less like an abandonment and more like a journey still unfinished.

But soon another thing began to happen. Dreams.

At first they were fragments—corridors twisting in impossible angles, footsteps echoing in halls of stone, a voice calling faintly. Then, one night, it became clear. He dreamed of his father, gaunt and shadowed, trapped within a labyrinth with walls that breathed like living things. His father's eyes, though dim with exhaustion, fixed on him with desperate urgency.

"Damian," the voice in the dream rasped, "find me... free me."

The boy woke drenched in sweat, his hands trembling as though he had touched those impossible walls. The image refused to leave him, clinging even in daylight.

And so the search, which had once been duty, began to burn like destiny.

The dreams came more often, and with them the same pressed urgency: corridors that narrowed just as he rounded them, his father's voice threaded through the stone like a rope, the single wordless insistence — remember, remember — until Damian woke with his heart a hollow drum.

This time the dream left something behind besides sweat. In the grey of morning, while the house still smelled faintly of last night's soup, he found the wooden spiral Miska had given him resting in the palm of his hand though he had not held it when he slept. The spiral's grooves were warm from his skin; he traced them with a finger and felt, absurdly, that the loop meant something more than a gift. In the dream his father's lips had brushed the same shape before the walls folded away.

That small, stubborn detail — the spiral — became the first hinge of a long, slow unravelling.

—

He began where everything he loved had begun: at his father's desk. The study was a map of Alaric's mind in stacks — journals tied with string, pamphlets whose corners had been thumbed to papers thin as wings, margin notes that shifted from careful script to a hurry of shorthand. Damian spread the papers on the floor and worked by the weak light of the lamp, taking care as if the pages themselves might break.

Alaric's handwriting changed as the pages marched on. Medical case notes, clinical observations, then, tucked among them, lines of speculation about perception: "labyrinths: external & internal — which opens the other?" In the margin beside a list of names was the tiny spiral again, drawn quickly, decisively, as if to underline a point. Nearby, a line in Latin: "Memor et mane" — remember and remain.

Damian traced the letters until they blurred.

He found a folded map in the back of a worn ledger, edges stained with travel grit. Someone — Alaric — had marked a small cluster of places along the west road with inked dots. One dot had a faint spiral stamped next to it. At the bottom margin someone had scrawled a single word: Meridian.

He took the map to the shed where the three of them kept their collected things and showed it to Choe, who at first tried to make a joke, then grew oddly still.

"So the old man had a hobby other than scaring the market," Choe said, but there was no mockery in his voice. "Meridian — that's beyond the next hill, isn't it? The scholars say there are old houses there. My uncle once told a story..."

"Stories aren't maps," Damian said, but his voice felt thin. "Still — it's a place to start."

They decided to go to the library. It was the natural next step: books could make patience into evidence. Miska walked with them, steady as always, clutching a list she'd made in small, precise handwriting: travel notices, visiting lecturers, institute ads, county records.

At the library, the smell of paper and dust was like a different weather. Mrs. Garrick — the librarian with a bun like a small stern planet — opened the ledger for them with the practiced economy of someone used to impatience and sorrow.

"You're looking for a Meridian?" she asked after Damian explained in halting sentences. She drew a slow breath. "There are places called Meridian in these old volumes. Also a conference once advertised under that name — a symposium about memory and mind. It passed through here many years ago."

She fetched newspapers, brittle pamphlets, an index of visiting lecturers. The three of them sat cross-legged on the floor, flipping pages. There were references enough to make a road of speculation: a professor who lectured on cognitive maps, a small institute that advertised experimental treatments, a travel notice listing a meeting at Meridian House. A photograph, grainy, showed a hall of columns; at its corner someone had printed a spiral as a mark of editorial note.

"That spiral again," Miska said softly, and the sound of her voice made the connection real.

They copied names into Miska's notebook. When the librarian's son came in, they bribed him with leftover pastry to make a quick run for any registry ledgers in the back. He returned with records: a Mr. Alaric, entry noted three years prior — a subscription to a monthly journal on Psychiatry & Social Mind, plus a short letter requesting references to Meridian House. The ledger handed back the marginalia: appointment confirmed — Professor Locke, 3ʳᵈ month. The handwriting matched one of the margins in Alaric's notebook.

A small, ordinary victory: a name, a date, a place.

—

The days became a cadence of small discoveries and larger anxieties. He copied down every reference. If a name in a pamphlet sounded unfamiliar he would walk to the apothecary and ask for local gossip. The apothecary's apprentice, a man with steady hands, listened and then laughed and told them a story about how intellectual men liked to travel to places where no one bothered them — settlements where the stone kept secrets because few visitors cared to ask.

"Your father was not the only one," the apprentice said finally, wiping his hands on his apron. "Men go searching for answers. Some answer back."

Choe, impatient with the slowness of books, went out to talk with the lamplighters and the ferrymen, who remembered a carriage that had passed on a moonless night with scholars and leather trunks. Each person gave them a piece of the night — a color of coat, a scent of pipe tobacco, an argument caught at a tavern's door. None of it was definitive, but together the fragments shaped a route.

At school, when their teacher praised neat arithmetic, Damian found his mind half in the ledger lines of old visitors. Once, a boy in the yard jeered, "He chases ghosts." Choe answered with a shove and a laugh; some things, Choe seemed to say, you defended with your hands as urgently as with words. Miska stayed beside him, an anchor.

—

He kept returning to the spiral. In Alaric's pocket journal he found it stamped again — on a tiny scrap from a visiting-card with the words Meridian House, Symposium of Mnemosyne and, oddly, the address of an inn in a city he'd only ever read about in a shipping manifest. The handwriting at the bottom of the card was Alaric's: If I do not return, look at the Ashwell bridge. The sentence was shorthand and thin, but it was a sentence.

Damian read it until the letters steadied. Ashwell Bridge was a place on the west road; the lamplighter had mentioned it as the last place a carriage had been spotted that night. He folded the card and placed it with the map in his pocket.

That night, the dream pressed closer. The labyrinth's walls dragged like cloth now; his father's face was sharper, younger and older at once. "Find the bridge," the voice rasped. "Follow the spiral."

He woke with the map in his fist. The lamp glittered on the wooden spiral around his neck. He felt, absurdly and suddenly, as if he were carrying a trail of breadcrumbs and had, at last, found the first crumb.

—

There were small resistances to his search. A neighbor — a widow used to the solidity of predictable days — told him bluntly at the market that he should be careful of men who followed ideas too far. "They do not always find answers," she said. "Sometimes you find only holes." Her words slammed into him like a cold gate but did not close. The constable, visiting with papers about the household, warned gently but firmly against riding off in winter without good reason. "You're a boy with debts and a roof," he said. "Mind those things or they will enfold you before you can leave them."

Miska and Choe argued with him once or twice about what to do next — with worry entering their play like a new, unwanted guest. "We can go with you," Choe insisted in the shed one night, all bravado, then softer: "We'll buy a horse even if I have to sell all my prank supplies."

Miska, pragmatic as ever, paced lately and then said, "First, we find a reason to go. We gather papers, money, someone who will vouch. We do not leap into fog because a dream tells you to." She was not cold in saying it; she was careful, which for Miska meant love.

Damian understood. He also knew he could not wait forever.

—

So he kept looking. He read Alaric's diaries in the small hours, copying out the words that seemed to return, over and over: spiral, Meridian, Ashwell, Mnemosyne, bridge. He made lists and pinned them above the hearth. He cross-checked names with the ledger at the library. He walked the west road at dawn, following the lamplighter's route, listening to the way the wind spoke through hedges as if it were telling him which way to turn.

Some nights he failed. He'd go to bed and find no answer in the margins, only the old ache of absence. The labyrinth in his head shifted each time the dream came, and the dream came more often, thicker now, as if the walls within it knew he hunted their seams.

When he found a place name, a smudged ticket stub, a remark in a visiting ledger that matched Alaric's handwriting, he treated it like a small mercy. He would wake Choe at dawn to read the note aloud, and they would plan in whispers over stale bread. Miska would tape the new scraps into her little book and label them with neat, irreversible letters.

"No hurry," she said once, reading his face. "But not idle." Her voice balanced him.

—

Weeks wound into months and the search did not end. The pattern shifted: small discoveries, nights of empty answers, the dream growing a shade clearer, then fading, then clearer again. Each scrap, each name, each spiral drew him onward by a slow, steady thread. He lived in margins and lists, in the smell of old ink and the creak of the lamplighter's boots.

At times he wondered whether he was being led by grief alone — by the hunger to patch absence — or whether there truly was a place where a man like his father could be found. The line between devotion and obsession blurred like ink in rain. But the spiral on his chest and the script in his father's notebook whispered the same counsel: follow the sign.

So Damian continued to follow it, step by patient step: reading, asking, listening, and, when the night came, dreaming the labyrinth thicker until the map of his waking world and the map in his sleep began to lie over one another, line for trembling line.

The first time Damian saw the word Shie, it was almost by accident. A brittle pamphlet, folded among a pile of conference notices at the library, carried the faint heading:

"Meridian Symposium, hosted in the city of Shie — Bogston Centre for Cognitive Inquiry."

The name struck him like a chime struck too hard. His eyes kept tracing it, back and forth, as though it might rearrange itself into something else. Shie. Bogston. A place he'd heard only in passing, half in awe — the world-renowned centre where the greatest minds gathered, where theories of memory and mind bent the future.

Yet something unsettled him. In the margin, in his father's handwriting, a note:

"Not by choice. Pulled."

The word pulled dug under Damian's skin. His father had not gone there in search of knowledge. He had been taken.

That night the dream came heavier. His father stood within the labyrinth again, but the walls now bore marks — spirals etched like burns, and above them a single word: Shie.

"Damian," his father rasped, voice breaking through the dream like glass under strain, "they did not invite me. They bound me. They opened my head. Do not let them do the same to you…"

Damian woke gasping, his fist curled around the spiral as though it had been seared there.

From that point, his path sharpened. The grief that had once slowed him became fuel. He knew what he had to do: not just search in the dark, but prepare. To enter Shie, to enter Bogston, he needed to become what they could not ignore.

"Psychology?" Choe had asked when Damian told him. "Mind sciences? That's years of books and greybeards and papers nobody reads. You want to bury yourself in that?"

Damian's answer was quiet but certain. "It's not burying. It's building. If Bogston is where they took him, then Bogston is where I'll stand. But I'll go in through the front doors, not dragged through the back like he was."

Miska's eyes lingered on him, long and steady. "Then you must outlast them. Learn their language better than they know it themselves. Otherwise you'll only repeat his fate."

So the years became discipline.

At eighteen, Damian left for the academy, carrying only his father's journals, the spiral, and the map. He studied psychology with a hunger that startled his teachers. Where others memorized, he dissected. Where others skimmed, he traced patterns through margins, searching for the places theory cracked into mystery.

He spent long nights hunched over case studies, annotating by candlelight, while the voice of his father's dream echoed faintly: remember, remember.

Professors began to notice. One, Dr. Harren, a stooped man with sharp spectacles, paused after Damian's presentation on "labyrinthine cognition."

"You speak as though the mind itself were a structure we could walk," Harren said. "As though dreams were not metaphor but blueprint."

Damian only inclined his head. "Maybe they are."

The class laughed, but Harren did not. Later, in private, he murmured, "If you keep walking this way, boy, you'll either fall off the map or draw a new one. Both are dangerous."

Damian smiled faintly. "Dangerous is already behind me, sir."

He completed his bachelor's with honors, his name whispered among the academy halls as "the one who thinks in spirals." By the time he entered his master's, he had carved a reputation for insight that leaned into obsession. He studied cognitive architecture, memory systems, the psychology of altered states — every subject that brushed against the idea of a labyrinth within the mind.

Miska wrote often, her letters neat, urging balance. Choe visited once, loudly proclaiming the city was too clean, too full of people who "never touched mud," but when he left, he clapped Damian on the shoulder with uncharacteristic solemnity. "Don't lose your fire, eh? Just... don't let it eat you whole."

The opportunity came on a rain-soaked afternoon. A letter arrived, stamped with the seal of Bogston itself.

"Mr. Damian of the South Quarter,
Your work in the field of labyrinthine cognition has drawn attention from our board. We invite you to present your thesis at the upcoming symposium in Shie, at the Bogston Centre."

His hands trembled as he held the letter. The very name that had haunted him now beckoned him through the front doors.

He went to the riverbank where he and his mother had once stood. He unfolded the letter, held it against the grey sky, and whispered to the absent air:

"I'm coming, father. Not as a boy looking for scraps. As a man who will walk where you were taken."

SIX

THE SPIRAL IN THE MARGIN

They met after the lecture in the same small chamber as before, the afternoon light slanting through the dusty panes and making the particles in the air look like a slow, constant decision. Reed came first, cheeks flushed from walking; Anesthesia followed, notebook under her arm, corners softened by use. Damian stood by the desk with his notes spread in a careful fan — the bunker sketches, the map of the lower passages, little arrows in his own hand.

He didn't need to say much. The three of them had that unspoken language now: a look, a tilt of the head, a single pen tapped against a page.

"We know the bunker wasn't it," Damian began, voice even. "Not the active experiments. The skeletons — a perimeter. A warning. Or a mistake from a generation ago. Either way, what we need are plans. The blueprints. Sketches of Bogston's service passages, access points, annexes — everything. If there's a hidden wing, it will show."

Reed swallowed. "Where do you even get blueprints for a place like this? The archives? Maintenance? Those doors are locked tighter than a sermon."

Anesthesia opened her notebook and smoothed a scrap of paper with two fingers. "The Map Room," she said. Her voice had a flatness to it — no excitement, only fact. "Old maps, building plans, alterations. It's in the administrative wing. I saw a cart bringing volumes through last month. But access... it's restricted. Faculty can request, staff can sign off, and the registrar is—" she shrugged. "The registrar is careful."

Damian looked at the page with his father's spiral drawn faintly in the margin, and let the urgency show only as a quiet set to his jaw. "Then we'll make a careful request. I will ask as faculty — a routine review of historical plans for a lecture. If they refuse we take another route. There are always routes."

They made lists. Reed's list was the shortest: "Distract the porter if necessary, bring a lantern, don't touch anything we can't carry." Anesthesia's was long and neat: names of clerks, times when the Map Room clerk took tea, the route of the map cart, the location of the keys. Damian's was pragmatic: the exact phrasing of the request he would make, which documents to ask for first, what to say if the registrar pressed.

They left in light rain, voices low, moving like people who had rehearsed small rebellions.

—

The administrative wing smelled of oil and old paper. Lamps hung in glass globes, their light steady and unsensational. At the door to the Map Room sat the registrar's office — a low, dignified room where a man named Torv kept the keys and the patience of the university. Torv was the sort who believed rules existed to be kept precisely; his hair was trimmed in the manner of a man who cut corners only where law had allowed it.

Damian presented himself at the window with polite gravity. "Registrar Torv," he said, showing his faculty card and a résumé of reasons. "I am compiling materials for a seminar on institutional memory. I require access to the historical building plans of Bogston. Specifically, plans of the lower service levels and annexes, circa the last fifty years."

Torv peered over the spectacles that hung at the end of his nose. "We do not loan original plans to faculty, Professor Damian. They are archive material. One may inspect them under supervision.

Who is assisting you?"

"I will be alone," Damian said, and let Reed and Anesthesia stand back in the corridor, visible but still distant. "For logistics I asked the Map Room to prepare copies. I will, of course, read under supervision and return them."

Torv made a soft, almost sympathetic noise. "The Map Room requires an application, signed by the head of department. They are particular about restricted annexes. There are names redacted in several of these plans. You understand."

Damian's throat tightened, but he kept his voice even. "I understand. Will you accept a written request today, pending Kael's endorsement? He knows my work."

Torv blinked. Kael's name was a key. It opened doors, blurred scrutiny. "Without Kael's signature, the application will not be processed," he said finally. "Regulations."

Damian studied Torv for a long second, then stepped back. "Thank you. I will—arrange it."

Outside, under the drizzle, the three of them folded into a tight plan. Kael's endorsement would be ideal — the clean path. But they had learned to expect that the clean path either wasn't available or led them somewhere else entirely. They had a second, slower plan: obtain partial plans through the Map Room's assistant at tea time; copy what they could; use the librarian's microfilm if necessary.

"That man trusts signatures," Anesthesia murmured. "But he also trusts routine. He hates surprises more than he hates falsehood."

Reed's answer was a grin that tried to be brave. "Then we'll be routine."

—

They split roles. Damian would, the next morning, stop at Kael's office under a pretext — a departmental question — and attempt to secure the signature. Reed would shadow Torv, make casual conversation and look for the assistant's tea-hour. Anesthesia would, in the meantime, charm the child who helped move the map cart and ask about the times the cart left the Map Room unlocked for sorting.

Their little network formed like barnacles on the day.

The first snag came sooner than they expected. Kael was not in his office. His door stood ajar and papers lay across his desk as if someone had left in a hurry. Damian found on the desk only a short slip of paper with the words: "Attend Heckrog — urgent. Back at dusk." No signature, no relaxation.

He penned a note and slid it under Kael's door instead. The absence made the path harder but not impossible.

Reed reported that Torv kept to habit — the assistant, a thin man named Belen, took tea precisely at three, and the map cart was sorted twice a week, late in the afternoon. Belen, Reed said, was fond of a joke and of the archivist's cat. "If you bring the cat a fish," Reed added with the reverence of a plan becoming mischief, "Belen will talk to anyone."

Anesthesia had her own discovery: the Map Room stored maintenance sketches not on the public shelves but in a maintenance drawer beneath the floorboards — the sort of place where custodians kept their private records. She found a small loose tile when she was alone in the corridor and noted its location with the exactness of someone used to finding paths by tiny features.

"Everything has a seam," she said when they met later. "We only need to find the right seam."

—

They executed the plan slowly. First, Reed's distraction: he borrowed a small fish from the kitchen—Old Nari's largish herring that would not be missed if promised a neat replacement. He walked the corridor with exaggerated steps, humming the tune of some student song until Belen the assistant appeared, curious. Reed knelt, produced the fish with a flourish and the cat, obligingly present, took to it with eager grace. Belen laughed — a brittle thing at first, then honest.

"You're wasting the poor cat's dignity," he grumbled, but his tone was easy. Reed's small questions slid in: "What time do the maintenance plans come out? Ever seen annexes redacted?"

Belen, who expected only harmless chatter, answered. "Maintenance plans are kept separate. Old blocks, service ducts, things that the architects forgot. We don't let students near them. But sometimes — sometimes — if there's an old sewer sketch or an extension note, I fetch it. It takes tea, or a favor. Who is asking?"

Reed lied poorly but persuasively. "A faculty member. He's writing a lecture on building memory. He asked me to ask you."

Belen, flattered, agreed to show them the maintenance drawer that afternoon when the Map Room was quiet. A small victory — if limited.

—

The next difficulty was Torv. When Damian returned the following morning, prepared with a gentler plea for a provisional review, Torv recited the regulations with the calm zeal of a man who had memorized the university's appetite for order.

"I cannot authorize transfers on verbal request. Kael's signature is still required," Torv said, but he left a small window open: "You may inspect materials in the Map Room if accompanied by an archivist. No copying. No removal."

Damian weighed it, then accepted. "Very well. We will inspect. If we find nothing, we will report it by the end of the week."

Torv's glance was thinly curious. "You understand what you take on, Professor? Maps are not only paper. They are stories and contracts. They show not only stairways but intentions."

Damian only nodded. "I understand."

—

They spent three afternoons in the Map Room, humbly seated beneath its glass lamp, while Belen rolled out sheets and produced bundles. The room smelled of glue and the cold paper tang of rooms seldom touched. The archivist watched them with a careful neutrality — a man paid to measure curiosity without encouraging it.

They traced service ducts, old drainage lines, and layers of additions to Bogston; they found whole wings removed from later editions. The maintenance drawer produced brittle, hand-drawn sketches: a floor plan for the north service passages with an unlabeled alcove; a schematic of ventilation shafts with a note in ancient ink: "—for observation, 19—." There was no neat label: "experiments" or "patients." What they found was the language of utility and omission.

At one table, Anesthesia found a faint stamp in the corner of a maintenance sketch — the same spiral Alaric had drawn a thousand times. Her fingers paused. "There," she whispered. "It's been used as an internal mark."

Reed leaned in, breath fogging the paper. "They mark what they want hidden," he said. "Like a library putting secrets in thin wrappers."

They tried to copy; the archivist refused a mechanical copy without permission. They took photographs of sketches with the excuse of referencing for a lecture — a grey area, but one the archivist allowed when Damian signed a form stating the images would be used for pedagogical purposes only. Each photograph was slow, precise, a legal trespass in the margins.

They left with a small bundle of photocopies and with the knowledge that Bogston's plans had been edited, redacted, and carefully laced with gaps. The skeletons in the bunker were not on the active plans; they were an earlier generation's omission. The maintenance sketches hinted at an annex, but the annotations were coded.

—

On the walk back, passing under the university's eaves, they stopped at a low wall to sort what they had read. Anesthesia spread out the photocopies, smoothing them with fingers that moved like someone laying out a small map of the day. Reed shuffled the papers into piles, trying to make sense of the annotations. Damian watched the spirals in the margins, then looked up at the stone itself.

"So the place isn't the bunker," he said finally. "But the bunker is related. It's a boundary. A buffer. Someone used it to bury the past. We need to find where the plans are redacted — who signed off on those deletions. That will point to the active annex."

"And the spiral?" Reed asked, voice careful. "Why mark it there?"

Anesthesia's eyes were steady. "A signature. Or a code. Someone tagging sites that matter. Meridian, Ashwell, Shie. Small marks in the margins — a breadcrumb trail only those who know the sign can follow."

They sat on the wet stones and made a new list. The list was longer now, threaded with names: Belen (assistant), Torv (registrar), the inspector who signed the redactions (a name in the margin — "Locke?"), and the professor who had been present at the original installations (a note: "Thane?"). They would follow signatures now, not only stairways.

Before they parted, Reed frowned at one of the maintenance pages. "There's a note about patient ventilation in the old ducts. It's dated. Whoever wrote that used a hand we've seen before." He tapped the letter with a nail. "Look."

Damian read the slanted script and felt a small, cold certainty: it was Alaric's handwriting. A name in the stitched margin, a date, and then — a terse line: "Transferred under patronage. Confidential."

"That's the hook," Damian said. "Alaric was not merely curious. He had access to their language. He signed into something. And then they took him."

They left the campus slow, the photocopies folded into Reed's coat. The rain had settled into a quiet, as if the university itself were mulling over their progress. Nothing dramatic had happened: no alarms, no dramatic confrontations, only a series of small permissions seized and a careful trail of ink. But their bundle of papers had given them a direction sharper than any night's fear.

Back in his chamber that night Damian spread the copies on the desk and traced the spiral with a finger until his nail left a faint line. The dream returned at the edges of thought, but this time it carried something else: the sense of movement, not only of loss. The labyrinth in his sleep and the plans in his hands were beginning to match, and that matching made the next steps clearer — though not safer.

"We go deeper," he told Reed and Anesthesia when they returned later to confer, voices hushed in the lamplight. "We follow the names, the signatures. We ask who had patronage for these transfers. We find the redactions and the signers. From there we'll locate the annex."

Anesthesia tapped her pen in agreement. "Slowly. Quietly. And watch for Torv's habits. He's careful, but he sleeps at the same hour."

Reed folded the last photocopy into his pocket and looked at them both, tired but resolved. "We do this together."

They sealed the plan with small, ordinary gestures — checks on lanterns, the clipping of lists, the drawing of new arrows on the map. They were no longer a scatter of frightened witnesses; they were a small, deliberate team.

Outside, Bogston's towers lifted into the night, indifferent and massive. Inside, on a narrow desk, the spiral in the margin and the inked redaction made an opening — a seam to be pried, a secret beginning at the slow, steady edge of maps and signatures.

In the map they found someything strange the old church was called crowhouse .They thpught of gping there to find out actual things out there.

———

They walked toward the church with the kind of quiet that has the weight of too many nights behind it. Rain had swept the city clean that afternoon; the alleyways were still slick and bright, and the low sun threaded through clouds like a promise that meant nothing. The old church crouched at the edge of a narrow square—stones blackened with moss, the wooden doors swollen and bowed. No congregation had entered there for years; the place smelled of cold stone and old incense.

Anesthesia pushed the door with the flat of her palm. It gave with a hesitant groan and showed them a nave littered with dust, collapsed hymnals, and a few pews that still held the ghosts of long-sitting worshippers. Light came in slatted bars through a high, broken window, slicing the dust into narrow columns. The altar was a ruin of candles long burned to stumps.

They spread out slowly, lanterns held low. Damian kept his steps careful, not wanting to kick old timber or disturb anything that might speak. Reed padded after him, face drawn, fingers white where they gripped the lantern. Anesthesia's notebook was open in her hand, but she did not write; she watched, cataloguing the place with her eyes.

"Nothing obvious," Reed murmured after a long minute, the lantern's halo turning over cracked tiles and a rusted censer. "No signs someone's been here recently."

"Look at the soot," Anesthesia said, pointing to a ragged patch along the back wall. "Someone burned a fire here long after the place fell to ruin. Marks are recent."

Damian crouched, tracing the whisper of ash with a fingertip. "They tried to keep warm. Or they used it for something else. Keep your eyes open. The plans hinted at auxiliary rooms beneath old churches—storage spaces, crypts, maintenance ducts."

They moved toward the chancel, slow as if the floor itself might remember footprints and recoil. The air grew cooler near the altar. Damian's lantern illuminated a shallow recess in the stone where the floor had been hewn away—an entrance to a narrow stair. The stone steps disappeared into shadow.

"Of course," Reed breathed. "A stair."

They debated briefly, voices hushed. Anesthesia wanted to call Torv — make the find official, summon caution. Reed wanted to descend, impatient and eager. Damian put up a palm.

"Not yet," he said. "We do not know who uses this or why. If someone is removing evidence, calling others risks walking into a sweep. We go carefully, together." He handed Reed the second, smaller lantern. "You first, on the rope."

They threaded a thin length of rope through a hook embedded in the wall — a precaution Anesthesia had insisted upon — and Reed descended, each step measured. The light below revealed a narrow cellar, more like a passage, with crates stacked along the walls and a smell of damp linen and iron.

He called up after a few paces. "Nothing but boxes and a rolled tapestry."

Damian eased down after him. The passage opened into a wider undercroft with low arches. Here the air was stiller, as if the stone held its breath. Then a drop—hard to locate in the dim—splattered on the paving. Reed glanced up, and his voice went thin.

"A drop of blood," he said.

They all followed that single bead, absurd and terrible in the quiet. Damian moved slowly, then stopped so suddenly Reed stumbled into him. There, in the shallow pool between two broken pillars, a darker stain marred the flagstones. The lantern light trembled on it and made it look like an answering wound in the stone.

"Who—" Reed started, then the sound of his own voice was swallowed.

From above them, something shifted. A long shadow detached itself from the beams and resolved into a body. It hung inverted from a rigging set into an old iron ring—face turned away, clothing sodden and dark. For a half-breath they all stared, as if waiting for the figure to move, to resume argument or song. It did not.

Anesthesia made a small, animal sound like a page torn. Reed's knees went slack; he crouched and clutched the flagstone with both hands. Damian felt the old, cold certainty settle into his stomach. The rope from which the figure hung had been knotted with a practiced hand. The sleeves were clerical—linen at the collar still held a thread of white.

"Father Athelston," Anesthesia said, voice flat as if reading a line from a ledger. "He's—"

The words fell. Reed's lantern wobbled hard enough to cast the body into a strobe of shadow and light; in one of those slices the face came into view—older than the man Damian had seen in the chapel years ago, cheeks slack, eyes closed. There was no dramatic blood spurt, no fevered movement—only the hush of finality and a slow, steady seep onto the stone. Another drop pinged from the cloak and landed on Reed's shoulder, warm and bright against his skin.

Reed jerked, the color gone from his face. "This is why—this is why he wasn't here the other day when we looked," he said, breathless and breaking. "I thought... I thought someone must have been here before."

Damian's throat tightened. He knelt, not to touch but to look for signs—wounds, bindings, anything to tell them whether this had been a ritual, a murder staged to look like something else, or an execution meant to send a message.

"This isn't accidental," he said slowly, the syllables measured as if testing iron. "Not staged by weather. This is deliberate."

Anesthesia's hand found her notebook, but she did not write. She only breathed and then said the thing that had lodged under Damian's ribs since the bunker: "They kill those who know."

The three of them stood very still, the church pressing in on all sides like a stone mouth. Footsteps from the street sounded distant, ordinary — someone closing a shop, a cart rolling. The normal noises of the city felt obscene.

"How many know?" Reed asked, voice small.

"Enough." Damian's reply was spare. "Enough for them to be careful about witnesses. We have to assume anyone who sees too much risks being silenced."

Panic rose around them in different ways. Reed began to pace, hands at his temples. Anesthesia leaned against a pillar and slid down until she sat, notebook unopened like a shield across her knees. Damian felt anger, cold and precise, and beneath it a new thing—fear braided with responsibility. Father Athelston had been a name used casually in the house and the chapel; here he was turned into a sign.

"We must leave," Damian said. "We do not touch anything more than we must. We document as best we can, quietly. We do not call the registrar yet. We must think who can be trusted — if anyone."

Reed's laugh had no joy. "Trust? After this? Who do you trust, Damian? Torv? Kael? Heckrog?"

"No," Damian said. "Not yet. We trust only ourselves and the evidence. We must cover the ground: note the rope, the knot, time—how long the body could have been here. Then we withdraw. If they patrol the area, we could be found and blamed. If we state the find publicly, we invite a sweep which could erase everything."

Anesthesia pressed her palms into her notebook until the paper rustled. "We also have a moral obligation to the dead," she said. Her voice was tired and sharp. "We cannot simply run. If we do not tell someone, the body will be removed and replaced by a story that hides everything."

Damian met her eyes. The decision weighed like a stone in his mouth. They argued in soft lines—what to tell, when to raise the alarm, who might listen without killing the trail. They tested options: the constable (trusted but likely to alert the university), a sympathetic priest (who might pray but do nothing), a public notice (which would call collectors, students, inspectors who would sweep clean).

"What if the murderer wanted him found?" Reed asked suddenly. "What if hanging him where we would find him is the point?"

"That is why we are careful," Damian said. "They are sending a message. The message is: do not pry. Our movement tonight confirms that message. We must respond without playing into it."

They took careful measurements. Damian stood at the base of the pillar and measured the length of rope looped to the ring. He noted the knot—expertly tied, a hitch used by sailors more than common hands—and the angle of suspension, which meant the body had been hoisted from a scaffold or rig above. Anesthesia crouched and traced the path of the drops, their spacing suggesting the body had been in position for hours. Reed found a scrap of torn cloth snagged on a nearby nail; a fragment of embroidered thread, ecclesiastical in nature.

"Someone staged him as a cleric," Reed whispered. "To make it obvious who he was. Or to make us assume something."

"And to warn," Damian said. "To warn anyone who remembers him, who knows something."

They did what they could without alerting the world: Anesthesia took three small, furtive photographs with her sleeve-clad hand;

Reed, trembling, sketched the layout on the back of a scrap torn from his pocket. Damian found a small corner of the altar cloth and folded it into his hand to carry as a sample. They sealed it in a scarf and tucked it away.

When they climbed back into the nave the light had shifted to a thin gray. A rat scuttled across the aisle and vanished beneath pews. For the first time since the body swung, voices came—two passersby, wondering aloud about the broken door, drawing nearer.

"We leave now," Damian said, voice hard. "Do not return. Do not speak about this in public. We tell no one but each other, and we write what we have learned in code. We are, for the moment, the keepers of this knowledge. If anyone else knows, they will die."

The words were bleak, and each of them felt the truth of them land like a stone.

They slipped out the way they had come, the church swallowing the quiet behind them. On the threshold Reed paused, looking back at the black mouth of the open door.

"If anyone asks," he said in a low voice, "I already told the constable I was at home all evening. He can vouch." His hands trembled. "I didn't come earlier because—" He stopped, unable to form the rest. It was an admission, as much a confession as anything else: he had been spared the sight by chance or by a private fear that led him away.

They walked away with the rain returning in thin threads, as if the sky tried to wash the place clean. At the corner, they stopped and read their list under the weak light of a gutter lamp: the knot, the rope, the embroidered thread, the ash marks in the chancel, the stair down. Each item was a small, careful fact that might build into truth.

Damian put his hand on Reed's shoulder, the contact brief but deliberate. "We keep the record. We move quieter. No more bold steps without a plan. We find out who had access to the church. We find who knew Father Athelston. We find who benefited from him being gone."

"No one should be alone tonight," Anesthesia said. "We keep watch in shifts. We mark the seam."

They arranged a slow plan before dispersing: Reed would check the constable's rounds that night from a distance, see who was making notes; Anesthesia would visit the library and the chapel in the morning to ask innocuous questions about who had been conducting rites and repairs; Damian would write down every name that appeared in the map-room redactions and cross it against church registers.

They left the square with the feeling of someone who had picked up a shard so sharp it could cut the hand that held it. The old church sank back into its shadow. Behind them, the city went on, unaware. Ahead lay the small, patient work of making a map of danger: names, times, habits, the seam by which the hidden annex—whatever it was—could be pried apart. They walked on, their steps slow, each knowing that the presence of horror had altered the rules. They would be careful now not out of cowardice but because they had learned the cost of being seen.

They all reached Damian's chamber.They shut the door softly behind them and let the room settle. Evening light slanted through the curtains and fell in a dull stripe across Damian's desk; the papers, the maps, the small pile of photocopies lay like a careful accusation. The three of them stood for a moment without speaking, the sound of the city a muffled far thing outside the window.

Anesthesia set her bag down and, deliberately, opened her notebook. She met each of their eyes in turn. "I have said my story," she said, voice steady though tight. "Now you two tell me yours."

Damian sat on the edge of the desk. His fingers played with the wooden spiral Miska had given him until the grooves left a pale ring on his thumb. He looked at Anesthesia and then at Reed.

"I'm not here to expose Bogston," he said slowly. "I'm not a crusader. I'm here because..." He stopped, searching for words that would not sound like a child's plea. "Because of my father. I get the dream—every night now. He's trapped in the maze. I know him; he was intelligent. He would not have vanished of his own choosing. He came here, and they took him under the pretense of study. I think he's still inside some part of this place. I'm here to find him and bring him back."

Reed's reply was shorter, quieter. He perched on a stool, hands in his lap. "I don't have a story like that," he said. "I'm just a student. I followed questions, curiosity—like most of us. I wanted to learn. I never expected... this." His eyes flicked to the photographs of the church hanging in Anesthesia's sleeve. "I was in the wrong place, I suppose, at the wrong time."

Anesthesia watched them, and for a breath there was the hush of an animal listening for wind. Then she closed the notebook, palms flat. "You still don't understand," she said. "Not fully." Her voice, until then careful, tightened into something more urgent. "We are not here by accident. None of us came purely by choice."

She leaned forward as if the room itself might lean nearer and lower her voice. "They bring people who are useful—bright minds, influential patients, the kinds who can be made to think certain ways. They offer scholarships, positions, the chance to be part of something greater. They offer families help, or secrets, or coin. When a man like your father, Damian, writes to them, they answer. They promise research and refuge. Then they take what they need, sometimes without return."

Damian's hands had stopped fidgeting. The spiral lay cold now on the desk. "You mean—" he began.

"I mean they recruit," Anesthesia said. "They lure. They buy loyalty and silence. Some come willingly, thinking they will be part of legitimate research. Some are coaxed—threats to a relative, a cupboard of debts settled, a letter saying 'help us and we'll help you.' Those who suspect too much are made examples of. You saw the church. That was not a private quarrel. That was a signal."

Reed's face went pale. "You mean Father Athelston... he was killed because he knew?"

"Either that," she said, "or because his very presence reminded someone of the smell of truth. Either way, he was left where we would see him. They wanted us to see." She rubbed her forehead, an impatient motion. "We must accept this if we are to act. We cannot go on thinking this is merely poor practice hidden in mortar. It is chosen."

Damian found his voice again, quieter than before but steadier. "If that's true—if Bogston markets itself as learning and cloaks something darker—then the question is how. Who pays? Who signs? Where are the board's minutes? Those redactions we found in the Map Room—someone approved them. Someone with power. If we follow signatures, we follow fingers, not footsteps."

Anesthesia nodded slowly. "Exactly. Names. Patrons. The small marks in margins. People like Torv, like Locke, like the registrar who rubber-stamps secrecy. But larger too—the ones who fund the work. They are the ones who prefer quiet corridors to public scrutiny."

Reed swallowed and then, in a voice that shook, brought up something they had not discussed. "If they recruit—if they use salaries, invitations—there are ledgers, payments. Records somewhere. Even those who do the dirty work must eat. Someone moves coin. If we can find records—offbooks donations, hush-money—maybe we can trace the line to a patron. And patrons leave traces: houses, clubs, names that recur in speeches."

Anesthesia reached for a blank page and, with a pencil, drew three small circles. "We make concentric work," she said simply. "First: safety. We protect ourselves. Second: names. We trace signatures and payments. Third: witnesses. We find people who have been made to disappear and speak to anyone who remembers an odd delivery or a sudden scholarship."

They argued tactics slowly, each suggestion chewed over like bread in the mouth. Damian wanted a direct approach—go to Torv, demand records—then realized, with a chill, that Torv would notify the university, and they would be watched. Reed offered to volunteer at the Map Room, to be eyes and hands among rolls of paper. Anesthesia suggested cultivating small allies: the librarian, Belen, the apothecary's apprentice—people who kept hours and habits and would let them move quietly.

The plans they sketched on scrap paper were small and cautious: a list of names to check, a schedule of who would watch which gate, a pattern of code words to use if one of them were detained. They wrote the word spiral in the margin of every page and gave the mark a new meaning: a token to represent shared knowledge, to signal when a note was genuine and untainted.

"You must promise me something," Anesthesia said at last, not without softness. "If you find a trace that leads to my father—if you find any living proof—do not hand it to the university immediately. Bring it to us first. Let us see it. Let us be some part of the chain."

Damian steadied his gaze. "I promise."

Reed, fidgeting, added, "And if I find something and I'm scared—tell me to hand it over. I need you both to be harder than I am."

They sat for a long time after that, the scratch of the pencil the only sound. Plans do not guarantee safety; they are only the attempt to make hazard legible. Yet the small circle of truth in Damian's chamber felt less like a shard and more like the first tool needed to pry a seam.

When they parted that night, each moved with the slow, careful steps of people carrying new knowledge. The city outside the window breathed and blinked as though nothing had happened. Inside, the lamp burned low, the spiral cool and steady on Damian's desk. He lay awake long after Anesthesia and Reed had gone, fingers drumming the grain of the spiral.

The dream did not come that night. Instead there was only a hard, steady promise—his father's voice not in the maze but in the margin of a page: find the names, follow the money, keep the people you love out of sight. Damian closed his eyes and listened to the sound of his own breath. Tomorrow they would begin again, slowly, and with care.

The next morning, Damian woke to the gray light spilling across his desk, the spiral still lying where he had left it. The city was quiet—too quiet, as though it waited for him to take the next step. He dressed slowly, each movement deliberate, listening for the faintest shift in the hall outside his door. There were no sounds, no footsteps. Just the wind scraping the corners of the old building.

He found Reed already at the Room, pretending to sort papers while his eyes flicked nervously toward the door. Anesthesia arrived a few minutes later, notebook clutched under her arm, eyes sharp despite the pale line of exhaustion under them. They now had made one extra man to support them .They got there in Map Room.

"First circle," Damian whispered as he closed the door behind them. "We go through the documents we have, double-check all the names and signatures we noted last night."

Reed's hands shook slightly as he opened the worn ledger. "I don't know if I can catch everything. They use initials, abbreviations... sometimes the same letter twice for different people."

"That's why we cross-reference," Anesthesia said, kneeling on the floor to lay out their collected photocopies. "Even small inconsistencies can tell us more than an exact match. A repeated mark, a misdated signature, a ledger that doesn't balance... those are breadcrumbs."

They worked in near silence, the only sound the scratch of pencils and the occasional soft sigh when a line didn't make sense. Hours passed, and the city remained muted outside the thick stone walls. Reed was the first to break the quiet.

"Look at this," he murmured, pointing to a series of donations listed under a name they had seen in the Map Room redactions. "These aren't registered. Not officially. They flow through an account I can't trace. It's... off the books. Someone is funneling coin quietly."

Anesthesia leaned over, lips tight. "This is what we needed to see. It confirms what I said last night. Whoever runs Bogston, the decisions are deliberate. Quiet coin, quiet deaths."

Damian's eyes darkened. "We have to know where it goes. Who benefits. Not just the ledger. Any mention in correspondence, letters, notes in the margins. They always leave a faint trace."

A sudden knock at the door made all three freeze. Damian's hand went to the doorframe. "Who is it?" he called quietly.

"Belen," one who helped them, a soft voice replied from outside. "I... I have something you might want to see. Very quietly."

Anesthesia's eyes narrowed. "Did anyone see you leave your post?"

"No," Belen whispered. "I came through the service corridor. No one was watching."

Damian nodded once. "Open the door."

Belen stepped in, holding a small bundle of papers, their corners yellowed and edges frayed. She set them on the desk with trembling hands. "I found these in the library archive, under old maps that were supposed to be discarded. I thought... you might know what they mean."

Anesthesia took the bundle, carefully untied the string. "Dates, amounts, signatures... partial notes. Look here," she said, pointing to one page, "this mentions a Father Corwin. That's not in our previous list. And see the annotation? 'Handled quietly, until observation complete.' They are... monitoring something. Someone."

Reed leaned closer, squinting. "Observation? Who? Why?"

"They always monitor before they act," Damian said softly, lips tight. "Before Athelston... before anyone disappears. This is how they manage the maze. People are watched. Notes are made. Signals are sent. And then the decision comes."

A long silence followed, heavy with understanding. The city outside had shifted slightly; a bell in the distance tolled, dull and uneven, as though marking the slow passage of an unseen clock.

"Then we are next if we are not careful," Reed said finally. "Every step we take, they could see. Every question we ask... they will know."

Anesthesia closed the bundle, her voice low but firm. "That is why we go slow. Every move we make must be deliberate. Every observation must be hidden. And we must test what is safe, what is a signal, what is a trap."

Damian pressed a hand to the spiral, now worn smooth from constant use. "We begin with observation tonight. Not interference.

We map the entrances, the exits, the likely corridors someone might use to move bodies, messages, or coin. And we watch the gates. Someone always arrives or leaves. Someone leaves a trace."

Reed swallowed, nodding slowly. "And if we see someone suspicious?"

"Then we don't confront," Anesthesia said sharply. "We follow at a distance, record what we can, and retreat if necessary. The moment they know we are aware... everything changes. They can remove evidence, silence witnesses, or—" her voice dropped to a whisper, "or punish us."

Damian's jaw tightened. "We will proceed as three, no separation. We test, we observe, we record. Nothing else. If we are discovered... we retreat. Survival is primary."

The room grew colder as evening crept in, shadows thickening against the walls. Each of them could feel the weight of unseen eyes pressing through stone and distance. Bogston was a maze not only of halls and hidden rooms, but of intentions and silent threats.

And as the first hints of night bled through the window, they knew that tonight would be their first real test: to step beyond observation and into the labyrinth without alerting the unseen masters of Bogston that they were awake.

SEVEN

INK BENEATH THE PLASTERS

They left the Map Room before dusk with the slow carefulness of people who know what silence costs. Each of them carried something small that mattered: a stack of photocopies, Belen's bundle, Reed's folded sketch of the church cellar. They split the practical tasks between them without fanfare — lanterns checked, spare twine coiled, pockets filled with chalk and a small knife. Nothing dramatic: just instruments for watching.

Their plan for the night sat on a single scrap of paper, scratched in Damian's neat hand:

* perimeter watch — two points (north gate, service alley)
* record arrivals — time, description, direction
* do not approach — follow at distance if possible
* rendezvous at three-quarters of the market (old fountain) if separated

They moved in pairs to their stations. Reed took the service alley because he knew the paving and could melt into shadow there. Anesthesia claimed the north gate — she liked angles and choke-points; she said people make mistakes when they can't choose an exit. Damian walked the market arc between them, a drifting presence, the eye between two hands.

Night fell with a blade-edge of cold. Lantern-glow pooled on flagstones; steam rose from the fishmonger's stall. The university felt alive and asleep at once — students clustering in taverns, a custodian rocking on the steps of the chemistry block, a carriage clopping slowly down the main way. Bogston's noises were normal noises, which made the quiet ones stand out all the more.

They reported in low phrases.

"Nothing yet," Reed whispered on the alley wall, his voice barely a breath. "But a dog's been worrying the bins for twenty minutes. Could be a rat, could be a messenger."

"Count each stray," Anesthesia answered from the gate by way of reply. "They'll see numbers before faces."

Damian watched the entrance to the old service lane. He tucked the spiral against his palm and let his attention spread like a net. He tried to be a small, patient man: a watcher, not a hero. He listened for key sounds — the bark of a hound, the scrape of a crate, the particular cadence of a carriage wheel on cobbles.

An hour in, they had nothing but small discomforts: a loose shutter that clattered at half-moon, a cluster of students who puffed past singing, a patrol that turned its head this way and that and then moved on. The tedium was its own threat; it frayed nerves.

At one in the morning, Reed signaled — a faint three taps against the stone in a rhythm they'd agreed on. Damian rounded the corner into the service alley. A single man moved there, hunched under a cloak, one arm holding a small crate. He walked with the kind of exactness that suggested habit; the crate's weight sat balanced, like money carried with care.

Damian did not move toward him. He did not step into light. Instead he walked parallel at a distance of two lanes over, keeping iron railings and store fronts between them. From the corner of his eye he watched the man pause at a gap between two warehouses, whisper to a shadow, and hand over the crate. The shadow accepted it. They exchanged no words that reached Damian; only the small click of metal and the rustle of fabric.

Anesthesia, who had come closer under a market awning, made a tiny sound and put a finger to her lips. Reed, behind them, had the smallest tremor in his shoulders; he was younger but learning to move like a shadow.

They followed at two paces behind, lightless, slow. The recipient moved into the deeper parts of the district — an area of lean houses and fell workshops where no gatekeeper lingered. The exchange looked routine, practiced. The man they had watched returned alone, his step unchanged, as if he had never moved at all.

When they were sure they could afford a mistake, Damian made a choice: they would not follow him into the workshop alleys. Instead they circled to the receiving side of the same block. There, half-hidden beneath a loose shutter, Damian found a strip of paper tucked into a crack in the stone — the sort of thing a gloved hand might have slipped there to mark the spot for a second collection. The strip bore a partial stamp: a spiral, cut in haste, and below it a notation — a pair of initials and a number.

He stuffed the paper into his palm and stepped away, heart thudding as if from a short run. This was small: a hint, not proof. But it was what they had come for.

Their near-miss happened because of breath. As they crossed the square to regroup, a cart came down the lane — one of the university's maintenance carts, loaded with coals and sacks. Its driver glanced at the three of them and then slowed more than necessary. The cart's lantern swung and in that swing threw their shadows long and indiscreetly across moonlit stone. Reed caught the light and flinched visibly. The driver's eyes sharpened.

Damian's training in waiting paid off: he flattened himself against a doorway, chin to collar, and made no movement. Anesthesia eased behind a stack of crates and faked busy study of a catalogue pulled from her bag. The driver, a man with tired eyelids, coughed and spat, and the cart creaked onward. They exhaled as one.

Small incidents wove through the night like stitches. A child lost his mitten and cried near the fountain; Damian stepped out and returned it, offering a mundane explanation for being awake, because ordinary acts are better alibis than silence. Reed tripped over a step and cursed softly; Anesthesia laughed once, bright and human, and Reed smiled through the fear. An old woman on the corner asked if they were students who had missed curfew; they nodded and she muttered a blessing and sent them on. It was small theatre — the necessary kind that preserves a shape of normality.

After three such runs of watch — the cart, the crate, the paper — they met at the fountain and compared notes in whispers.

"I saw the handover," Damian said, laying the scrap flat between them. "They use code marks. The spirals are not decorative. The initials are likely clerical references, or patron IDs. The number could be a crate index. That man's gait — regular, not anxious — suggests he does this with permission."

"Permission, or confidence," Anesthesia said. "They aren't covering their tracks by sneaking. They're marking with arrogance."

Reed's voice was small but steadier than it had been the week before. "The paper's damp but readable. The initials are H.L. — could be 'H. Locke' we saw in the margins, or someone else. The number is 7. If it's inventory, we need to see what their crates contain."

Damian folded the paper into the spiral and put both back into his pocket. "We map and we match," he said. "We'll cross-reference H.L. and crate 7 with the donor ledgers. If money goes, the ledger will show notes. If things come in, the stores will show receipt."

They split again — different routes, different covers. Damian returned to the Map Room at dawn with the paper in his pocket and a burnt-out coil in his chest. He watched Torv move between his office and the stacks, neutral, then disappear into a meeting room. He left a question at Kael's door tucked with a copy of the photograph from the church; no answer came yet.

In the late morning, Belen—quiet, trusting in small ways—met them at the librarian's side door with something else: a list of carriage movements from the warehouse manifests. He smoothed the paper like a man ashamed of what it contained and said in a whisper, "I don't like these names, but they come often."

Among the manifest entries was a recurring sender: a private house in the south quarter that showed the same mark in the ledger, the same spiral scratched faintly at the corner. Names repeated: a "Patron H.L." in one column, "Meridian" scrawled in another. A shorthand code for "observational equipment." Nothing outrageous on its face until you fit the pieces together.

They sat in Damian's chamber that afternoon as rain began again and made the world grey and flat. The scrap from the alley, the manifest, the crates, the spiral — together they looked less like fragments and more like a door. They spread their papers and read slowly, aloud sometimes, parsing a ledger's syntax the way men read scripture.

Anesthesia's voice was level, but an undercurrent of anger hummed through it. "They are not only moving bodies; they are moving things that make bodies observable. We are not dealing with an institution of learning anymore. We are dealing with logistics — racks, vents, machines."

"Then the annex is a workshop," Reed said. "Not a ward. Machines need space and power. They move crates, they hide their receipts, they co-opt clerics and make examples when necessary."

Damian pushed his chair back and stood, hands on the window sill. He watched the rain stitch itself into the glass. "We have a lead on H.L. and crate 7. We have a pattern of deliveries out of a south-house tied to Meridian and a spiral. We have proof that Athelston was silenced for knowing. That's enough to open a new circle: who signs for the crates? Which faculty name appears in the receipt logs?"

They made a plan that smelled of more waiting. Reed would ask at the stores where deliveries were logged — as an eager student seeking employment in stores, a plausible cover. Anesthesia planned to sit in the chapel that day and listen for remarks, to place subtle questions and plant the impression she was simply a diligent practitioner. Damian, meanwhile, arranged to see the ledger clerk again, using a modest lecture proposal as a route to request access to more manifests.

They moved in slow, deliberate pieces.

That night, sleep came in pockets and not as a whole. Damian dreamed less of the maze than of receipts and signatures — lines becoming corridors, columns of numbers folding into halls. His father's voice, when it came, was not a call but a cautionary whisper: follow what is routine; the routine is a map.

In the days that followed they collected small things: a ledger line that mismatched, the name of an auxiliary clerk that turned up in two places, a signature that Alaric's handwriting matched in curl. Sometimes the work felt like archaeology — careful, painstaking, and half-lit — and sometimes like surveillance, which gnawed at them because surveillance sharpened fear into action.

They moved slower than their urgency demanded. They had learned, in the church, what price hurriedness could exact. Each night of watching taught them how to stand still when the city turned its head. Each small discovery hardened them — not into belligerence, but into a tempered patience born of necessity.

At the edge of every day, when they reconvened in Damian's chamber and stacked the night's scraps into a new order, they added another line to the map: H.L., crate 7, south house, Meridian notation, patron mention, manifest slip. Little by little the web tightened.

"Next," Anesthesia would say, tapping the newest note, "we see who signs receipts at that house. We watch the deliveries again. We learn the faces that bring the goods."

"And we do not forget Athelston," Reed would answer. "We write down his name in full on the first line of every page so we don't lose what this is about."

Damian would close his eyes and draw a faint spiral on the corner of a fresh sheet, then press the tip of his pencil so the mark imprinted slightly. The spiral had become their password, their promise, and each faint echo of it felt like a small, stubborn light in a place that preferred shadows.

They were still small; they were still vulnerable. But they had begun to make the country of secrecy legible, page by patient page. And the map — ragged, incomplete, and carefully guarded — grew with them.

The next monday they meant to meet at dusk; Jonas Reed did not show.

At first Damian thought he was late—Reed had a way of running after small errands, of detouring into a lane to barter a favor or to return a borrowed book. When the hour on the fountain clock slid past their agreed time, Damian let the lamp burn a little brighter and waited. Anesthesia arrived with the same steady, taut line to her face; she set her satchel down and asked once, quietly, "He rang?"

Damian shook his head. "No." The answer came out too small.

They set themselves to the obvious things first. Reed had a small room off the north stair — a narrow bed, a shelf with a limp row of textbooks, a folded coat on the peg. Damian led the way. The door gave with the same sigh it always did; the room smelled of wax and someone else's breath. Reed's bed was unmade, the blanket kicked half off as if he had left in a hurry. The lantern on the stool was cold.

Anesthesia moved with the practiced eye of someone who read traces the way others read books. She opened the small drawer where Jonas kept his notebooks. The drawer was empty except for a folded scrap — a tiny ticket stub from the market and a grain of sand that did not belong inside an attic room. "He packed light," she said. "Or something took the light for him."

Damian checked the cot; the mattress had an imprint at one corner, as if Reed had sat there and then been pulled away. Under the bed they found a single thing — a pencil rolled to the edge of the floorboard, its point blunt and smudged with graphite. Reed's sketch of the church cellar, the folded paper they'd used as clandestine evidence, was gone.

"His sketch," Damian said. The words were a kind of small apology to the air. "He never leaves that behind."

They moved through his room like people closing small doors. On the table, in a neat line, were a pair of gloves; on the peg a scarf. His satchel was gone. There was no sign of violence, no overturned chair. It looked, in the tight light, as if Reed had simply left — but the room's silence said otherwise.

They split, the way trained teams do, but with no formal training to steady them: Anesthesia went to the Map Room to see if Reed had returned or been seen; Damian checked Torv's office and the registrar's corridor; both of them sent quiet questions along the stone paths of the university. Reed's usual rounds — the pillared cloister, the fishmonger's corner, the archivist's dim window — were checked by the hour; students were asked with soft urgency: had anyone seen Jonas Reed? A few faces furrowed in memory, a few shrugged and said no.

Belen—who had been their small, steady ally in the Map Room—came with the first useful thing: a list of who had left that night, signed for last-minute tasks. He produced it like a man ashamed and apologetic. "He left at one, sir," he said, voice low. "Said he'd do the alley watch for practice. He took his lantern. He never came back to return it."

Damian felt something uncoil in him. He asked Belen for more: did Reed speak with anyone? Belen hesitated. "A man with a cloak came past the gate at half after midnight," he said slowly. "He and Jonas spoke for a moment. Then Jonas went on. The man turned back and moved different. I thought nothing of it then. I thought it was just two students passing."

They checked the alley. The lantern Jonas had carried — the small second one, battered and reliable — was missing. The slate where he'd made notes last night was gone too. At the very mouth of the alley they found a small thing stuck in a crack: a scrap of cloth, red at one corner. Not enough to cry over, Anesthesia said. Not yet. But enough to prick their skin.

They widened their search as daylight lifted into a thin, anxious morning. The constable would not immediately commit men to comb every lane—officials are wary of conspiracies and of being routed into trouble—but he did send two town watchmen to check the river path and the wharves. Damian supplied them with the folded scrap of paper from the alley, with the H.L. and crate 7 notation, and with a small description of what Reed had been doing. The constable's eyebrows drew together when he heard the name of the old church and the mention of Father Athelston.

"If you suspect foul play," he said, careful and blunt, "you must file it. And plausibly." He set the tone of the official world: cautious, legal, sometimes slow enough to hurt.

They asked Reed's acquaintances. A thin student in the dorm had seen him last night crossing the square toward the fish-stalls, muttering to himself. An older boy shrugged: "He's a wanderer. He works odd hours. We assumed he'd be in his bed." Nobody had seen him after the alley.

Anesthesia returned from the Map Room with a face that looked like someone who had swallowed ash. "Reed's name isn't on any out-list for the warehouse tonight," she said. "No sign he signed a crate out. No record of him at the stores."

Damian sat, the map on the desk seeming suddenly brittle, like paper over a pit. He drew, without thinking, the spiral again, darker than he'd meant. "If they took him," he said, very quiet, "they took him clean. No scuffle, no trace. They knew how to make him walk."

"Or he thought he was going willingly," Anesthesia said, and her voice was sharper than a blade. "Baits leave a line. A face, a favor, a promise. We must accept both possibilities. He could be taken. Or he could have gone, believing — and then found it was a lie."

They went back to Reed's room a second time, looking for a missed sign. On the shelf behind a jar of ink was Jonas's thin wallet, closed, with the coin they knew he never spent; inside, a pressed ticket stub from the baker where he favored the pastry; a small scrap of paper with a list of ledger names he had been copying at Damian's request. Nothing in it suggested departure. His watch was still looped in the drawer.

Panic enters like a fog: it changes voices. Reed's mother—if he had one in town—could not be found; he'd been an orphan of routines, living in rooms lent by a landlord. They'd not known where else he might have gone.

At noon, Damian and Anesthesia went to the river. People came and nodded with quiet sympathy. An old ferryman, who knew every face that crossed his launch, said he'd seen a boy with Jonas's coat moving toward the west road late the night before—no, he corrected himself—he'd seen a procession of cloaks, someone moving quickly, but the low light made it hard to tell. The ferryman looked at Damian with tired eyes full of salt. "Too many things move in a night," he said. "The river takes note, but it keeps most of what it sees."

They reported to Belen, who had another scrap: a folded map found where a clerk had stashed things — a note Jonas had left for himself that read, in a small hurried hand, "check H.L. deliveries—alley—1 AM." The handwriting was jagged where the ink had smeared. It was proof he had gone deliberately to the alley to watch. It deepened the guilt. They'd assigned him that watch.

Damian's voice when he spoke to Reed's absence was flat with an ache that made it feel like a wound. "He volunteered," he said. "He wanted to be part of this. I put him in the service alley because I thought it was easy to hide. I thought he'd be safe."

"You were keeping him close," Anesthesia answered, and there was no accusation in it—only an observation that cut both ways. "You thought you could shield him."

That afternoon they asked the registrar, Torv, for help. Torv's face stayed a practiced neutrality until Damian mentioned Athelston and the crate manifests. Then a thin thread of something — worry, curiosity, maybe fear — drew in his expression.

"You're asking for trouble," Torv said softly. "A missing student draws attention. The university will want to investigate, and the university means the council, and the council will close rooms. You understand."

"Yes," Damian said. "We understand the risks. But we can't find him ourselves."

Torv's hand rested on the ledger. "I will make inquiries," he said finally, and the tone of the promise made them uneasy because it sounded like someone buying time. "I will speak to the watch. But you would also do well to give me anything you have that points to the wrong-doers. Evidence changes urgency."

They left his office without Reed.

What moved them was not official apathy but the slowness of the gears. The university had procedures; the procedures required formalities. They were small people with small scraps of paper and the urgent ache of missing flesh. The apparatus of power moved through bureaucracy.

As the day sloped toward evening, they widened the search beyond official channels. Anesthesia spoke to the priest at the smaller chapel — one who had once known Father Athelston personally — and the priest's eyes filled with a slow sorrow. "Athelston had enemies," he said quietly. "Not for what he did but for what he said. If Jonas is gone... bring me word if you find anything. I will say masses. I will also light a lamp tonight. Sometimes small lights call attention."

They combed the city: the market, the wharves, the back lanes. They tapped at doors whose owners might have seen a hooded figure crossing late. A grocer recalled a boy with Jonas's gait — quick, attentive — passing the stall and keeping to the shadows. A lamplighter remembered seeing two lanterns moving in the same direction an hour before dawn. Nothing definitive. Their net held only guesses and thin threads.

That night they returned to Damian's chamber in a bone-deep tiredness. The city had given them only silence.

They did not sleep. They made lists. They pinned the new facts to the map with small careful marks: last seen — service alley — 1:30 a.m.; scrap with spiral found near receiving block; manifest shows south house marked to "H.L." crate 7; Reed's sketchbook missing. They wrote Jonas Reed's name in heavy strokes on the top of the paper. It felt, for reasons that were not purely rational, like a prayer.

"You think they took him because of what he knew?" Anesthesia asked finally, the question both a hypothesis and a demand.

"Either what he knew or what they feared he might tell," Damian said. "He had the church sketch. He had the maps. He was close to things we don't have a right to touch."

"He's also young," Anesthesia said, and in her voice was a tenderness that meant they were both fierce now, like parents. "Young people go missing more easily. They think they can talk their way through a danger and are sometimes swallowed for it."

They decided reluctantly to tell one person beyond their circle: Belen, who had proved loyal in small ways. If Reed had been taken by people who watched the Map Room, perhaps Belen could find a notch in the manifest ledger they had not seen. Belen came with a face that had been grown old by fear. He offered what knowledge he had: a ledger page, a name that repeated across three manifests, and a detail — a house belonging to a minor patron with the initials H.L. The house was the same south-house on the manifests. Belen's fingers trembled when he spoke.

"People whisper about it," he said. "They say men go there at night and leave with empty hands or with heads bowed. But nobody likes to say the name aloud. They say it's bad luck."

Damian walked the line of houses in the south quarter that night and stopped at the door with the iron ring the ledger suggested. The ring was cold in his hand; the door itself was in darkness, as if the house had been chosen to be invisible. He listened at the stones and thought of Reed's hand touching the rope in the church, of the body that had been hung so everyone could see, and felt a low, rising violence that was not simply emotion but a harness of resolve.

They placed a small, coded thing — a scrap bearing the spiral folded twice — in the hollow beneath the front step of the south-house, a message meant for Jonas if he was alive and being kept close: we look. Do not panic. It was a stupid, brave thing: a scrap in a stone. But they had nothing else to offer him.

On the third day of searching, the watch reported a rumor — a whisper that Reed had been seen bundled into a vehicle with two men near the river at dawn. Each rumor tasted like salt and mud: possible, terrible, and unprovable. The constable promised to run down the rumor. He came back with nothing but a list of four other rumors and the complaint that such things multiply like rats in the dark.

Every step they took after Reed vanished felt more hazardous. Where once their work had been patient, archival, it turned toward urgency, toward the taste of a hunt. Their careful sentences shortened. They began to sleep in the Map Room in turns: Anesthesia by the ledger table, Damian on the narrow couch, Belen at the desk. They left small notes pinned with the spiral so that Reed — if he was kept but could escape or read their signs — might know they had not forgotten.

At the end of a week their trail ran cold. There were more leads, but each dissolved into bureaucratic fog or into the careful unbelief of those who do not want to know. The university, when pressed, tended toward closure: declared missing, suggested travel, recommended patience. It was a protection and an erasure at once.

In the small hours of a grey morning, Damian found himself at the church again—not the old abandoned place that had been Crowhouse, but the little chapel where the priest had promised a lamp. He stood alone in the nave under the thin light and spoke Jonas Reed's name aloud. The name hung in the air and then sank into the dust.

"You did not leave," he told the empty benches. "If you did, you left too little."

His voice sounded like a boy's in the echo. He did not know whether he spoke to God or to the absent man or to the stone.

When he returned to the Map Room his hands were steady but his eyes were raw. "We cannot file this in official channels and expect justice or speed," he said, eyes on Anesthesia. "We have to accept we are on our own timeline now. We must find H.L., the south house, the patrons behind Meridian. We must find out who benefits from silence."

Anesthesia nodded slowly. "We also must be careful," she reminded him. "Every move costs. If they took Jonas to silence knowledge, they might already know we look. If they took him for other reasons—perhaps a message—it's even more urgent."

They wrote his name again at the top of the ledger box, penciled it in heavy strokes. Then they added the spiral beside it and pressed the pencil so deep the mark dented the paper.

They did not sleep that day either. Their small slow work had become a rescue. They operated now by urgency and by the rules they had first set in the chapel: watch, record, do not approach without plan. But the rules had shifted their meaning: a watch was no longer merely observation; it was a way to keep one missing from being forgotten.

And somewhere—somewhere they could not reach—Jonas Reed was a name they could not erase from their mouths. They kept calling it, mapping what they knew, and moving in the small patient hope that pieces of paper, lists of names, and the stubborn spiral might one day be enough to pry open a door and bring him back.

———

They only began to suspect Belen slowly — a drift of small things that, piled together, felt like a tide.

It was a misremembered appointment, first: Belen had told them he'd seen a delivery cart pass the Map Room at one in the morning, then a ledger clerk corrected him later to half past midnight. Then there were the pauses: when Damian asked how the maintenance drawer was inventoried, Belen blinked and said, "We don't always note everything," in a tone that read as practiced omission. Finally, Anesthesia, who had learned to read the tremor in a man's fingers the way others read a line on a map, caught the way he watched his own hands while they spoke, as if expecting someone to step in the doorway at any minute.

They argued about it for an hour in Damian's chamber. Words were sharpened and softened in turns.

"He's a clerk," Reed objected before he disappeared. "He liked us. He brought us things."

"He also keeps the keys," Damian answered. "If someone is slipping notes under tiles, he knows which ones are loose. If we are watched through manifest logs, he sees the signature flow."

Anesthesia did not want to believe it. "Belen is small against the university. He helps where he can. You think he's betraying Jonas?" Her voice was incredulous but not naïve; she wanted proof, as she always did.

They had none that satisfied the better angels of their hearts — only friction, gaps, the way small stories rearranged themselves if you looked at them from a certain angle. Desperation, they told themselves, makes a bad map of a man.

Still: Reed's absence had already sharpened every edge. Hours of sleep had unraveled into a single thread of panic. The spiral on the map felt suddenly inadequate. Damian, who had weighed risk and plan in a way that felt like religion to him, found patience empty. He found an ugly certitude growing where carefully charted caution had belonged.

They invited Belen to the chamber with the cordial stiffness they used when asking questions of people who had previously been kind. He came without a coat — a sign of trust, or of having nothing to put on in a hurry. The Map Room clerk tried to be casual, handing them a small packet of papers and smiling too broadly. "Thought you might want these," he said. "Found a misfiled manifest."

Damian closed the door and lit the lamp. The three of them sat in a small, tight geometry that made the room feel like a trap. They gave Belen tea, because politeness is brittle armor in interrogations, and because Anesthesia could not bring herself to begin otherwise.

At first their questions were normal: who signed this, where did the crates go, did anyone check the south house's receipts? Belen answered in his habitual halting way, but the answers repeated that same song of incompleteness. "I... I only move the carts," he told them. "I write what I'm told. I'm not—" his voice broke and he swallowed. "I'm not the head."

Something in Damian snapped — not rationally, but in the long, animal way that grief and fear do. He had promised Reed he would bring him back. He had promised Liora he would keep the house safe. Promises had weight; promises pushed a man into acts he would not have otherwise done.

He rose then, and the change was small at first — a hand on the table, fingers curling. "Where were you at one a.m.?" he asked. The question was quiet. Belen named an alley; his voice was even until he said the name of the alley that matched the scrap of paper Damian had found. "I walked the lane," he said. "I helped a delivery. There were men. I left. They told me not to tell."

Damian's hand found the edge of the desk and then the skin under Belen's ear. The next moments were not cinematic, only close, ugly: a shove, a chair scraping back, then a push that sent Belen to his knees. Words tumbled into the small room like thrown things. Damian wanted names, times, the needle point of truth; Belen gave him sentences that wandered and circled, answers that invited more force.

Anesthesia stood, then sat, then stood again. "Stop," she said once, voice thin. "This will not work."

But it had already begun. Inexperience and fury make bad interrogators but ferocious ones. Damian shook the man — not with the methodical cruelty of an executioner, but with the animal impatience of someone trying to wrench open a box that would not yield. He grabbed at wrists, demanded, threatened in a voice he'd never used before. He slammed fists on the table to make the room listen. He leaned close and told Belen about Jonas — about the sketch that had gone missing, about the boy's laugh, about the empty bed. The images were small torments, and they were meant to wound.

Anesthesia tried again to pull him back. "You promised you would not make this beast of yourself," she whispered, not to Belen but to the man she had come to trust as their slow, unflinching center. Her hand on his arm was a plea. "Think. If you break him, we lose a source. If you—"

Damian did not hear the last of it. Desperation makes you deaf in certain registers. When he struck out, when he used the kind of pressure no law allows — he did not catalogue his actions later. Memory compresses violence. On some things you cannot think closely.

Belen's answers changed from sentences to noises. He coughed, inhaled, hissed. He did not yield a name. He did not point a finger. Sometimes a person closes against pain by closing their mouth, and Belen's mouth had the tightness of a man who had chosen a silence that no blow would unloose.

Anesthesia could not bear it much longer. She grabbed Damian's arm, pulling with a force that surprised them both. "Stop!" she said, once, then again, louder. Her knuckles were white. She was not, in that moment, a neutral observer. She wanted to help her friend hold to the thing he still was — reasonable, careful, principled. She also wanted Reed alive. The contradiction hollowed her.

They stopped because Anesthesia made them stop, not because their cause had been justified. Damian's chest heaved. Belen slumped on the floor with a wet, animal sound in his throat. He had the blue-black of a man who had been forced through more than fear — the look of somebody pressed to the edge. His face was bruised. His shirt had tears at the collar. There were marks on his wrists.

"Tell us," Damian whispered, voice spent. "Who signs for crate seven? Who is H.L.?"

Belen's eyes opened and closed like a slow slit. His lips moved, and no sound came out, as if whatever held his voice had become a stone lodged in his throat. He did not speak.

They waited until the room had emptied of the noise of struggle and then, with hands that would not be steady for days, cleaned the worst of the marks from the table. Anesthesia tore a strip from a sheet and made a bandage for Belen's bleeding lip. She worked with the kind of meticulous care she had once used to catalog evidence. She tried to make the room whole again with quiet tasks; mending is a kind of atonement.

Belen did not, that night or the next, offer a clue. He told them nothing beyond the same small, fumbled sentences he had offered before: "I do what they tell me. I sign what I'm told." He would not name a patron; he would not point to a door. When they pressed, he simply went silent, his eyes distant as if he were already somewhere else.

They left him with a blanket and a candle and a rawness that no bandage could hide. Anesthesia sat for a long time afterward on the opposite chair and refused to meet Damian's eyes. When she finally spoke it was not to him but into the quiet room, to the paper maps and the small, stubborn spiral on the desk.

"We have no right," she said. "We have no right to become what we hunt."

Damian could only answer with a thin, animal sound that passed for a laugh and for nothing more. "I promised him," he said. "I promised Jonas."

That promise did not sanctify what had been done. It did not make the bruises on Belen less. It did not strip away the fact that they'd forced a human being — someone who had shown them a sliver of kindness — into a silence by which they hoped to buy another life.

In the days that followed, the chamber smelled of damp and iron. Belen did not leave the Map Room to work; he sat with his head down and let others bring him bread. Rumors would mottle the university's gossip for weeks — that Jonas had been taken by men with cloaks, that Reed had run off, that the Map Room clerk had grown unreliable. No one named the beating. No one put together the pattern for what it was: the first time desperation had been answered with cruelty from their side.

That silence — Belen's continued refusal, their failure to get what they wanted — settled over them like a second winter. It was not only that hope had not returned with a name. It was that something in them had shifted. Anesthesia grew colder in ways that were different from resolve: a small cynicism in her tenderness. Damian carried a new hardness behind his eyes. Reed's absence, already a wound, had become a bone-deep thorn: they had mistaken force for efficacy, and it had not worked.

They dreamt that night in fragments: Jonas's face in a doorway; Belen's eyes as if losing a color. The spiral they carried between them — once a promise and a sign of solidarity — felt for a while like a stain at the edge of paper. They had crossed a line and found nothing on the other side.

When they pinned new notes to the ledger the next morning, they left a line scratched around Belen's name: no cooperation. They circled it twice with their pencil like a damp seal. It read as facts are often forced to read: a ledger entry, cool and neutral and not quite able to hold the weight of what it meant.

They continued. They had to. There was a boy out there with his name written heavy on their tongues. But the memory of the room — the small lamp, the bruised cheek, the stubborn silence — did not leave them. It sat in their chests as a measure they did not want to keep: the cost of retrieval laid bare in the quiet of a man who had not spoken a single useful word.

And in the evenings, when Anesthesia and Damian sat across from each other to plot their next careful move, both of them touched the spiral on the map before they began, as if to remind themselves of what they had been and of what they had been foolish enough to become.

For three days after Belen's silence, the city felt narrower—its alleys closer, its doors heavier. They moved in that small orbit the way men move when a weight has settled on their shoulders: careful, habitual, each step measured by the ledger on the desk.

Anesthesia kept to the work of small repairs. She patched Belen's shirt where it had torn, boiled herbs for his bruised jaw, and sat with him while he stared at a wall and refused even the consolation of a muttered grief. Caring, she believed, was an action as much as an argument; it was how she paid for the moment when she had been unable to stop what happened. Damian could not look at her when she brought the cloth. He busied himself with maps, with the slow arithmetic of tracing initials through manifests. The spiral in the corner of each page felt like a stitch in something that might otherwise come apart.

They argued more now, too—not loudly, but the pinprick kind of quarrel that lasts all day: about risk, about whether to go to Torv, about whether to widen the net of people they involved. Damian wanted speed; Anesthesia wanted patience. Each held the other's fear like a mirror.

"We cannot do what they do to us and call it justice," she said once, near dusk, while they spread manifests across the desk. Her voice was steady but small. "If Jonas is alive we need a way to pull him without becoming what hides bodies in plain sight."

Damian's hands were in a paper-tangle. "We are not them, Ani," he answered, using the name like an anchor. "But we are not gods either. Jonas is out there. If there is the smallest chance Belen knows—if he can point us even a finger—then we do what must be done."

"You promised you would not strike again," she said, and the memory of the bruised face in the lamp's glow made a quiet ferocity in her. "You promised me."

He looked at her, and for a long breath the two of them looked like people who had been carved from the same stone and then placed back together with a new seam. "I promised Reed," he said finally. "I promised Liora. I will keep those first."

They did not decide anything in heat. They repeated their options like a litany: ask Torv (slow, public), push Belen harder (ineffective and morally bankrupt), follow manifests to the south-house (risky, direct), plant a watcher in the warehouse (practical, needs a face). Every plan had a cost. Every cost tightened the knot in Damian's stomach.

That evening, Anesthesia walked back to the Map Room with a tray of bread and soup. Belen sat in the corner by the ledger-shelf, hands folded like a boy's. He would not look at her when she entered. She set the tray gently and sat across, keeping her eyes on her own hands as she spoke of nothing: the weather, the new shipment of binding thread, the librarian's cat that had learned to steal the best pages from the atlas. It was the kind of harmless talk that, if you could keep it flowing, let someone float above the memories they had been pressed into.

Halfway through the bowl, Belen stirred. He reached into the inner pocket of his jacket with a slow, furtive motion and extracted a folded scrap of paper. He placed it in Anesthesia's hand without a word and then turned his face away. She unfolded it with fingers that did not tremble though her pulse had quickened. The scrap was small, scribbled—perhaps hurriedly, perhaps with fear—but legible enough. Two lines, a letter and a number and a place:

> H.L. — 7. South door, dusk. Cellar key: ring 3.

Anesthesia's throat made a sound that might have been a laugh or a sob. She looked up. Belen's eyes were wet and far away; he did not meet her. He mouthed something like sorry and nothing more.

She sat for a long moment with the paper between her palms, feeling its weight like a new, sudden fact. It was not a confession. It was not a full map. But it was a mark in the dark: a direction that might lead to Reed, or at least to the anatomy of the place that had taken Athelston. It was the sort of thing a terrified man might dare hand to someone he trusted if he was trying to atone for a silence that had felt like survival.

She went to Damian without walking. He was at the desk, pushing pins into the wall map where manifests and alley scraps had been placed. When she put the scrap before him his breath was short and precise and, for once, without the hard bite of anger. He read it twice, then three times, the letters making a small geometry on his tongue.

"This is something," he said finally. "It's small, but it is something." For a moment his voice lost the rasp that had sharpened over the past week. "If it's true — if H.L. signs for crate seven at dusk — we can watch. We can learn who carries the key, who takes the crate into the cellar. We don't confront. We only see. We trace the hand."

Anesthesia put her hand on his arm. "We do it right. No more breaking men. If Belen tried to give this, he did it knowing the cost. We owe him that much."

They planned on paper and in small conversation. There were practicalities to arrange: who would keep the long watch, who would approach the south-house gate under ordinary cover, what phrases to use should suspicion rise. They practiced being invisible: the way you stand lit by a lantern without looking like you stand to light, the way you fold your gloves into your pockets so it looks like a man who has simply come to pass. Reed's absence weighed every move like a stone on a scale.

Night folded over the city like cloth. They took positions with the same slow precision they had used before. Damian found a shadow by the bakery, a place where he could see the south-house gate and remain, in the outward city, nothing more than a shape in the dark. Anesthesia stationed herself at the opposite side where stone steps made an easy seat and a line of sight to the side entrance. Belen lingered nearby—his presence was an ember of something between hope and penance—and kept his head down while they did their watching.

Dusk came and with it the small rituals of the neighborhood. A boy chased a hoop down the lane, and a woman called him home; a cart rattled past carrying coal, its driver singing. Nothing obvious. Then, as the light thinned, two men in cloaks came up the street, each carrying a crate like a thing of ordinary work. The smaller of the two had the gait of someone who hauled things often; the other's hand was quick to the ring on the gate.

They did not move toward the house. They paused at the door and spoke in low voices—a single line from which Damian could not hear more than a few words. The smaller man produced a key and, with a practiced ease, turned the lock. He lifted the ring on the step and, as if retrieving something left for him, dropped it into a small hollow in the stone.

Damian's chest tightened. The hollow: ring 3. The scrap from Belen had been right.

The men crossed the threshold and the lantern light dimmed behind the shutter. For a long minute nothing else happened. Then a long, muffled sound—the creak of wood, the placement of a crate—came from inside. The smaller man stayed at the doorway as if on habit; the larger one moved back into the lane and then vanished into deeper shadow.

Across the road, a door opened and closed with a sound like a secret. A girl, the housemaid perhaps, passed with a bucket and did not look up. The world continued to be the sort of place that allowed dreadful things because they were disguised as ordinary.

Damian felt the old animal impatience rising: to move, to fight, to tear open the door. He felt also Anesthesia's hand on his sleeve: still, she mouthed, watch. They could not risk a confrontation, not with the university sleeping one street over.

From the angle of her observation, Anesthesia made a precise note in her book—a shorthand of timing, of the man's height, of the sound and direction of the footfalls. Belen, who had crept closer while the men were inside, breathed like someone who had just woken. His face was ashen as paper. He had given them a line and now they had to follow it the way hunters follow a scent.

They did not force the door that night. They would not risk being the sound that erased Reed's trail. Instead, they withdrew with what they had: the time, the description, the knowledge that the crate had entered that cellar and that ring three had been the marker.

On the walk back the rain began again, slow and fine, as if the sky were washing its hands. Damian's shoulders felt simultaneously lighter and heavier; the scrap in his pocket was small but it was a path. Anesthesia kept her notebook closed and her eyes on the stones. Belen trailed behind, a thin figure who carried a secret like an ember.

They returned to the chamber and wrote what they had seen in a new ledger—dates, times, the shape of the crate, the ring. Each entry was a small promise. Reed's name sat at the top of the list, heavy as lead. They had a place to go now, a hinge.

They went to bed tired in a way that felt honest. In the dark, Damian thought of the church and of Athelston's body, of Belen's bruised face, and of Jonas's missing sketch. He did not sleep long, but when he slept he dreamt of narrow stairs and of ringed keys.

The labyrinth in his dreams had walls that were more map than stone now, and for the first time in a long while a path in that map had a next step.

They had found a door. They would open it, slowly, in the morning.

———

They left before dawn, the city still in that soft half-dark when noises are muffled and decisions sound louder than they will in daylight. Damp wrapped the lanes like a second skin; breath came in white puffs that vanished almost as soon as it formed. Each of them moved with the deliberate slowness of people who know haste will only make them clumsy.

Belen led them down a route that avoided the main stones: service alleys, a gardener's back lane, a gate whose latch could be lifted from the inside if one knew how. His hands trembled when he weighed the little hollow in the step and drew from it the ring they'd watched the night before. For a moment he stood as if the ring had the whole of his courage on it. He slid it into Damian's palm like a thing that demanded payment.

"Don't make noise," he said. The voice came out a husk. "If there's anyone here awake, they'll hear."

They worked in pairs. Damian and Anesthesia moved across the threshold together; Belen remained outside as promised, his head bent like a man paying penance by watching. The door did not resist. Inside, the south-house smelled of coal and old varnish and a faint chemical tang that made Damian frown. It was, in its living-room ordinary way, arranged to deny secrets—carpets, a lamp on a side table, a clock that ticked so loudly in the silence it felt accusatory.

Light from their lanterns found the inner door to the cellar: stout oak, iron-bolted. The key turned with a reluctant sigh. A breeze moved the dust motes in the stairwell like confetti. They went down.

The cellar was not large. Crates were stacked against one wall, labeled in neat stencilled caps that read, blandly, "SUPPLIES." There were hooks on the beams and, in one corner, a table with tools—pliers, pumps, a coil of rubber tubing. A single oil-lamp guttered on a shelf as if someone had put it out hastily. The air was colder below; breath made small clouds. Damian's lantern swept the room in a slow, methodical arc.

"Nothing," Reed's absence echoed before they said it aloud. The word was a small blow.

They checked systematically. Anesthesia opened every crate wide and smelled them, made notes in her book.

Damian glanced at the book. A half-smile tugged at his lips as he finally asked, "Why do you always carry a book with you?"

Ani shifted the book closer to his chest, as if guarding it from the question itself. "It's... required," he answered simply, his tone carrying both necessity and secrecy.

For a moment, silence lingered between them. Then Damian's gaze drifted past him, lost somewhere in memory. "You know," he murmured, "I once had a friend, back when I was younger. She, too, always carried a book—just like you."

The continue to check them systematically .Only she and Damian understood—"no linens; mechanical parts; faint scent of solvent; no bedding." One crate held glass vials nested in straw; another contained cast-iron parts, old and oiled. There was a narrow wooden frame—an armature of sorts—that made Damian's stomach pull. The things they found were consistent with what they had feared: equipment rather than bodies, observation rather than care.

They found tracks. Mud smeared the flagstones near the back wall; a single boot print was clearer than the rest, the tread of a small, service-style boot. Fresh straw had been dragged aside in one small place; the straw glistened with the slow sheen of something wiped up and not entirely gone. There were marks on the beams where ropes had rubbed, as if something had been hoisted not long ago.

They found no Reed.

Anesthesia crouched and pressed the pad of her finger into a smear at the lip of a crate. "They moved something through here recently," she said. "Not long before we came. Probably within the night." Her voice was quiet; the fact became a small blame.

Damian went to the far wall and found, tucked into a seam of the stonework, a scrap of paper folded small. He expected—hoped—a message, a map, a name. He unfolded it with the same kind of unhurry he used on fragile manuscripts.

It was nothing Jonas would have written. It was a receipt: "Crate 7 — delivered to Meridian Lab. Signed: H.L." The ink blurred at the corner as if a hand had been wet. It was proof that the crate had a destination beyond the cellar, and proof that the line between house and annex was a corridor of commerce. It was also, painfully, confirmation that their night watch had been right about the crate and very wrong about the audience it would yield.

They checked again. A narrow hatch beneath a stack of crates squeaked when Anesthesia eased it open; it led to a low crawlspace under the floor that terminated, after a foot's length, in a blocked bit of wall and a pall of old, stagnant air. Whoever had left the place had no intention of hiding a sleeping man there to be found. Whoever had taken someone had not wanted him left in a place anyone could see by morning.

"Maybe they took him upstairs to a room," Belen whispered from the step, and the sound of his voice, tight and small, made both of them stop. He had the look of a man who had given a scrap of truth and paid for it in fear.

They reconstructed possibilities the way someone might build a small bridge from thin planks: he had gone in with the crate; he had seen something; they had taken him beyond the crate's destination; the crate itself was misdirection. Every hypothesis left a space where a man could be lost.

They left the cellar as quietly as they had entered and closed the door behind them. Belen's face, when they looked at him from the street, was unreadable. He did not meet Damian's eyes. He had given them a route; he had not given them a boy.

They returned to the chamber with a slow, hollow silence between them. The wind had picked up; rain had begun again as if the city wanted to rinse the morning clean. The map on Damian's desk looked like a small domestic violence when set against the absence they carried.

They sat with the receipts and the crate labels spread across the table as if they were bones someone else had named. The thing they had: proof the crate moved onward; traces that someone had been in the cellar; no Reed. It felt like a hand slipping through their fingers. Disappointment moved through them in layers: the practical failure of the search; the deeper, gnawing sense that their map was still a map of shadows.

Anesthesia's voice broke first. "We went in and found rooms and not the child," she said, and the word came out like a small, shameful thing. "We look like fools."

"You did not go in to be fooled," Damian said, though the words were thin and did not quite hold. His fingers smoothed a fold in the receipt until the paper creased. "We have progress. H.L. is real on paper. Meridian Lab had a crate. The south-house is a node."

"You wanted Jonas to be in a crate," Belen said suddenly, the sentence a small, raw sound. "I—" He cut himself off as if a further confession would topple him.

Damian looked at him. "We wanted him home," he said. "We wanted that more than we wanted anything else."

Silence gathered again. The three of them circled the same small set of facts as if trying to warm themselves by them.

"We check the manifests in detail," Anesthesia said finally, letting resolve patch the holes in her voice. "We check transport routes. Crate 7 went to Meridian — find who signed for it on the Meridian side. If there are carriage logs, there's a driver. If there's a driver, he remembers hands. We will find the path the crate walked."

"And we watch the south-house tonight again," Damian added. "If they're moving goods at dawn, they move people by dusk. If they move in patterns, we can learn the rhythm and find the gap."

Belen's hands finally stopped trembling enough to fold into one another. "I will show you the ledger entries I do not touch," he said. "I will show you the columns I never read. I can—" his voice broke on the last word.

"No more violence," Anesthesia said quietly, and her eyes bore into Damian as if to re-anchor him. "We do not put our hands into other men's skin and expect truth to ooze out. We use what we have. We watch, we trace, we force no one into silence."

Damian bowed his head. "I promise," he said, and the promise was small and meant to be kept.

They spent the day in quieter work: Anesthesia cross-checked ledger entries with the receipt they had found; Damian copied names and initials into a clean folio; Belen, when he could, pointed out the clerk's shorthand and the times when crates were listed as "consolidated." Their progress was granular, made of small recognitions rather than dramatic revelations. Each tiny match felt like the scraping of flint: sparks, not fire.

Toward afternoon the constable's assistant—noisy with good intentions—arrived at their door with a formal note: "We have increased rounds near the south quarter." It was, in effect, a public announcement that someone official had finally acknowledged a pattern. It was also a risk; anyone connected to the south-house might now become more cautious, or more violent.

"That may push them to move Jonas," Belen said, all the hope of a man who had given up almost everything. "To move him away from prying eyes."

"Or to hide deeper," Anesthesia answered. "Both are possibilities."

They did not sleep that night. They took turns in the Map Room—Anesthesia with the ledgers, Damian pacing the map pinned to the wall, Belen sitting with his head on his arms and the line of his shoulders finally slackening enough to weep without shame. At dawn Damian watched the south-house again, his eyes hollow with fatigue. Men came and went with the same ordinary faces; a child sold birds at a window; the maid carried coal. Nothing in the outward life of that street gave away the inward violence.

When the day closed in and they met once more to plan, Damian felt the small, unyielding press of guilt like a weight at his throat.

Reed was a hole not in paper or in ledger but in them: a gap where a laugh had been; a name that would not stop asking.

"We mapped a node," Anesthesia summed up. "We did not rescue a boy. But nodes make networks. We follow the receipts; we follow the hands that sign for crates at Meridian; we follow the drivers. We do it with care and with witnesses—people who will not vanish from hunger for a week."

Damian nodded. "We find the driver. We trace the crate's path to Meridian. We test whether crate 7 is the kind that moves people or the kind that moves machines. We watch patterns and wait for the moment the pattern breaks."

They wrote out tasks in the tight, economical script that had become their ritual: who watches which gate, who queries which clerk, who will make a note of names and times. Each entry was a small, faithful oath.

Before they left the chamber that night, Anesthesia stood and placed her hand—brief, decisive—on Belen's shoulder. "You did what you could," she said softly. "You will not have to carry the next step alone."

Belen's lip trembled. "If Jonas is harmed because of me—" he began.

"Then we will answer it together," Damian said. It was not an answer that could undo the past. It was, however, a promise that they would attempt the one thing the university had not: keep human beings at the center of everything they did.

They left the ledger spread open on the desk and the spiral they used as a seal pressed into the corner of a fresh page. Outside, Bogston's towers rose indifferent. Inside, the three of them moved like people remaking themselves, not into heroes but into watchers who had learned the cost of being seen.

They had not found Jonas Reed. They had, instead, found a corridor that might yet lead to him. The disappointment was a flavor that sat in their mouths all the next day: bitter, persistent, and a spur. They would follow the route the paper suggested, and they would keep their hands clean of new cruelty. It would not be quick.

It would not be easy. But it was a path, and in that country they had at last learned to walk—together, slowly, and with all the care grief had taught them.

EIGHT

THE LABYRINTH'S REFUSAL

That night, the dream returned—his father's face rising once more from the haze of sleep. But this time it was different. The old silence had broken; his father carried a message.

He stepped forward, eyes heavy with a sorrow that seemed older than death itself. "My son," he said, his voice carrying both warmth and warning, "I had wished for you to come here and set me free. But now, I tell you this—" his tone deepened, like stone cracking under pressure—"it is you who are being trapped. You must save yourself."

The words echoed long after the figure dissolved into darkness, leaving the air weighted with urgency.

He woke with the taste of iron and paper in his mouth and with a small, terrible certainty. It sat in him like a stone you cannot shift: if Bogston swallowed everyone who reached too near, there would be no one left to pull Reed back. If he did not go—now, while the door between cellar and Meridian was still warm—others might take the path and vanish, and the thing that ate them would remain untraced. He told himself the dream was a warning; he told himself it was a permission. Either way, it conspired with the ledger in his hands.

He found Anesthesia at the map, elbows deep in manifest columns, eyes rimmed like a scholar who had not closed a book for days. She looked up when he entered the room and did not smile when she saw him. Her face read the same line he felt at the center of his chest: perhaps this could end badly.

"We need to save ourselves and go from here," he said without preamble. The words sounded loud in the narrow chamber.

For a moment she only stared. Then disappointment, old and hot, came to the surface of her voice. "How can you say that?" she asked. "How can you leave Jonas—leave me—when he's out there? We are tethered to him now. We did this together."

Damian sat opposite her. He had rehearsed the speech in shreds through the night and found it always too small. "I'm not abandoning him," he said carefully. "I'm not refusing to look for him. But if the place is trying to swallow everyone who searches... if they are making a net—then one of us going farther, learning the bounds, surviving to map it, is the only way we bring anyone back. I—" he paused. The wooden spiral in his palm felt like a pulse. "You come along me."

Her laugh was a brittle thing. "You think I will walk away from the city that keeps its mouths shut? You think I will let you become the only voice who remembers?" Her hands clenched the map. "No. If you go alone, you go alone. I will not be an accomplice to a single man's flight."

He could see the exact moment her resolve set like ice. It was the same look he had seen in his mother when she first refused to let Alaric break him. Different speech, same stubbornness. It steadied him—and made him guilty.

"Then I go alone," Damian said, and his voice broke in the small way it had when he cleaned his mother's face. "My father came in the dream. He told me to save myself. I—Ani, I believe he is right. If I go, I keep the map. I keep the ledger. I keep Reed's name alive on paper. I can follow Meridian further; I can press beyond the university's reach. I can come back with tools, witnesses—if I survive."

Anesthesia's face crumpled, not in anger now but in a sorrow that smelled of long winters. "You are not the only one with promises, Damian. You promised Jonas, too." She reached across the desk and put her palm on his knot of fingers. Her hand was warm and steady. "If you go, you will fracture what we are. You will make me carry the ledgers alone. You will make Belen... whoever he becomes, carry more than he has strength for. If you go, you leave me to be the one who waits with the list."

He looked at her and found only truth: she would not stop him if he would not listen to her; she would not follow if he would not ask. Their faces, close across the map, were the faces of two people forced into the same grief and given different answers.

Belen came in then, hesitant on the threshold with a small bundle—extra boots, a flask, a coil of thread and a folded spare cloak. He had the awful, careful look of someone who has handed over what he can and expects the worst.

"If you go," he said, voice small, "take more than you need. Take a knife that cuts rope, not a blade for striking. Take food that keeps. And promise me—promise Ani you will leave a trail not of paper but of people to call out if you fail." The request was a public shame—an admission that they could not do everything alone.

Damian nodded. He took the cloak and the coil and the knife. He set the spiral into his palm like a charm. He tried in that motion to put all the promises he could make into one small imprint.

Anesthesia did not change her mind. She did not throw him out, either. She made instead a different kind of preparation: she taught him how to fold paper so it would not betray him in the rain, how to map a footfall by the angle of a boot tread, and how to listen for the absence of bird song—something the old ferryman had taught her once, and which, in Bogston, was the sound that warned of human traps.

Before he left, Damian found himself alone at the window, the city stretched into a map of low lights. He pressed the spiral to the glass and whispered to the air—not to the dream, not exactly to his father, but to whatever small mechanics of memory still did him the favor of listening. "If I survive," he said, "I come back. If I don't—find Jonas for both of us." The sentence was ragged; the promise felt like a stitched seam in his insides.

They left at dawn. No grand farewells—only a knot of glances, a sealed ledger left under Anesthesia's hand, and a small scrap pinned to Reed's name on the wall so that anyone who entered the chamber would know they had not given up. Belen walked with them to the edge of town and then turned back, the weight of his own fear making the distance between them an ache.

The biggest problem, as Damian had said: the Cursed Forest. It sat like a dark lung between Bogston and the west roads, a place of twisted trunks and roots like ribs where the undergrowth refused to die or yield. The town's older men told stories of people who went in for a day and found years had gone by; they spoke of children who ran screaming from the edge and of hounds that would not cross the first root. And guarding that living wall were the medmica.

They were not soldiers. They were not beasts in the way a farmer's hound is a beast. The medmica were slender, almost too light, with faces pale like damp bark and eyes that reflected light as if water were held in them. Old women called them "sentinels made of patience," because they never ran and they never shouted. They watched. They wove between trunks and seemed to be grafted to roots. Their fingers moved as if pruning the air. Men who had met a medmica and survived said the things that passed for their speech were not with words but with the sudden turning of your own name inside you. Those who tried to stride through the wood found themselves mislaid—footsteps folding back onto themselves, bearings rearranged, and the medmica appearing where you had not seen them come.

No living soul, the elders agreed, had ever crossed the forest and returned with the same face. The stories were not all horror; some spoke of a man who left with a different manner and a head full of strange grammar, as if the medmica lent a different language to those who passed and took back something in payment. Others said the forest was a seam between thought and place—an old experiment gone wrong, or else an old boundary meant to keep something from wandering out.

Damian listened to all of it, not as a child who collects ghost stories but as a man who needed to know how the world would resist him. He unrolled the copy of an old shipping ledger they'd found in the archives and traced with a pencil the line that led from the south-house, through a lane, toward the forest's edge. He marked the place where the trees loomed like a wall: a knot of names circled like a bruise.

"How do you cross it?" he asked, because he had to know if any wisdom could be turned into a plan.

"You don't," Belen said bluntly, and the bluntness was honest. "You go at the right hour when the medmica are busy, if there is a right hour. You move like you belong there. You don't call; you don't think loud. Dreams... dreams help some. They say if you walk with a question that isn't yours the forest will offer a wrong path. If you walk with a name—" His voice broke on that. He could not finish the sentence.

Anesthesia shook her head. "It isn't superstition," she said. "It's behavior. The wood responds to patterns—quiet, rhythm, the kind of steady weight you cannot fake. There are ways to imitate belonging: mimic the footfall of a woodcutter, carry as if you are a merchant who pays tithes. But imitation risks being discovered as false."

Damian folded the map and put it into his inner coat. He fastened the spiral under his shirt and let its grain press against his sternum. He had no recipe for crossing a place guarded by medmica. He had only the ledger, a dream that had told him to survive, and an oath to a missing boy.

"Then I go," he said softly. "If I cross, I go for Reed. If I fail, tell the story in the ledger so someone else can follow the next seam." The sentence should have been arrogant. Instead it sounded like someone arranging his pockets before winter.

Anesthesia did not stop him at the gate. She did not come with him. She tied a small scrap of paper—one of their coded spirals—into the knot of his cloak, pressed it to his chest. "If you meet a medmica," she said, voice stripped of bravado, "do not try to speak its language. Walk like the kind of man who has nothing to hide and everything to lose. Come back."

He left without looking back more than once. The last image he carried of the chamber was the ledger with Jonas's name at the top and Anesthesia's hand pressed flat on it like a benediction.

At the forest's edge the trees stood like a wall. Light changed there; the air felt a degree colder, and the birds were silent as if taking breath. Roots knotted like hands across the path; leaves shivered without wind. Damian took his first step into shade and, as he did, felt the world rearrange itself in the small, intimate way maps can do when you fold them wrong. Somewhere a twig cracked, a footfall that was not his. A shape moved inside the trunks, barely a notch of movement, and the medmica's eye—if it was an eye—opened like a coin into his skin.

He straightened his shoulders and kept his pace slow and even, thinking of ledger lines and of the spiral pressed to his heart, and of Reed's laugh, and of a father's voice that had told him, in a place between sleep and waking, to be alive. The medmica watched. The forest listened. And the path ahead, braided with roots and silence, pulled him deeper where no man had gone and returned unchanged.

He made his heart and decided to cross the cursed forest.The forest changed when he crossed the last root. The light went thin and green, and the underbrush closed with an almost apologetic hush, as if apologizing for the noise men made in other places. At first Damian moved like a thief — soft-footed, trying to make himself small against the trunks — because the stories of medmica had taught him the usefulness of not being noticed. He kept his head down, his breath even, the small coil of thread Belen had given him coiled in his fist.

It did not feel like magic for long. After an hour of walking, the trees thinned, and the ground underfoot went from leaf-mulch to something harder, colder. Beneath the moss and the woven roots was metal.

He stopped so abruptly his lungs burned. A patch of the earth had been sheared away and, beneath the green, a ring of dark metal reflected his lantern like a calm eye. He crouched, fingers numb from the cold, and swept the moss off the rim with the blade he'd been given. The dust came away in a ribbon and left a pattern beneath it: grooves and ridges in the shape of a maze — not a carved labyrinth as a symbol, but a map laid into the metal itself, channel lines turned into narrow troughs, the whole thing like a sundial for lost people.

He knelt and brushed harder until the grooves were bare and the concentric paths showed. The design grabbed at the corners of his memory: his father's sketches, the spirals Alaric had left in margins, the great wheel of his childhood drawings. This metal floor was a plan made literal.

A sound whispered under his palms then — minute and mechanical, like a gear finding its tooth. He should have left at that sound. Instead he pressed a fingertip into one channel and felt the metal pulse, a faint vibration that answered his skin and then went still. The pulse stirred something deeper; somewhere below, something shifted as if doors had been unlocked in the dark.

He remembered, with the sudden clarity of an ache, the phrase from his father's notes: memor et mane — remember and remain. The sentence had felt like a riddle before; now it felt like a protocol. He stuck the spiral — the wooden charm Miska had given him — into the pattern, as one might set a compass needle into a map. For a moment nothing happened. Then the metal took a soft, obedient sound and a seam opened in the floor at his fingertips. The sound was not violent. It was the sound of something made to wait.

He had found an entrance into the labyrinth.

The first corridor smelled of oil and old rain. Panels of metal rose like the walls of a ship's hull; their seams clicked when his lantern light struck them. He took a breath that tasted of iron and pushed through. He dropped a length of thread from the coil as he went, knotting it at intervals to mark his passage — a habit Anesthesia had insisted on: map what you can leave, leave no permanent mark. The thread hung in the green gloom like a faint constellation.

At first it felt like an old shelter. There were racks of broken instruments, jars lined up like teeth, and on a narrow table a pile of notebooks with faded handwriting. He recognized Alaric's spidery ink not by name but by cadence: the slow tilting run of letters, slanted, confident. Pages crinkled under his thumb; diagrams of mazes, experiments detailed in the clinical voice of a man who had once believed that the mind could be measured and contained. In the margins — the spiral, again and again.

A lamp sputtered at the far end. A figure moved there — a man no older than a clerk, quick to check the door and quick to look away. The person's hands were steady, and for an instant Damian thought he had been discovered. The man vanished through a hatch and the lamp winked out.

He followed.

The hatch led him into the heart of the metal labyrinth, and the labyrinth answered his presence with those small, methodical changes that make a place actively puzzling. Corridors narrowed after he'd chosen an angle; a path he had just walked closed with a soft hydraulic sigh and became a wall of cold metal. The map under his boots — the metal ring at the forest's edge — was not a map you read passively. It was a machine that rearranged itself when it was walked upon.

He cursed softly and scrabbled at the seam where the floor had closed. It would not give. When he pulled back his hand there was blood on his knuckles — metal is honest and does not pretend to be kind.

Panic is a small heat that spreads quickly; he felt it like the prick of fever. The labyrinth was not a simple test: it was a controlled environment, an experiment in disorientation. Somewhere above the root-and-wood ceiling, the medmica were not acting like guardians so much as like curators of fear: their stories, their presence at the edge of the tree-line, had done the work of scaring ordinary folk away, but here, hidden and deliberate, men with instruments watched those who were caught inside like scientists reading pulses on a screen.

He tried to call. His voice died on the metal. Sound behaved differently here, folding back as if the walls remembered and did not like repetition. He walked in tight circles for a while, following the thread that trailed from his wrist. The thread ran dry after a few yards — the spool had been smaller than he thought. He cursed again, in a voice that surprised him: rougher than the one he had used in the chamber. He tied a strip of his cloak to the end of the thread and secured the tail in a notch, an attempt to make the trail more permanent.

It did not hold. When he doubled back to where the thread should have nested, the knot he had left was a clean seam in the metal. The wall stood where the knot was supposed to be, indifferent.

He began to chart in his head, the slow arithmetic that had comforted him since childhood: left, right, four steps, count, mark. He scratched marks — shallow, with the knife — when the metal allowed it, and when it did not, he bit the leather of his glove to leave an imprint. Memory became a tool: he remembered the angles of corners, the sound a certain seam made when the light hit it from the left. He kept repeating to himself the things Anesthesia had taught him: count your paces by the echo, feel the slope of the floor under your toes, note the small changes in smell. The maze answered with trickery: passages that once went left now leaned right; steps he had counted before felt shorter. Time smeared.

He found other traces of human passage: a faint smear of soot on a beam where someone had dragged a lamp, a bootprint in a patch of damp dust with a tread matching the one he had seen in the south-house cellar. Each find both warmed him and hollowed him out: someone else had been here; they might have come this way and not returned; they might have unfolded into the same clinical curiosity that had taken Alaric.

Fatigue arrived as a slow pressure. He ate a small ration and the bread tasted like the riverbank where he had run as a child — dry, wholesome, ordinary, and impossibly far away. He set his spiral in a hollow and tried to rest his head on his knees. When he closed his eyes his father's voice threaded in: remember and remain. He did not know if the voice was from sleep or memory. He could not say whether it helped or was only another layer of the experiment.

He put his hand to the wall and tried to make a map by touch: seams, rivets, the long run of bolts that defined an axis. Memory was his only map. He began to mark cadence in his feet — press with the ball of the foot on each step, three beats before a turn — a rhythm he hoped the mind would hold when the walls tried to steal the sense of direction.

Then, as if the labyrinth had grown tired of subtlety, it shifted.

He was crossing a low corridor when the floor under his feet slotted into a new angle and fell away. Damian had the singular moment of a man who knows falling will come and cannot stop it; wind took his lantern, and he dropped, palms slashing, heart pounding. He landed in a round pit with metal ribs along the wall and a single shaft of light above, like the eye of a watchtower. Dust filled his mouth. The thread he had left lagged to the side as if the seam ate it; the last knot hung on a lip that was now a foot above him.

He spat, tasting iron, and hauled himself up. The pit was not deep enough to be a grave, but it was a trap. A narrow collar of space, a ring where voice would echo and logic would loop. He tried the knife on seams and found them stubborn. He tried the coil as a rope and the cord slipped through his wet fingers, fraying at the edge of the metal where something chewed at thread like a rat. He barked a laugh — and listened to it come back thin and unhelpful.

The air here was warmer; a low thrum moved through the ribs as if the labyrinth's heart were an engine. He crouched, pressed his forehead to the cool metal, and tried to think. Panic had sharpened into a single bright thing: he would not be useful if he died here. He owed Jonas and he owed Liora and he owed a promise to keep going.

He thought of the spiral again, the way Alaric had drawn it not simply as a diversion but as a signature. He reached a hand to the wood charm he still wore under his shirt and felt its grain steady his fingers. The charm was small and from a different life; still, he pressed it to the metal edge and felt, foolishly at first, that it fit the groove near his knees. It slid into a notch and caught.

Something hummed deeper in the structure — a single, low note — and then a seam loosened above him. A thin hatch slid aside with a slow, obedient scrape and a shaft of cooler air breathed down. He clambered up, hands slick, and hauled himself through the narrow opening into a corridor that smelled of something alive: green rot, oil, and a faint antiseptic.

He thought he had escaped then. He rounded a corner and found himself looking into a chamber that did not belong in any natural wood: a room of glass panels, racks of instruments, and a chair bolted to the floor like a surgeon's throne. The chair had leather straps. The glass reflected his face and a dozen other faces like echoes. On a shelf a notebook lay open where someone had fallen mid-sentence: "—participant disoriented on day three. Increased stimulus matrix. Spiral imprint functional as key. Subject's kin reported. Recommendation: maintain isolation."

His mouth went dry. He sat down with the trembling of someone suddenly tired enough to drop. This place was not a myth of roots and spirits. It was a clinical theatre for minds.

A noise — human and immediate — made him start. A voice spoke from behind the glass in a language he did not know, and then, nearer, a sound like a door sighing. Through the glass two figures moved, their faces hidden behind masks, hands bare and precise. They were not medmica exactly; they were the men who used the medmica's fear as a curtain. They spoke softly, their words clipped, and one of them put down a vial with an amber liquid.

He should have fled then. He should have hidden in the shadow and let the men go. Instead he stepped forward — a motion half-driven by foolish courage, half-driven by the iron that had anchored him since his mother's death: the need to do something when someone else might not.

The men looked up and, with a calm almost theatrical, one pressed a small panel and the glass slid like a page across. The taller of the two inclined his head, not with alarm but with businesslike curiosity.

"You're not in any register," the taller said in a low voice with no accent Damian recognized. "You're not a participant. How did you come?"

Damian's throat worked. He could have lied. He could have said he was a scavenger who found an old hatch. Instead he said the truth simply: "I came from Bogston. My name is Damian. I follow a trail. I'm looking for a boy named Jonas Reed. I—" The sentence ended thinly.

The men regarded him with the kind of silence people use when they are cataloguing a specimen. The taller one — he carried something at his belt that looked like a ledger of names in metal — tapped it with an index finger.

"You are not the first to come with a name," he said. "Names bring others. The forest is full of names. Some of them fit and some do not."

Damian swallowed hard. "What is this place?"

"A study," the man said. "A place for observation. Memory is a mechanism that can be turned. We watch what turns. We measure what moves."

The other man — quieter, with ink on the cuff of his sleeve — looked at the empty chair and nodded. "Locke will be pleased to know you opened the hatch without request."

Damian heard the name — Locke — and it made his mouth a dry thing. He recalled the ledger note: Professor Locke. The same name in Alaric's margins. He thought suddenly, terribly, of the bracketed sentence in his father's paper: transferred under patronage. Confidential.

"Did you bring any instruments?" the taller man asked. It was not a question about tools, but about credentials. In that room credentials mattered more than fists.

Damian thought of the coil of thread in his pocket and the knife at his belt. He thought of the spiral under his shirt. He thought of Liora's face. He told them, plainly, "No. I have a charm and a ledger that says crate 7, Meridian."

The men spoke to each other in a low, precise whisper, their words like the closing of a book. Then, without a needless motion, they moved to the far panel and released a latch. The taller man smiled, the expression small and clinical. "You are interesting," he said to Damian. "You will make good data."

The glass shutter closed behind him with the finality of a judge's hammer.

He had been trapped. The labyrinth, the forest, the medmica's fear, the men with masks — all of it a net. He pressed his palms to the cool glass and felt, for the first time since his mother's death, the hard, hot press of a real, human panic: the bright, sharp need for air and for light and for someone to break the door.

He crouched on the cold floor and drew his knees up and, because memory is a weapon as much as it is a map, he began to whisper the names he had been carrying. Jonas. Liora. Alaric. He whispered them into his palms so they would not dissolve, counted steps in his head, traced the labyrinth in the soft scrape of his nail along the metal. He would try every seam, every lever, every small thing the men had prepared for experiment. He would not be a specimen without dragging his captors into the ledger with him.

Outside, beyond the glass, the taller man wrote in a notebook and the other refilled a vial. The lab was quiet and patient and very professional. It smelled of old paper and sterilizing alcohol and the way rules smell when men convince themselves they serve something higher than fear.

Damian pressed his forehead to the clear surface and dared to imagine the moment he might pry free the seam that held him. He felt absurd, stubborn, and not nearly clever enough. But he also felt something older than the fear: the small, steady bell of promise in his chest — the spiral's grain against his sternum. In the murmur of the lab, over the hiss of instruments and the soft clack of pens, he said Jonas Reed's name again and began, slowly and with the terrible concentration of someone who has been given only the edge of time, to work.

For a long time the labyrinth simply would not let him leave.

At first he tried the obvious things. He pushed and shoved at the glass with the palms of his hands until his knuckles stung; he leaned his shoulder into the sealed panel and felt the cool resistance of metal that had been built to keep things in. He hammered at seams with the butt of his knife until the sound echoed back as if the metal itself were laughing. Nothing yielded. The men on the other side moved with a calm that made his own franticness feel obscene; he could see them through the glass sometimes, silhouettes bending toward instruments, and every time they turned away he felt the hollow of being watched like a cold coin in his gut.

Days — or what he guessed were days — passed in the slow calculus of a man counting small elements to keep his mind from unravelling. He had no watch and time in the labyrinth contracted and elongated with the mood of the hum. He rationed the crumbs he had left, sipped tepid water only when the pit of thirst became a shout, and slept in staccato naps with his head against rusted ribs so that the metal might press his heartbeat into a steadier rhythm. He memorized the sound of the engines: a thrum that rose and fell on a roughly even cycle, a note like a faraway bell. That cadence became his clock.

He tried every seam he could find. He filed at rivets with the small knife until the blade was nicked and dull; he dug fingernails into crevices until the skin under them bled and yet the seams held. He shut his eyes and drew triangles and spirals in the sweat on his palm and told himself the designs were maps until the shapes blurred and turned into something else. He pressed the wooden spiral against metal where the groove looked like it might take it — as he had once by the ring at the forest's edge — and sometimes, almost shamelessly, the metal would answer with a faint vibration. But the answers were local and specific; they opened cupboards and small service panels into storage, not the wide exit of a stair well. Each small success was a cut of hope; each failure taught him how the place did not want him.

If he spoke, it was to the names he had carried in his pocket. He said Jonas's name until it stopped being a plea and became a tool to brace his tongue. He read passages from his father's notebooks aloud — the lines about memory as an architecture — because the cadences steadied him. Once, half delirious, he laughed at himself for treating prose like a rope. The sound made him hate the silence all the more.

On the fifth long stretch between sleep and waking he found the notebooks more carefully. They had been left on a table as if flung aside. He sat and read by the sputtering lamp: notes on the "stimulus matrix," diagrams of observation screens, and, in a margin his father would have recognized as decisively Alaric's, a tight sentence that read like instruction: maintenance windows: vents open @ 03:20 cycle; access to sub-floor via panel C4-3. Keep spiral to hand.

The sentence was a compass. It gave him a rhythm to hitch to the engine's music. He listened for shifts in the thrum and learned to mark them. At 03:20 — the numbers later proved oddly exact — the hum in the metal rose a quarter tone and then steadied. It was the cadence of valves cycling, of pressure equalizing. When the tone came he climbed, hands raw, to the panel C4-3 indicated by the map he had sketched from the notebook's diagrams. The panel was narrow, bolted with flat-headed screws that had been designed for a screwdriver, not a blunt knife. Damian had no screwdriver. He had only patience and his teeth and an old knife tempered by effort.

He worked the blade at the slot, tiny, desperate rotations that took the skin from his knuckles. The metal grated. The lab hummed. Above him he heard the thin, patent sound of a door opening into a service corridor — a sound that made his heart hammer so hard he feared it would burst his ribs. He slipped the spiral into the notch the way he had at the forest ring, and this time the charm was not merely ornamental. It caught on a small peg and depressed it. A soft, mechanical click answered.

He was not thinking of heroics. He was thinking of leverage. He wedged the blade and then, with an animal groan, levered. One screw turned, then another, each movement a theft from sleep and metal. Sweat soaked his shirt. He tasted copper. The panel let go with a sound like a held breath released, and a narrow passage breathed cold air into his face.

He squeezed into the crawlspace. It was a low tunnel lined with ducts and warm to his touch. For a moment he felt ridiculous — a man contorting himself between pipes like a child hiding in cupboard — and then a lightness he had not had since Liora's bedside filled his limbs. He dragged his knife and the last of his thread, knotting the end to a bolt he left as a tracer. The tunnel moved down at an angle; at one point he had to shimmy through an elbow of ductwork that scraped his ribs and made him retch. Twice he jammed his shoulder against a bracket and thought angrily of the men who had designed this place as if inconvenience were part of a lesson.

He emerged not into open air but into a maintenance access under the floor of a long corridor. He lay there on the cool metal for a long while, listening. The world beyond the corridor was muffled and yet alive: the patter of distant feet, the soft scrape of a cart, the far-off argument of voices that did not look at him with curiosity but with the businesslike disinterest of people doing their jobs. He slid along the shadow of the wall until he found a ladder descending into a service yard that smelled sharply of sap and damp iron. At the bottom was a narrow hatch that led, by a steep, winding stair, toward a grate he could feel with his hands as a change in the air, a suggestion of sky.

The stairway was old and wobbled. He climbed it in fits, pausing to listen at each landing. Once he heard a foot pass above and held his breath until the soles rattled away. Once a door opened and a shape paused in the light — and in that pause he felt the animal truth of being hunted: his body made itself small and the shape never noticed. Had he been a step sooner the silhouette might have seen him, and the climb would have been a story of failure. He told himself a hundred small thank-yous for the shape's inattentiveness.

At the top of the stair the hatch was fastened with a deadbolt rusted to stubbornness by damp. His hands had no strength left but his resolve did. He used the knife to scrape away the rust until a line of metal freed its tooth. It took him three tries, a cut on the palm, and a muttered prayer to no one in particular. The bolt moved with a scream of grain and metal. The hatch lifted on a hinge that protested like an old man; he pushed it and felt the first breath of outside air on his face.

For a moment — just one small, shimmering moment — the forest smelled like Liora's soap, like the river market, like a life he had promised to keep. He hauled himself up onto the grass and lay on his back and laughed with a sound that was half sob. The sky was a thin, pale thing above the treetops. Dawn had only just begun to stitch light through leaves. He could not tell how much time had passed; his beard, if it had any claim to time, felt longer. He cupped his hand over his face and let the air that was not sterilized by metal fill him.

He did not run. He sat and warmed, letting his limbs remember that the world could be soft at the edges. The labyrinth in the metal had not released him because it was merciful; it had released him because he had found the pattern it used to keep its heart. He crawled back to the hatch, pulled the spiral from where it had been wedged, and pressed his palm to it until the wood warmed to his skin. It felt then not only like a key but like a promise kept.

He stumbled back through trees that smelled of sap and loam, each step a small triumph. In the dim he thought he saw a shape move in the undergrowth — pale, patient, like bark. He did not stop to look. He moved away from the metal ring he had found and toward the path that led out of the forest and, eventually, toward Meridian and what might come after: questions, witnesses, ledger lines that might be followed into daylight.

He had escaped the labyrinth, but the metal had left a map on his hands: scratches, a smear of grease that would not wash off easily, a small scar across one knuckle. In his pocket the receipt for crate 7 burned with its plainness. In his chest the spiral's impression pulsed like a kept vow.

When he finally pushed back through the last root-line and the sentinel trees closed behind him, the forest felt both the same and not: the medmica's watch, he understood then, had been partly a guard and partly theater. It had made the town look away while the true work went on in metal and glass. He held that knowledge like a knife and a condolence both — dangerous, hard, necessary.

He walked back toward Bogston with a slow, deliberate gait. The dawn laid the town out in pale light. He was alive. He had seen the laboratory and the chair and the notebook and the way the spiral had been used like a small mechanical truth. He carried that truth in the hollow of his ribs as he moved, and in that hollow was the sound of Jonas's name, which he said aloud into the morning as if calling someone down from a roof.

He was out. He had not found Jonas yet. But he had found a seam to pull, and he had learned, in the small soft cruel hours of the metal labyrinth, how to pry.

For a long time the labyrinth simply would not let him leave.

At first he tried the obvious things. He pushed and shoved at the glass with the palms of his hands until his knuckles stung; he leaned his shoulder into the sealed panel and felt the cool resistance of metal that had been built to keep things in. He hammered at seams with the butt of his knife until the sound echoed back as if the metal itself were laughing. Nothing yielded. The men on the other side moved with a calm that made his own franticness feel obscene; he could see them through the glass sometimes, silhouettes bending toward instruments, and every time they turned away he felt the hollow of being watched like a cold coin in his gut.

Days — or what he guessed were days — passed in the slow calculus of a man counting small elements to keep his mind from unravelling. He had no watch and time in the labyrinth contracted and elongated with the mood of the hum. He rationed the crumbs he had left, sipped tepid water only when the pit of thirst became a shout, and slept in staccato naps with his head against rusted ribs so that the metal might press his heartbeat into a steadier rhythm. He memorized the sound of the engines: a thrum that rose and fell on a roughly even cycle, a note like a faraway bell. That cadence became his clock.

He tried every seam he could find. He filed at rivets with the small knife until the blade was nicked and dull; he dug fingernails into crevices until the skin under them bled and yet the seams held. He shut his eyes and drew triangles and spirals in the sweat on his palm and told himself the designs were maps until the shapes blurred and turned into something else. He pressed the wooden spiral against metal where the groove looked like it might take it — as he had once by the ring at the forest's edge — and sometimes, almost shamelessly, the metal would answer with a faint vibration. But the answers were local and specific; they opened cupboards and small service panels into storage, not the wide exit of a stair well. Each small success was a cut of hope; each failure taught him how the place did not want him.

If he spoke, it was to the names he had carried in his pocket. He said Jonas's name until it stopped being a plea and became a tool to brace his tongue. He read passages from his father's notebooks aloud — the lines about memory as an architecture — because the cadences steadied him. Once, half delirious, he laughed at himself for treating prose like a rope. The sound made him hate the silence all the more.

On the fifth long stretch between sleep and waking he found the notebooks more carefully. They had been left on a table as if flung aside. He sat and read by the sputtering lamp: notes on the "stimulus matrix," diagrams of observation screens, and, in a margin his father would have recognized as decisively Alaric's, a tight sentence that read like instruction: maintenance windows: vents open @ 03:20 cycle; access to sub-floor via panel C4-3. Keep spiral to hand.

The sentence was a compass. It gave him a rhythm to hitch to the engine's music. He listened for shifts in the thrum and learned to mark them. At 03:20 — the numbers later proved oddly exact — the hum in the metal rose a quarter tone and then steadied. It was the cadence of valves cycling, of pressure equalizing. When the tone came he climbed, hands raw, to the panel C4-3 indicated by the map he had sketched from the notebook's diagrams. The panel was narrow, bolted with flat-headed screws that had been designed for a screwdriver, not a blunt knife. Damian had no screwdriver. He had only patience and his teeth and an old knife tempered by effort.

He worked the blade at the slot, tiny, desperate rotations that took the skin from his knuckles. The metal grated. The lab hummed. Above him he heard the thin, patent sound of a door opening into a service corridor — a sound that made his heart hammer so hard he feared it would burst his ribs. He slipped the spiral into the notch the way he had at the forest ring, and this time the charm was not merely ornamental. It caught on a small peg and depressed it. A soft, mechanical click answered.

He was not thinking of heroics. He was thinking of leverage. He wedged the blade and then, with an animal groan, levered. One screw turned, then another, each movement a theft from sleep and metal. Sweat soaked his shirt. He tasted copper. The panel let go with a sound like a held breath released, and a narrow passage breathed cold air into his face.

He squeezed into the crawlspace. It was a low tunnel lined with ducts and warm to his touch. For a moment he felt ridiculous — a man contorting himself between pipes like a child hiding in cupboard — and then a lightness he had not had since Liora's bedside filled his limbs. He dragged his knife and the last of his thread, knotting the end to a bolt he left as a tracer. The tunnel moved down at an angle; at one point he had to shimmy through an elbow of ductwork that scraped his ribs and made him retch. Twice he jammed his shoulder against a bracket and thought angrily of the men who had designed this place as if inconvenience were part of a lesson.

He emerged not into open air but into a maintenance access under the floor of a long corridor. He lay there on the cool metal for a long while, listening. The world beyond the corridor was muffled and yet alive: the patter of distant feet, the soft scrape of a cart, the far-off argument of voices that did not look at him with curiosity but with the businesslike disinterest of people doing their jobs. He slid along the shadow of the wall until he found a ladder descending into a service yard that smelled sharply of sap and damp iron. At the bottom was a narrow hatch that led, by a steep, winding stair, toward a grate he could feel with his hands as a change in the air, a suggestion of sky.

The stairway was old and wobbled. He climbed it in fits, pausing to listen at each landing. Once he heard a foot pass above and held his breath until the soles rattled away. Once a door opened and a shape paused in the light — and in that pause he felt the animal truth of being hunted: his body made itself small and the shape never noticed. Had he been a step sooner the silhouette might have seen him, and the climb would have been a story of failure. He told himself a hundred small thank-yous for the shape's inattentiveness.

At the top of the stair the hatch was fastened with a deadbolt rusted to stubbornness by damp. His hands had no strength left but his resolve did. He used the knife to scrape away the rust until a line of metal freed its tooth. It took him three tries, a cut on the palm, and a muttered prayer to no one in particular. The bolt moved with a scream of grain and metal. The hatch lifted on a hinge that protested like an old man; he pushed it and felt the first breath of outside air on his face.

For a moment — just one small, shimmering moment — the forest smelled like Liora's soap, like the river market, like a life he had promised to keep. He hauled himself up onto the grass and lay on his back and laughed with a sound that was half sob. The sky was a thin, pale thing above the treetops. Dawn had only just begun to stitch light through leaves. He could not tell how much time had passed; his beard, if it had any claim to time, felt longer. He cupped his hand over his face and let the air that was not sterilized by metal fill him.

He did not run. He sat and warmed, letting his limbs remember that the world could be soft at the edges. The labyrinth in the metal had not released him because it was merciful; it had released him because he had found the pattern it used to keep its heart. He crawled back to the hatch, pulled the spiral from where it had been wedged, and pressed his palm to it until the wood warmed to his skin. It felt then not only like a key but like a promise kept.

He stumbled back through trees that smelled of sap and loam, each step a small triumph. In the dim he thought he saw a shape move in the undergrowth — pale, patient, like bark. He did not stop to look. He moved away from the metal ring he had found and toward the path that led out of the forest and, eventually, toward Meridian and what might come after: questions, witnesses, ledger lines that might be followed into daylight.

He had escaped the labyrinth, but the metal had left a map on his hands: scratches, a smear of grease that would not wash off easily, a small scar across one knuckle. In his pocket the receipt for crate 7 burned with its plainness. In his chest the spiral's impression pulsed like a kept vow.

When he finally pushed back through the last root-line and the sentinel trees closed behind him, the forest felt both the same and not: the medmica's watch, he understood then, had been partly a guard and partly theater. It had made the town look away while the true work went on in metal and glass. He held that knowledge like a knife and a condolence both — dangerous, hard, necessary.

He walked back toward Bogston with a slow, deliberate gait. The dawn laid the town out in pale light. He was alive. He had seen the laboratory and the chair and the notebook and the way the spiral had been used like a small mechanical truth. He carried that truth in the hollow of his ribs as he moved, and in that hollow was the sound of Jonas's name, which he said aloud into the morning as if calling someone down from a roof.

He was out. He had not found Jonas yet. But he had found a seam to pull, and he had learned, in the small soft cruel hours of the metal labyrinth, how to pry.

He should have gone back to Bogston. The logic of the town—names on ledgers, witnesses, people who could sign statements—argued for returning at once: to tell Anesthesia what he had seen in the metal rooms, to gather men who would not be so easily frightened by stories of medmica and spirals. But there is a small, stubborn code that lives in certain griefs: you follow the seam you have found as far as you can before you show the wound to anyone else. Damian had crawled out of the labyrinth with metal under his nails and the knowledge that Meridian was not a rumor. The seam demanded a pull.

So he went deeper.

He left the path he knew. The forest there was stranger than the edge suggested. Where the sentinel trunks had been regular and spaced, the interior crowded: trunks braided into arches, bracken that rose to his knees and then curled back as if to examine him. Light came through in green shards and pooled under leaves that were impossibly broad. The air smelled of loam and something clinical — the faint ghost of alcohol and copper that followed him from the lab — as if the ground itself absorbed the experiments and kept a memory of them.

He moved slow because haste in a place built to misplace men is simply a way of stepping into the teeth of a trap. He measured each footfall, remembered the rhythm that had let him find the panel C4-3, and used it again: three soft steps, the heel slightly turned inward at the third, a pause to let the sound of his own breath settle. He left no paper markers this time; thread would have been eaten by seams. Instead he pressed tiny notches with the knife into the underside of broken branches, a code only he would read.

The medmica watched him, as they always watched. Not a single one stepped into his path; they did not need to. Sometimes he saw the pale disk of a face pivot like a slow moon through branches; sometimes a hand, pale and rootlike, would appear behind a trunk and draw a slow figure in the air as if pruning the mood. Once, when he stopped to retie a bootlace, a medmica's face was only a few paces away, half-hidden in fern. Its eyes—if they were eyes—reflected his lantern like two wet stones. He felt, as he always did, a vertigo of being read. He did not speak. He did not look long enough to be noticed. He tied the lace and stepped away.

Incidents accumulated not as drama but as small, precise difficulties that eat at a man's resolve. A fallen oak had created a shallow pool whose surface trembled with the echo of something below; he waded through and found the soles of his boots clogged with a black silt that came away in long gray ribbons. A web of thin metallic wire lay coiled under a bramble and sprang at his sleeve like a young thing; he snipped it with the knife and set it aside — not as a hazard but as proof that someone had been there wiring the trees. A fox slunk past him, small and gnarled, with a ribbon of cloth tied round its tail: a human marker, or a trap bait, he could not tell.

Midday shifted into the peculiar dusk of the forest, where the light thinned but the green did not darken entirely. Damian found, half-buried in moss and leaf litter, a stone that had been carved into a shallow basin. Someone long ago had set it as an altar and then abandoned it. The basin still held rainwater; the water's surface shimmered like oil. Around the basin, the ground was scoured of leaves as if feet had been kept off it. On the stone rim someone—carefully, with a small hand—had incised a line: not a spiral but a single straight line, deep and precise, running like a seam. The line looked like a threshold drawn in stone.

He examined the basin with the scientist's careful eye that had been taught by Alaric and honed by his own nightmare: patterns, repetitions, mechanical intent. When he ran a finger in the water a subtle electric taste prickled the skin of his tongue. The water shivered at the touch of his finger as if expecting a coin. He drew his hand back and listened: a low, distant chord rose in the wood, a vibration like bees in a bell.

He walked around the basin and found that the straight stone line continued. It was not only on the basin; other trees bore it faintly, as if a blade had traced a path through bark across a swath of trunks. Where the line ran, the underbrush was thinner; the leaves lay oddly still.

He had the absurd, sudden certainty that the stone and the line and the wire and the medmica were not disparate things but a single device, an edge cut through the forest to mark a boundary.

A divine line, he thought—an apt, ridiculous naming for something that felt intentionally sacred: a threshold maintained by men who wanted one part of the world to remain other.

He stepped toward the line.

He wanted to pause, to make three soft steps and catch the rhythm of whatever lay beyond. But curiosity is a hard thing to temper when you think a human life might be beyond it. He put his boot over the carved groove and let his weight fall forward.

At first nothing seemed to happen. The leaf litter crunched. A bird two branches over took flight and made a small, surprised sound. Then, as his foot left the groove and his other foot crossed, the world answered.

The sound struck like being hit in the chest by a bell of compressed air. It was a high, thin note that seemed to originate all around him and yet to be inside his skull itself. It was not a noise that one could place on a scale: it vibrated the teeth in his jaw, it made his fillings hum. It lasted less than a second but that second stretched wide and blunt. His ears filled with a pressure that was not only sound—the sensation was of a closed room shrinking; his skull seemed to fold inward like a paper cup being crushed.

Pain came after the sound as a white bloom. His right ear let loose a hot, metallic flood of blood that tasted of iron on his tongue. His left ear followed. A thin stream found the bridge of his nose; he felt the sticky, clotted heat on his upper lip. The world became a smear of red and green and the sound did not leave. Tinnitus howled, a constant needle in both ears, and he clutched at his head with both hands as if he could hold the sound in.

For a heartbeat he thought he would vomit. The forest lurched around him; the trunks leaned like towers. He tried to stumble back but his legs forgot to obey the plan. The medmica forms uncoiled from the moss they had been folded in and moved toward him with a slowness that was not pity but certainty; they did not shout or touch. One reached the rim of the carved line and paused, fingers tracing the groove without contact, as if measuring how wide the wound in the air had become.

He fell on his knees where the line had crossed him. Blood filled his mouth from the nose and the pressure in his skull made the letters of the world smear. He thought dimly of the lab's chair and the notebook that had said spiral imprint functional as key. A pulse hammered beneath his sternum — the spiral's pressure against bone — and he had the childish urge to call for his father, though he had never relied on that comfort before. The world tilted; the ferned floor spun.

His hands went numb. He tried to speak Jonas's name but only a dry rasp left his throat. The medmica watched without the slightest expression; their presence felt like weather. Above him the trees hummed in the same tone that had struck his ears, and for a moment materials and living things were the same instrument.

Then the lights at the edge of his vision ran like beads and the forest turned its back on him.

The last thing Damian felt before the world closed was the wooden spiral's warmth where it rested under his shirt — a tiny, defiant heat — and the sense that he had crossed a boundary that was both physical and ceremonial, a line men had paid for in wire and coin and silence. The forest and its keepers had answered his passage with a sound that was not merely protective but punitive. He folded into the earth and the leather of his cloak absorbed the taste of iron as consciousness drained away like water running through fingers.

NINE

SHIE 1777

The city of Shie rose each morning as if remembering itself anew: roofs exhaled the night's chill, shutters creaked open like eyelids, and the river that divided the town from its lowlands moved in the same patient, indifferent way it had for a thousand ordinary mornings. Atop the highest rise, the whitewashed walls of King Edmund's hall caught the pale light and held it, a quiet promise that law and ceremony were near — but below, where lanes twisted and courtyards opened like small lungs, life was measured in the smaller acts that make a city live: the first loaf drawn steaming from an oven, the soft knock of a potter's wheel, the bargaining of a woman who knows exactly how much a thing is worth and will not be rushed. Thomas Whitaker woke before the market bell with hands already smelling of flour in dreams. His wife Mary lay for a moment longer, listening to the sound of his boots on the stair as he went to shove open the oven. Thomas knew the exact moment to turn the loaves; he had learned it from his father, and his father from his. He learned the way light menaces the crust at dawn, how a baker's morning moves like clockwork and like prayer. Outside, the lane carried the smell of yeast and the distant clank of John Fletcher's hammer where the coppersmith worked in a small yard patched together from timber and goodwill.

By the time the eastern market stuttered into life, girls with baskets on their heads threaded between stalls, and Margaret Hale, who sold spices in neat paper cones, arranged turmeric, cumin, and dried ginger like bright, edible jewels. She liked to see customers pause and breathe in the spices as if inhaling stories. Opposite her stall Oliver Carter, the potter, kept one hand on his eldest daughter's shoulder and the other on a fresh bowl, tapping its rim to judge its voice. Conversation in the market moved at a pace like measured breath. "How goes the kiln?" Mary asked Oliver when she passed with a tray of loaves. He smiled, pride threaded with exhaustion. "Three nights and one moon," he said. "If the damp keeps to itself, I will have a dozen for the festival."

There was always an incident waiting to be noticed; Shie collected such things as other cities collect dust. A stray goat, thin and brazen, slipped its tether near the fishmongers and launched itself at a pile of discarded bread. It toppled a basket of salted herrings and sent the vendor spluttering, his apron dotted with brine. Peter Clarke, who owned the boat with a crooked oar and the laugh of someone who has made peace with the river, grabbed a string and re-tied the goat with a consolation of stale bread and a reprimand in the language of men who feed animals daily. Children shrieked and laughed; a small, instant audience assembled and then dissipated. These were the warm, trivial combustions that kept the market from being merely trade.

In the courts beneath the king's hall, where the colors of office hung with sober dignity, King Edmund received petitions that day — a dispute over a boundary, a plea for a widow's exemption from a levy, a request to have a road mended where the rain made the mud impassable. Minister Robert carried the petitions with inked fingers; Samuel, the scribe, had a careful hand and a way of pausing before he wrote a name, as if names themselves deserved consideration. The king listened and asked small questions, the kind that unknotted things: who had last tended the post, who saw the men on the boundary, what was the father's name. He did not speak for theater. He measured, he weighed, and then he gave judgments that were meant to be equitable in the small ways that matter most — a debt adjusted by a week of labor, a post returned, a levy postponed until the harvest. People liked to tell the story afterward as if justice were a thing that fell like rain and refreshed the city. They liked to imagine the king's face as they recounted it, and sometimes their versions were sweeter than the reality.

Captain Henry, who kept an eye on the western moorings and whose duties seemed sometimes to mingle with the private boyish pleasure of watching people, came into the market with a line of men behind him and an expression like a man who had not slept. He had found, the morning before, a plank broken on the bank and a small sealed barrel with a mark none of them could read. It was the sort of thing that collected the attention of townsfolk without meaning to: a foreign coin here, a strange scrap of cloth there, a fish-hook shaped like nothing any of them owned. Rumor bloomed: a sloop had been sighted, a man in odd clothes had been seen making notes on the quay. But the city itself took these as it took everything else — with curiosity threaded through caution. Captain Henry did the sensible thing: he sent for translators from the traders who frequented the docks and asked that no one turn suspicion into violence. In Shie, suspicion became trouble only when people failed to speak.

The day went on in its careful, noisy way. William Brown, whose art was shaping metal until it held light, debated the right curve for a lantern with Elizabeth Ford, a widow who had the steadiness of someone who had learned to measure grief and make it practical. "Light must not be too arrogant," she said, touching a willow handle with a thoughtful thumb. "It must be willing to bend." William laughed at the phrase and added a small flourish to the lantern's rim. They argued about craftsmanship and children and the price of coal like neighbors will, with the intimacy of people who see one another daily.

Afternoon stretched, and the market moved through its slow seasons of bargaining, lull, and bustle. A boy named Charles Lane — quick with a grin and quicker with a snatch — attempted to lift a small purse from beneath a stall while the vendor turned to haggle. He failed not because his fingers were clumsy but because Margaret

Hale's sharp-eyed apprentice, Judith, noticed the movement and called, not with accusation but with a sharp sound of surprise designed to catch only the thief's attention. The sound unstitched Charles's courage; embarrassment and the sudden, genuine shame of being caught stopped him in his tracks. His mother, Anne Lane, arrived panting from the other lane, scolding and relieved all at once, and when Charles's cheeks were flushed with contrition she held him in public and admonished him in a voice that had always been kinder than the streets. The vendor laughed, Charles promised to fetch extra loaves to repay the trouble, and the city accepted the small restitution as if it were an offering. These small repentances stitched the fabric together.

As evening approached, the smell of frying spices and baked bread mixed with the sweet smoke of incense a woman named Margaret—no relation to the spice seller—offered at her doorway for a private prayer. Light gathered in the windows as families lit lamps and set a place at the table, even when the table was little more than a plank. Thomas and Mary ate slowly, counting bread and listening to the distant sound of a fiddler practicing for the festival. Mary spoke then, in the low language of long familiarity, of a new idea: a bowl with a thinner rim to please a customer from the king's court. Thomas worried at the seam of his thumb where flour gathered. "If you make it," she said, "I will carry it to the court myself." He looked at her as if only now seeing the plan. They agreed on the shape and on the slow work of practice.

At night, a small fire began in a granary at the edge of town — a careless lamp overturned by a cat, perhaps, or a smoldering that caught on old straw. The alarm was the simplest, most communal thing: a bell rung by a neighbor, hands passing buckets of water in a chain that moved like a living thing. Captain Henry abandoned his formal duties and took his place in the line, and when fumes stung and sweat mingled with ash, even the king's own courier carried a pail. Old Alice Grey, who had been midwife to a generation, scolded everyone as if they were children and then ordered them to stop shivering and act. The fire was put out before dawn; only a corner of the barn blackened, and the city woke with a story to trade over morning porridge. In the aftermath, concession was ordinary: a lad who had dropped the lamp offered to work a week in the granary to pay for what was ruined, and the granary master accepted, partly for the work and partly because accepting made a kind of peace.

Days slipped into one another without great fanfare. A messenger arrived from a neighboring town seeking help to mend a bridge; King Edmund ordered carpenters and promised a portion of grain. A traveling weaver from the west — George Fletcher — traded a length of cloth for a dozen bowls and a loaf and spent an evening telling stories of highways and inns in a voice that made the children press closer. Elizabeth the widow received a letter from a distant cousin and passed it around the small circle in her kitchen like a secret: the cousin had a notion of marriage for her niece and asked if Elizabeth knew any eligible and steady-hearted men. They all smiled, even the men, because town matchmaking liked the idea of practical decisions clothed in romance.

A small council met in the king's hall to discuss the river tolls. Nothing dramatic happened there. Minister Robert unfolded papers and read numbers aloud; Samuel annotated the margins with a neat, black hand. King Edmund asked if the tolls might be adjusted seasonally, and someone suggested a sliding rate to keep fishermen from having to sell at ruinous prices at the lean times. They made a plan that pleased no one entirely and soothed many a little; in Shie, the art of ruling was to make enough people feel heard that the city did not tear at its seams.

The festival came slow as a tide. Lamps were made, and Thomas spent a night shaping the rim of his new bowl until his fingers vibrated. Mary sewed a strip of blue into her apron for luck. Children practiced a step that involved a small bow and the presentation of flowers. When the night of the festival arrived, the river held the reflection of a thousand lamps, and King Edmund stood with his hands unclenched and watched the city he governed — not merely as an adjudicator, but as someone who liked the way light settled into people's faces. He did not make proclamations that night; he walked instead, quietly, and gave a coin to a musician for a tune that made the younger people dance.

And so the days were ordinary and therefore endless in their value: small trespasses forgiven, a goat tethered again, a boy who learned not to steal, the potter whose bowl found favor, the sailor who brought a strange coin and taught them a fragment of another tongue, the midwife who soothed a fever, the baker who shaped a perfect crust. In the slow turning of Shie, none of these incidents was a climactic event; they were the stitches by which the city kept itself whole. King Edmund kept his hall and his judgments, Captain Henry kept watch and lent a hand where needed, and the people below continued their repeated, steady motions — making bread, mending roofs, trading, applauding a tune — all of them, in their small, careful ways, living the ordinary days that made Shie a place to remember.

The city had not been given to suddenness, and even the threat that arrived on a salt wind and a broken plank could not at first force it into panic. Rumor moved first, as it always did: a fisherman named Peter Clarke returned to the quay at dawn with his boat smelling of tar and something foreign and a small barrel stamped with a mark none of them knew. He told, breathless and salt-stiff, of long, low ships with dragon-head prows that appeared at the mouth of the river before first light, their oars rising like a forest. "They rowed like men with no sleep," he said. "Their voices were rough as the net-lines. They scoured the banks with iron." The word they used—Vikings—was older than anyone in Shie wanted to think about, but the picture Peter painted fit the thing in their bones: a violent, quick strike that took and left nothing but ruin.

King Edmund read the message from Peter in the morning light and did not flinch. He had the way of a man who had been given many small emergencies; he could sit with one and see which of its threads mattered. He called Captain Henry and Minister Robert and Samuel the scribe and told them to send riders to the western watch and to summon the carpenters and blacksmiths. "Do not name fear before it is formed," he said quietly. "Name only what we will do."

They met in the king's low chamber where a map lay across a table like a patient thing. The river curved at the mouth into a narrow throat before it opened into the wide salt. It was good ground for people who knew how to use it. Captain Henry ran his finger along the riverbank. "They will not come dressed as couriers," he said. "They will try for speed and surprise. We must close the mouth and force them into the shallows."

Nathaniel Rhodes, who had been in the city only three years though he spoke of Corinth and of ports that smelled of olives and smoke, leaned forward. He carried himself like a man familiar with other tides and with how to turn a small fleet into a statement. Nathaniel owned a trading sloop and a handful of men who had learned the river's moods and the sea's temper; the men called them Greeks when they meant seafarers from the farther Mediterranean, though their names were English enough and their speech had taken the city's cadence. Nathaniel had a map of his own—sketched by his helmsman—and he pointed to the submerged bar that waited under the mouth at low tide. "We can set a chain," he said, "and hide nets in the shallows. We can have fire rafts ready. If they come by night and we make them think it is only a trick of darkness, we can force them to run where we want."

King Edmund's thin smile touched his mouth. "We are no strangers to tricks," he said. "Prepare what you will. Captain Henry, you will have command of the men on the bank. Nathaniel, take the boats. Minister Robert, see that the granaries are secured and that women and children away from the quay have a place to shelter."

By afternoon the city that had been slow and ordinary all morning acquired a purposeful speed. William Brown hammered pikes long and blunt enough to hold against boarding, and he fashioned iron hooks that might catch oars. Oliver Carter made clay pots with thick necks to hold pitch and tar; his eldest daughter rolled the rims smooth until the pots sang in her hands. Thomas Whitaker, whose hands were used to flour and oven heat, began to bake for different reasons: bread for the men who would stand in the cold and for the families who needed comfort. "Bread steadies the mind," Mary told him, and he packed loaves into baskets, his shoulders set in a new line.

The docks filled with men who were not soldiers by trade. Fishermen strapping strips of leather into their wrists to help row faster, coopers fashioning floaters out of old barrels, boys who had been stealing purses the week before laying ropes and looking at the water as if learning it anew. Captain Henry drilled them with a calm that was becoming him: how to form a line along the bank, how to hold pikes until the muscles remembered the weight, how to lean into the river when a boat listed. "Remember where you stand," he kept saying. "One step forward and the current fills a man's mouth with regret."

At dusk the first scouts returned with sight of prows on the salt, long shadows that slid with the waves. The Viking force drew a line on the horizon: longships with overlapping shields along their flanks, hulks of muscle and oars, and men who moved with the efficiency of fearsome certainty. The people of Shie watched from the parapets and felt the old small city-prickling of adrenaline. Children who did not know the meaning of the word 'raid' were called inside. Old Alice Grey, who had been midwife and healer and a figure like a cliff, moved through the lanes gathering linens and poultices as if this were another kind of birth—only now the results might be flesh torn rather than babies born.

Nathaniel Rhodes stood by the river with his men, his small fleet of flat boats hidden behind a low sandbar, ropes coiled like sleeping serpents. He spoke to Captain Henry in a quiet voice, the two of them bending over the plan as if it were a joint prayer. "We will make them think the river is an easy prize," Nathaniel said. "When they think so, they will not watch their flanks. We force them into the throat where the shoals will slow their oars. Then we singe them."

"What will singe them?" King Edmund asked, appearing on the quay as if drawn by the river's own concern.

Nathaniel's thumb brushed the map where the channel squeezed. "Fire pots, tar, and a chain. We will tether a raft with barrels and pitch loaded and set it loose when they are in the throat. The Greeks—my helmsmen—know how to aim a raft to catch a hull. They will think it a trick of wind. They will not know the river will be our weapon." He used the word 'Greeks' as if it named a long list of things—fire, salt, cunning—rather than particular people. The men around him understood he referred to the seafarers who had learned Mediterranean craft: angled oars, the subtle use of wind, the ways to make an enemy's hull drink flame.

The first clash came in the small hours, when fog hugged the river like a long, thin cloth. Longships, black and patient, crept into the mouth and tried to widen as if to swallow the city's throat. Shie's chain was a humble thing at first, a length of iron fastened to two barges and lowered to the water with men on either side ready to heave. They did not expect it to hold much more than a slow and clanking surprise, but when the Viking leader—Eric Hawke, a man whose name the traders had learned—ordered his ships to push through, the chain bit and a longship shuddered and listened as if waking to pain. Oars came out of rhythm. Shouts rose like blackbirds.

Nathaniel pushed his raft into the river with such care that it seemed he launched a portion of the night itself. He had loaded the raft with barrels of pitch and loose straw, and Oliver Carter had helped him set smaller jars of oil in carved wooden boxes. The idea was not simply to burn the ships—some of them would burn like thatched roofs—but to make the narrow channel a coffin of fire and confusion. When the longships became entangled on the chain and the shoals took their keels, Nathaniel touched a flare to the fuse. The raft answered like a slow beast and spilled a smear of flame along the water. Men on the Viking hulls screamed as flame found tarred planks; the shout of steel and burning cloth and splintered oar filled the throat.

But the Vikings were not only a force of terror; they were practiced at boarding and at turning chaos into advantage. One longship, its prow high and terrible, cut through the confusion and came to within grappling distance of the quay. Men leapt with hooks and ropes, leather boots finding purchase on wet stone. Captain Henry met them there and the clash became a handful of fierce, close moments: shield against pike, the smell of iron, a cry, a man falling into the mud. He moved with a kind of odd grace, his sword an extension of his arm, and his men followed because they trusted his steadiness more than their own fear. "Hold the line!" he roared, and the cry bounced off the warehouses and made the lamps tremble.

At that very edge of combat, William Brown stood with a pair of men and a wagon of iron. He threw down hooks and spikes that would make boarding ungentle, and he drove a small, crude cannon—more a loud, smoking thing—at the mouth of the quay; its shot tore through a mast and sent men into the water. There was the smell of powder like the smell of last year's thunder, and for a breath the Vikings reeled at being met by noise they had not expected in such an ancient place.

Amidst the battle there were small human scenes that the city carried afterward like stones in a pocket: Thomas Whitaker, who had not thought himself a fighter, took his linen apron off and wrapped a bandage around the arm of a boy cut by a fallen oar; Mary held a lantern high on the quay and held her breath and kept it when she saw Thomas's face; Elizabeth Ford knelt in the mud and washed a head wound and murmured prayers Old Alice Grey had taught her. Nathaniel himself was at the prow of one of the small boats, barking orders not with arrogance but with the same measured voice he used with his helmsmen. He moved among the men as if he were a brother and they, when taken with fire and sword, followed him like a tide.

The Greeks—Nathaniel's helmsmen and their kind—used more than flame. They rowed small boats fast into the flanks of those Vikings who were hopelessly beached by the shoals. They ran lines to cut oars, to pry shields off, to shove poles under hulls and make them list. The city's people, too, played their part in ways that were ordinary and therefore desperate: women poured boiling water from the parapets onto decks; boys with slings launched stones that found heads; old men who had lied about their strength all their lives now gripped pikes like children gripping a toy that at last mattered.

It was not a single turning point but a braided one: where flame licked, where chain held, where men shoveled and pushed against boarding, where Nathaniel's boats circled to make a noose. Eric Hawke, his beard singed and his face set in something like disbelief, saw that his longships could not slide free of the shoals nor escape the narrow mouth. He beat his shield and called for retreat, which those able to move did with oars frenzied and disordered. A final raft—one set with the most combustible of Oliver's clay jars—caught the stern of a flagship and sent it into a bonfire that glowed like an unholy dawn. When the smoke cleared and the fog thinned, the river was a black thing licked with embers and floating planks. Bodies were taken from water, men clung to wreckage, and the tide washed small things ashore: a carved whistle from a child's pocket, a coin with a strange face, a length of fur.

The price they paid was visible and heavy. Shie's quay had been torn; warehouses burned in corners; a baker's oven collapsed under smoke and heat. Names were given to grief: Peter Clarke's younger brother had rowed with Nathaniel and would not come home; Charles Lane—who had once tried to steal a purse—had a wound in his thigh that would not stop bleeding until Alice Grey worked with a silvered needle. There were funerals in the days that followed, carried out with the quiet solemnity the city reserved for those who had been taken into the ground. King Edmund stood among the mourners and said nothing grand; he walked, he touched shoulders, he listened to names and promised, measuredly, to remember. "We will build again," he said to those who needed it not as a command but as a small comfort.

Victory changed faces in small ways. Captain Henry came back with soot in his beard and a limp that he hid beneath his boot-stiff gait; Nathaniel Rhodes had a scraped cheek and a laugh that tasted like smoke but a new kind of place in the city. He and King Edmund walked the quay together and spoke of trade and of naval support and of how the Greeks could teach some of the carpenters to fashion better hulls that took less on the shoals. "We owe you a debt," Edmund told him, and the words were small and honest. Nathaniel shrugged as if to say he had been paid by the song of the river and the city's welcome.

The weeks after the battle were not a parade but a slow repair. Oliver Carter's kiln was rebuilt with help from the men who had cut their oars in the fight; his daughter, with a scar on her knuckle, set the new pots to dry and watched the sky as if learning weather again. Thomas Whitaker baked a bread called Victory Loaf—rough, salted, and large—and gave the first slices to the men who had returned. Mary sewed a blue stripe into a child's coat to mark that he had been in the line and come out blinking. William Brown made small iron crosses for those who had fallen, and Samuel the scribe wrote names on a clean sheet and propped it under glass to sit in the king's hall. The craftspeople who had forged weapons turned their hands back to ploughshares and candlesticks and lantern rims; the city was not a place content to be defined by its scars, but neither did it bleach them away.

There were practical arrangements that the victory demanded. King Edmund and Nathaniel Rhodes arranged for a small flotilla to be kept at the mouth for two seasons, a guard not of soldiers only but of tradesmen who could sail and men who could read the wind. The Greeks taught some of the Shie boatmen better knots, better sails for times when wind could be trusted, how to lash a raft so it would burn or sink as needed. In the market the talk slowly returned to bread and spice and flange and kiln, though now everything carried undercurrent—an awareness that the river could be a hand that gave but could also sometimes strike.

Victory did not remove fear. There were nights when mothers kept children close and the sound of distant waves made them uneasy, but there were also nights when Nathaniel's small trading sloop sailed in with cargo from a distant harbor and the sight of her hull and the faces on her deck—English names but with the eyes of men who had seen olive groves and basalt cliffs—felt like an assurance that there were other kinds of travel and commerce to come. Small tokens of gratitude changed hands: a carved whistle given to a Greek helmsman by a boy who had been pulled from the water; a length of fine cloth gifted by Nathaniel to Elizabeth Ford for sewing bandages; a coffer of sugar that Mary opened only for festivals.

The festival that year took on a quieter, fiercer tone. Lamps were made not only as ornaments but as statements that the city still knew how to make light where darkness tried to take ground. On the night when the river would again reflect a thousand timid flames, King Edmund did not stand alone. Nathaniel Rhodes stood near him on the parapet, his hand on the rail, and Captain Henry watched from below with his men. There was music—an old fiddler who had played before the battle and whose callused fingers seemed to hold memory like a second skin. There were names spoken aloud in a circle, small acts of remembering that made the dead part of the city's body rather than only an absence. Children offered flowers to the river and, in secret, to Nathaniel who had taught them how to make boats bob in the shallows safely.

When the crowd dispersed and the lamps guttered and the river took the last of the reflections, Shie was different in quiet ways: the quay had been patched with new timbers forged by men who had looked at broken boards and decided they would make new ones better; the granary had a stone corner to keep it from catching so easily; Oliver's kiln had a flap to damp smoke. People moved with an extra care when they crossed the quay; they did not forget the shape of the night when flame had come near. Yet the day-to-day heart of the city—the bread, the potter's wheel, the market's barter—reasserted itself because living demanded it. Thomas Whitaker continued to wake before the bell, smelling of yeast and the oven's hearth; Mary still stitched and kept worry folded into apron-pleats; Captain Henry still walked the western moorings though he now glanced at the horizon differently; and Nathaniel

Rhodes, who had been a stranger and had become an ally, set up his sloop with a small flag that was half his and half Shie's, and sold olive oil in summer and taught the children to knot ropes that would hold in storms.

Victory had been paid for with the city's own mettle. The Vikings had been driven back not only by fire and chain and plan but by the city's ordinary courage—the midwife's calm hands, the boy's quick sacrifice, the potter's stubbornness, the baker's bread—and by the allies who knew a thing or two about using the sea like a tool. In taverns and gateways people told the story as if it were a jewel: how the raft burned like a comet, how Nathaniel's men rowed too close to the bow and pried an oar loose, how Captain Henry held a gap with a grin like a blade. Each storyteller salted the tale with his own small pride because in the end victory belonged not to the king or to the Greeks alone but to the city that had learned to take the unusual and temper it with the ordinary.

Months later, when rains returned and the mud on the lanes was again a familiar grievance, Shie had its wounds but also its new habits. The city had a small flotilla at the mouth, a teacher for seamanship for the young, and a new respect for hands that worked both in the fields and on the oar. King Edmund and Nathaniel Rhodes spoke quietly of trade routes and repair for the quay; Captain Henry trained men who had never thought themselves soldiers to stand steady in the tide; Thomas Whitaker baked victory loaves for weddings as well as for the men who still bore scars. When children asked why the river sometimes shone like oil at dawn, their parents would tell them a smaller story than the ballads: a story of chains and rafts and of how ordinary people, with the help of some odd allies, turned a violent tide into a thing that taught the city how to breathe again.

Shie had won, and in the winning it became, as it always was, a city of slow recoveries and steady stitches—ordinary days repaired into an extraordinary whole. The river went on flowing, indifferent and patient, but now those who lived on its banks knew how to listen to both its kindness and its threat. They would remember the night of flame and the smell of pitch, and they would also remember how Nathaniel Rhodes taught a boy to tie his first knot, how Alice Grey hummed a lullaby while tugging thread through a mangled sleeve, how Captain Henry, begrimed and blinking, offered his hand to a stranger whose name he did not yet know. In that handclasp the city saw the future: alliances made not for conquest but for keeping the ordinary days—bread, pots, markets, lullabies—safe for another morning.

The lamps guttered and the river took the last of the reflections, and for a long time the city slept with the quiet of people who had been through something and were learning to breathe again. That breathing would, over the next year, reshape itself into something no one in Shie had expected. The allies who had bled beside them—the seafarers Nathaniel Rhodes had called "Greeks" for the way they spoke of olives and wind and the soft ordinances of other harbors—had settled into the city like lodgers. They taught knots and sail-trimming; they repaired hulls and showed a handful of Shie's boys how to read a sky for a coming storm. They were paid in bread, in barrels of fish, in hospitality; they were repaid in stories and a place at the quay. For a while that was enough. Friendship, after all, had its own economy.

But debts are patient things, and favors grow teeth when unpaid. What began as small discomforts—new men asking where the better moorings were, more voices in the tavern, a helmsman offering to "improve" the docks—met the old frictions the city always carried. King Edmund, who had been both the judge and the slow heart of Shie, found his counsel sharpened by an arithmetic he had not wanted: the cost of keeping a flotilla, promises made to families of the lost, the price of rebuilding warehouses with oak instead of salvage. He argued that Shie must remain a city governed by its own table of law and not by men who had come with sails and smaller allegiances. Nathaniel, who had interceded with rope and raft when the longships came, spoke then with the coolness of a man who had seen ports where commerce carried law like a knife.

"We ask only that our men be paid for their watch," he said in the king's low room, and when he said 'paid' he did not look like a man who wanted to be paid in mere coin.

Discussion became demand. The Greeks—those who had bound their lives for seasons to Nathaniel's sloop and to the sea—began to speak of 'contracts' and of 'rights to berth'. They wanted a quarter of the harbor for their own stores, a yard where they could mend ships without the constant worry of local levies. The merchants from Shie, who lived by the market's modest arithmetic of give and take, bristled at language that smelled suspiciously like annexation. Captain Henry argued that the quay was the city's throat and could not be surrendered in parts. He argued with the blunt earnestness of someone who had learned to trust his hands more than foreign rhetoric. "We gave them a place in hardship," he said one night to the king. "We gave them bread and fire. We cannot both house them and hand them the city."

Nathaniel's expression did not harden then; he simply folded his hands and said, "I ask for safety for my men. The quay is not a thing you can leave to chance when war has been nearby twice in a year." He had men around him who nodded as if Nathaniel's language made sense. Somewhere between the language of safety and the want of a harbor, motives braided. There were whispers—about trade debts, about payments promised and not yet paid, about a wealthy merchant in a distant port who had offered Nathaniel advantage if only his men could be given reliable berthing and a certain share of customs. These were the kinds of whispers that have long, slow teeth.

The first real incident that pushed talk into action was small and sharp. A night of rain, when the river boiled with the run-off and the docks smelled like wet rope and iron, a group of Nathaniel's men—led by a helmsman called Simon Harrow, broad-shouldered and abrupt—laid new planks along a neglected jetty without asking. They hammered in oak salvaged from a wreck; they lashed lanterns on new posts and set a small, unmarked bell to clang when a ship cut the mouth. The city woke to the noise and the sight: a neat, private quarter where there had been only public mooring. Minister Robert, who kept the king's accounts and watched borders more closely than some watched their children, stormed down to the quay with his ledger and a voice like a bell. "Who laid these planks?" he demanded.

Simon Harrow answered with a kind of blunt civility. "We did. We thought it would help. We pay for the timber." The minister's eyes narrowed. "You cannot pay for a public piece. This is theft by another name."

The argument that followed was not violent that night, but it left a bruise. Nathaniel came down and smoothed edges with talk of compensation; he promised to register the repair and to pay a fine to the town coffers. The fine was paid, but the new planks remained, and the bell hung on its post. Small authorities are porous things when the man with oars and trade is insistent, when he has taught half the boys to tie knots and when his helmsmen can carry a wagon more quickly than the official cooper. The bell chimed with a neighborly note at dawn and at dusk, and the sight of it, so ordinary in the morning, made some uneasy in the night.

Weeks and months stretched on in that way—petty seizures and compromises, trades that shifted a tax and navigational light whose maintenance seemed, by habit, to fall to Nathaniel's people. Captain Henry protested to the king and to the council more than once. He gathered men in the name of watchfulness—men who, during the victory, had learned to lean into oars and hold lines. They patrolled and logged and wrote lists of minor offenses. Nathaniel answered in the nether language of commerce; he paid for storehouses and claimed, in contract language that sounded slick and foreign in the hall, that the men had rights to shelter and to guard. The city's markets discussed the matter between weighing scales and evening ale. Stories were told that made Nathaniel's motives more mythical than factual: he was called hero, merchant, savior, usurper in turn, depending on whether the teller had sold pots that season or bought grain at harvest.

What finally broke the tie between negotiation and conflict was a smaller, crueller arithmetic: a wealthy convoy at sea needed a safe quay to unload, and Nathaniel wanted, it was said, preferential treatment for those ships in exchange for a guarantee of protection he claimed the king could not afford. The council refused. Edmund, who had always been cautious with the city's soul, hesitated to bind Shie's future to a single merchant's fleet. He said no to exclusive rights and offered instead a rotating berth schedule that would favor no single party. Nathaniel's face, in the council's dim light, lost something of its easy courtesy. "You ask us to risk men and flame for nothing in return," he said finally. "Then we will find what return we can."

They found it not in words but in movement. Nathaniel had friends along coasts where cities were made and remade by treaties and by force. Among his men and their contacts were captains of a small confederation—seafarers who kept to a certain law of the sea: when the harbor promised profit, it might be seized if the sovereign proved unwilling to bargain. They came not all at once but like a tide: a pair of coracles one week, a sloop that night, more hands every dawn. By the time the council understood it, the Greeks had bows in the alleys—men who had been taught to be useful in peace but who were not strangers to violence. Nathaniel did not at first show his full hand; he spoke of persuasion and of honor and tried, perhaps in the last minutes of decency, to find a compromise. The king, who had lost men and sleep already, pleaded for calm. Captain Henry readied his men on the quay and in the gatehouses.

The attack came like a sequence of small betrayals. At noon, when the market was at its breath, a band of armed men—Nathaniel's helmsmen among them—moved through the outer lanes and took the eastern gate by surprise. They did not shout immediately. They moved with the dexterity of men who knew a town's small muscles: a lock slipped, a night-watch bribed into idleness for a bowl of stew, a ladder thrown quietly to a roof. In the court beneath the king's hall, Minister Robert tried to warn Edmund as the bell of the eastern gate—set that morning by Simon

Harrow—took its second, different toll. Soldiers poured into the square not with the rhythm of the city guard but with the precise, disciplined step of men who had sailed in formation and who took orders without the city's old tenderness.

Captain Henry fought where he could. He met men at narrow points—bridges and alleys—where Shie's knowledge of its lanes told him he could make numbers count. He called out the names of men who had served beside him, imploring them to choose. Some chose the city; others, who had been paid by Nathaniel and had families who depended on his wages, faltered. A friend he had taught to hold pikes stepped aside, and the line snapped. In the king's courtyard there was a small, terrible moment when Captain Henry and Nathaniel found themselves face to face, the air between them filled with the clang of distant metal and the cries of men.

"Nathaniel," Henry said, voice rough. "Why—after what we shared?"

Nathaniel looked at him as if at an old rope, frayed but useful. "Because survival wears a different coat now," he answered. "Because I cannot watch my men die for a quay that pays less than our losses. Because the world pays in favors and in ports, and if we do not claim it, someone else will."

"You will put your flag over their doors," Henry said, as if it were a plain sentence.

"I will make the quay work," Nathaniel said. "And I will ensure my men are fed. I will not starve the hands that pulled me through."

There was no time for more. Coffers were broken into; keys were taken; the king's banners were cut from their mounts and folded, and in the morning the flag that flew above the quay was not Shie's but a new pennant tied with salt-stiff rope. The Greeks—Nathaniel's people among them—held the mouth of the river and the warehouses. They installed guards and decreed tolls. King Edmund was not slain in the first hour; he was taken under guard, his hall sealed, and his voice was allowed for a time to speak only in measured, supervised audiences. Captain Henry, bloodied and betrayed, was offered exile with a choice: leave for a neighboring town with those who would follow him, or stay and swear an oath to the new masters. He chose exile after a night in which he walked the quay and pressed a hand to the worn stones as if memorizing them.

The city in the days after the coup lived as one learns a new language—awkwardly and under duress. Curfews were set; foreign words were used in the market to name prices; a guard at the quay kept a ledger of every ship that came in and out. Nathaniel and his circle declared, with legal papers that smelled faintly of ink and of pressure, that they would govern trade to stabilize Shie's economy and to protect it from future raids. They placed their men as overseers at the granary, at the market, at the coinhouse. Taxes were rearranged; preferential berthing was enforced by the strike of a halberd. Some craftsmen found work building the Greeks' stores and were paid well. Some families found it prudent to appear collaborative. Some closed doors and said nothing.

Resistance did not die but it shifted. The midwife Alice Grey stitched bandages for those who pulled ropes in hidden night raids and whispered plans to boys who learned, at last, how to move silently. Thomas Whitaker kept his oven but sold breads not only to his neighbors but to the helmsmen who had commandeered the west quay, and he did so because his hands fed a family and because survival sharpened decisions into necessity. Mary sewed a blue thread not for luck now but to mark her eldest as someone who had been born under the old peace. Elizabeth Ford moved quietly through alleys, carrying news as she moved, and Samuel the scribe wrote, under duress, the decrees of a city that had been subsumed.

Over the months the Greeks reshaped the city in small ways that added up. The quay's timbers grew stronger where their hands had worked. The law courts continued, but their rulings now hesitated as if tasting a new salt. Local leaders who resisted found themselves fined or removed. Loyalists—men who had stood with Captain Henry and who refused a new oath—were offered a choice and sometimes dragged in the night to boats bound for ports where few asked about past allegiances. There were show trials, small ones, when a baker was accused of withholding supplies and fined to the point of ruin. There were times when Nathaniel—who sometimes walked the market and sometimes did not—appeared at the king's hall and spoke softly to Edmund of trade and peace and rebuilding. Edmund listened and, in the privacy of the closed hall, watched the flag he had once raised lowered and replaced.

People adapted. Children still learned to shape pots; mothers still mended stockings; the fiddler with the callused fingers found a new patron in a helmsman who liked old tunes. But in the quiet places the city kept an ache. The river moved as it always had, indifferent and patient, but it reflected now the sheen of new flags and the shadow of guards. Old songs changed their cadence. Laughter, when it came, was more cautious, as if measured against a ledger. The memory of the night of flame—the victory and the friends who had come to their aid—became complicated in people's mouths. They remembered Nathaniel's hands that had once steadied a raft and now, later, held the ledger that taxed their boats.

There were moments of private grace, small resistances that did not overthrow an occupying power but kept the city's soul from being wholly smothered. Alice Grey, in the market one morning, pushed a loaf of bread into the hands of a boy who whispered of a raid planned on a supply wagon and said, "Eat, and remember the shape of your hand on a rope." Thomas Whitaker, one evening, shaped a bowl with a rim so thin it might have pleased a court customer in any hall, and tucked it beneath his bench. In time, its thin lip would be shown to a child as a thing made under pressure: "We make beautiful things still," Mary told the child, "even when men make ugly choices."

Nathaniel did not, in his final decisions, wear the ferocity of a conqueror. He wrote letters, he paid for repairs, he signed decrees that made trade smoother for some and harsher for others. The city's loss was not a single burnished moment but a thousand small recalibrations. Shie had been taken, and it changed into a place that bore both the neatness of improved docks and the slow bruise of their occupation. A city that had once turned strangers into allies found, with a cruel irony, that the help it welcomed had learned a taste for permanence.

In the square where the market bell had hung, a new bell tolled for the first time on a morning the city did not expect. It was not the bell that had once signaled bread or festivals; it signaled curfew, the new hour of closing, the new rhythm imposed from a hand that claimed to care for order. People paused, hands on baskets, and then kept moving: a woman rearranged a pile of cloth; a child tugged at his mother's skirt. They learned to watch the river with a new kind of eye—one that could note both the generosity of its tide and the possibility that a flag on its bank might change the shape of the dawn.

Shie had been a city of slow recoveries and steady stitches; the stitches now held different seams. The river still flowed, indifferent and patient, and in its current the city's small everyday acts—bread, pots, markets, lullabies—found ways to continue beneath a new oversight. But where once alliances had been remembered as a story of shared courage, now they echoed also as a caution: that favors could become claims, that men who rowed with you in one tide might anchor their own claim at the next, and that the ordinary days one labored to protect could, in time, be governed by voices you had once called friends.

TEN

THE AWAKENED YOUTH

The bell at the quay had learned a new duty, and the city moved now to its clanging like a heart that had been taught a different rhythm. That change spilled into smaller things until the texture of life itself felt altered: a cart that once passed at any hour now waited at the gate for the guard's nod; a child who had been allowed to chase gulls along the mouth was stopped by a helmsman's stern hand; women who used to gather mushrooms from the edge of the wood came home with baskets that tasted of reluctance and worry. The Greeks—who had arrived with songs of olives and wind—had settled so thoroughly that their quarrels and their conveniences had begun to look like law. They were not all brutality and banners; many were careful, good craftsmen who mended hulls and taught a useful knot. But power, once it took root, grows small branches that sink into the soil and change which flowers can grow there.

They brought with them, in time, a thing the city had not been ready for: a name, a habit, and a place in the forest no one could cross. They called it Medmica. At first Medmica was a word said in low voice, like a rumor you did not want to give weight to. Then the word had a shape—a carved figure, dark and seated, breeches of bronze and a mask polished to a sober shine; then it had priests, men in robes who spoke with accents and with hands that moved as if they were smoothing a sail. The Greeks led a small procession one damp morning and set Medmica in a hollow of the wood where two old paths met. They moored small lanterns on posts, they strung a rope high across the entrance, and they declared the hollow a sanctum. "It protects the mouth of the river," Nathaniel announced before a small crowd that had gathered for the novelty. "Medmica keeps the woods safe for those who ask, and it keeps invaders from hiding there." His voice was careful—the voice of a man arranging an accounting.

That arrangement would come with rules. No one could cross the rope. No one could cut wood within a certain span of the hollow. No one could take herbs without permission from Medmica's priest. The priests kept lists and licenses written in an angular hand and stamped with a small emblem. These small emblems—stamped on paper, on wrist-bands, on the lids of boxes—came to be checked at the forest's edge by a guard who would not, for coin or for pleading, allow a passage.

At first people attempted to shrug: the wood was wide and other trees were plenty. But the forest had corners where the good timber grew, where the mushrooms the cooks prized waited under leaf-litter, where herbs with bitter-sweet smell cured fever and stilled coughs. Old Alice Grey, whose hands had healed more mouths than the city had houses, found that the satchel she had carried for decades—full of mugwort and yarrow and a thin silver needle—felt suddenly lighter where it counted. She came to the cordon one morning with the city's plaintive dignity and found the priest—a lean man called Marcus by the Greeks, who had learned to speak the local tongue with a measured gentleness—standing beside the bell they had hung there to summon the faithful.

"Good priest," Alice said, not in supplication but in the plainness of a woman who had spent a life in service. "My patient has a fever and the yarrow grows under that oak in the hollow. I ask only a handful."

Marcus's eyes were polite but closed like a lidded cup. "The grove is set aside," he said. "Medmica forbids plucking without an offering. We protect the grove so that we may protect the river. If all take as they please, nothing will be left."

"An offering is not a coin," Alice said. "A mother needs her child. She will offer a prayer, will you take that in place of coin?"

Marcus hesitated as if balancing ledgers in his mind. He let the space between them stretch. "Bring the mother," he said at last. "We will see if Medmica is moved by prayer."

So Alice returned with a bent woman whose son lay feverish and burning under his own breath. The priest moved with ritual: he laid a small cloth, he muttered a phrase that threaded between Greek and Shie dialects, and he allowed Alice a handful of yarrow. The herbs were given with the intensity of a bargain and the woman left with a mixture of gratitude and humiliation that sat heavy beside her thanks. The ritual was a door with a price paid in posture as much as in coin.

Word spread. Small things hardened into rules. Merchant carts that used to take the shorter path through the wood to save an hour were turned away and fined if they tried again. A woodcutter named Robert Mills, who had split oak by the bank for his family's warmth all his life, discovered one morning that his favorite coppice lay just within the cordon. He went to find the priest and asked for a license. "I cannot pay," Robert said, holding out his hand, nails deep with sap. "I have a wife, a boy to feed."

Marcus — or whatever name he used that morning — looked at Robert's hands and then at the ledger he kept tucked under his arm. "We have allowed some venality," he said. "There are wages for guild work. There are tasks for those who would mend the quay. We will place you where your hand is best used."

Robert left affronted and with no wood. That night his boy shivered beneath blankets thin as a promise. Robert went at dawn to the quay where men who had been paid to build new jetties and new houses loaded planks into the Greeks' wagons. He watched hands steady with coin and thought how coin had made a law where none had been before.

There were incidents that were neither law nor ritual but cruelty phrased as necessary action. A shepherd named John Ames tried to take his flock across a small hollow that had always been a short cut to good pasture. A guard called Elias — once a friendly face in the market—seized the flock and drove it back with blows until the bleating animal broke into a panic and three sheep were lost to the river's mud. John, who had been gentle and soft-spoken all his life, confronted Elias in the lane later, not with sword but with a voice that shook. "You have no right," he said. "You have stolen my season."

Elias's answer was not a defense but a repetition of the new language he had learned: "Medmica protects the wood. We enforce peace. If you cross you risk the river and you risk the peace."

"Peace?" John spat, his grief a raw stone in his throat. "You call this peace? You keep our wood, our herbs, and you hang a god in the hollow. You call that peace?"

Elias looked away. The guard's uniform—an added sash and a halberd at his side—felt heavier on him than the words he had been taught. He had children who ate the rations Nathaniel's overseers provided, and when you counted coin and hunger in the same breath, decisions changed their shape.

The market's cadence altered accordingly. Margaret Hale watched small merchants return with less spice and more silver, or with fewer bundles of mushroom and many more coins paid as fines. She kept a ledger of her own, not for the city but for her conscience: who had been forced to buy licenses, who had been fined for crossing an invisible line. She wrote a note to Minister Robert—who still came to the market sometimes under watch—and left it folded into the seam of a basket. It read, in her firm hand: We trade in openness, not in gates. Remember the men who cut oars for our safety. Robert took the basket, read the note, and buttoned it against his chest as if the paper were a keepsake he could not deliver.

There were added humiliations that pushed the city's patience thin. The Greeks set a tax on those who had once been exempt—widows who sold small bowls at market now saw a coin demanded at the quay entrance. A baker who delivered fuel to a priest's hearth was accused, wrongly, of hoarding flour. He was dragged before a makeshift tribunal and fined into the loss of his oven's repair. The punishment was public, made into an example the way thunder is made into a lesson for superstitious children. The man's wife cried in the lane and the fiddler — who had a new patron and therefore less appetite for trouble — played a tune that sounded like a sigh.

Resistance continued in ways that were small and cunning. Boys who had learned knots from Nathaniel still knew another kind of knot, one taught by Captain Henry that slipped a latch when pulled just so. They left those knots in the thicket near the cordon, a private map for men to follow toward supply wagons or to unhook a tether when necessary. Alice Grey's bandages travelled at night under the cover of onion sacks. Thomas Whitaker's oven, which had baked victory loaves, now also baked flatbreads with tucked messages inside—notes like thin leaves that told of times when a gate was less watched. These acts were not triumphs; they were stitches in a resistance that kept heat in the city's belly.

Then there were tragedies that turned private sorrow into public anger. A young girl named Lydia Barnes — who had been running in the lane and who lived with a cough that had been mild until the winter shook it — needed a certain root that grew on the far side of the wood. Her mother, Margaret Barnes, offered coin to a priest who at first shook his head and then, when the coin was fatter, allowed a passage so long as Lydia's family swore they would come to morning prayers for a month. Lydia left with hands clasped, hope and shame braided, and the priest blessed her in a voice that sang of obligation as much as of mercy. The medicine helped for a time, and Lydia's cough eased. But the family's debt to the sanctum made them outsiders in a way that was sharper than the cordon. Margaret told the story in the market quarter with a voice that smelled like salt: she had paid for a favor the city used to give without offense. People who listened shifted uneasily, because the price of safety had been rewritten.

There were also moments when the Greeks' religious pageantry turned into a public humiliation for those who had once stood with them. A festival of Medmica took place in which Marcus and his acolytes gathered offerings: jars of oil, bowls of figs, a small carved oar set at the god's feet. They paraded through lanes where old women had once pelted children with orange peels and where now they dropped coins into a plate beneath the god's feet. Nathaniel stood with the priests and spoke about protection and order and the god that watched the river's mouth; the speech was elegant, and many nodded because the sound of it was pleasing. But among the crowd were those who remembered the night the Greeks had rowed with them and who now felt the turn of gratitude into a leash. A boy in the crowd—Charles Lane, who had once tried to pick pockets and had been given a chance to mend—threw a small carved whistle toward the shrine. It landed at the base and bounced like a small, stubborn heartbeat. The whistle was not offered as tribute but as remembrance: of a hand that had once saved him from water. A priest picked it up and placed it into a bowl of offerings, and the crowd clapped in a murmur that did not reach the corners of the square where the old songs had lived.

In private, Nathaniel spoke with Marcus and with the more senior of his captains about tightening the sanctum's rules. "We cannot have smugglers," he said. "We cannot have men cutting the oak and trading it with others. Medmica is not a fence to make us feeble. It is a claim to the sea." His men nodded and their faces were set like carved wood. They heard in his words their own stomachs and their own families. They remembered storms and the nights when Shie had needed a foreign hand to steady a raft. In the ledger of survival, they had written their line: protection now in exchange for passage and profit.

King Edmund watched all of this from a parlor that had once been his own and which was now shadowed by a guard who was careful what he allowed the old man to see. Edmund still asked for small courtesies: a messenger allowed to visit a sick man, a bread ration increased for a widow. He wrote letters—delicate, measured—that asked for moderation and for an appeal to the common sense of men who had once shared a rope. Nathaniel replied in a way that was both courteous and absolute: protection required order; order required rules; rules required enforcement. There was, in his letters, an economy of concern that had less room for the intangible debts of sympathy. Edmund pressed his pen a little harder and returned to listening to the river, which flowed on like an indifferent judge.

As seasons turned, the forest became a presence that radiated rules outward. The path that had once been a short cut now required a passport of sorts—an emblem stamped by the priest. A mortuary tradition that had used a grove past the hollow for certain rites was now forbidden and another place chosen that lay farther and costlier. Weddings that had once scattered petals in the wood were rerouted to courtyards that lay under the observation of the Greeks' sentries. The old dances felt smaller. The children still played, because children play where they must, and sometimes they crept to the edge of the rope and watched the lanterns swing like patient eyes. They left small things at the cordon—a ribbon, a wooden tooth—secret offerings that meant nothing to the priests and everything to a child who wanted to mark that the place was still theirs in some small, private way.

There were whispered meetings, too, that brought together men who had not previously spoken together: a fisherman who had once rowed with Nathaniel, a cooper whose ribs had been split in the raid, a potter who now feared losing his kiln because of fines. They met by the quay where planks were being laid for new stores and they spoke in low voices about what could be done, about sending a petition to a neighboring port, about asking Captain Henry—if he were willing—to return and teach a few boys more than knots: how to read a tide for an ambush, how to hide a raft, how to build a small bell that rang for warning rather than for curfew. These plans were not swift rebellions; they were the slow, careful inventions of people who had learned the cost of being hurried. They sewed their own secrecy into knots the boys would learn and taught children to carry messages baked into flatbreads. They were not yet a force; they were a network of warmth that might become something else if rubbed long enough.

And always the forest and Medmica were there: a hollow with a polished figure seated upon a plinth, ropes across the entrance, guards pacing like metronomes. People bowed sometimes because they were frightened. They bowed sometimes because they thought obedience might buy mercy. They bowed sometimes because under that leaning of head they kept a private, stubborn prayer that the city would find a way to be whole again. The Greeks had brought protection in one season and possession in another, and the city learned by small degrees what it meant when aid turns also into rule.

In the evenings, when the tide lay flat and the lamps along the quay reflected like coins scattered on black velvet, Thomas Whitaker would shape his loaves and think of earlier nights when Nathaniel's boat had been a promise and not a claim. Mary would sit at his side and stitch while she listened to the market's distant talk. "We will teach our boy to knot two ways," she said once quietly, as if telling the future to a child not yet born. "One way to bind and one to slip." Thomas nodded because he understood that a people learns survival in craft as much as in courage. Outside their door a child would whistle the tune Nathaniel's helmsmen had once hummed, and Thomas would feel, in the music, the subtle bruise of a city learning what friendship can become.

Medmica sat in the wood and watched the slow human arithmetic on its rim: favors given and unpaid, children's toys left like confessions at its feet, herbs bartered for prayers, a flag raised where a home once flew. The god was not the only cause of fear—the ledger and the halberd and the guard's resolved silence were as much instruments of control—but Medmica provided a face to the change, a visible, uncanny boundary that people could point to when telling the story of the moment their ordinary days began to carry new burdens.

Time stretched and the city adjusted in one piece and then in another, like a woven cloth mended with a thread of different color. The stitches showed. They would be noticed by later generations, who would ask how a town so used to being slow and careful had allowed such seams to be rethreaded with the hands of men who had once been friends. For now, in the thin hours before dawn, there were still small rebellions: a plank loosened by a boy and replaced in the night, a priest given a loaf from a baker who made sure the bread was slightly burnt on one side as a signal. There were also compromises: a widow accepted a license in return for teaching a helmsman to bake, and the helmsman's child learned to say the name of the city in a voice that was not yet lost to other accents.

Shie, which had always been patient with the river and with its people's own small failings, learned now to be patient with a different cruelty—the slow kind that eats away edges until what remains is unrecognizable. The river flowed, indifferent and patient, and the forest held its god, its bell, its rope. Men kept watch on the quay and in the lanes; women mended and unmade. The ordinary days continued, but they were threaded now with the new knowledge that sometimes a friend's hand, once trusted in storm, might later reach to close a door. And in the hollow where Medmica sat, the priests wrote lists and the guards kept names, and the city lived beneath the shadow of a sanctum that had once promised protection and now promised only exclusion.

When the new bell tolled and the ropes of the forest corded off what had once been common ground, something else began to grow in Shie in the spaces between fear and habit: a quiet architecture of people who would not be quiet. It began in the church, as most things did here — not in any sudden sermon but in small gatherings that felt at first like shelter. The pews had always been places for the city's breath to find order: widows sat together, fishermen muttered prayers that smelled of tar, potters folded their callused hands and thought of clay as a thing that took shape under slow pressure. Now the church's low lamps also held the faces of those who wanted more than food and momentary comfort. They wanted an answer that would not be rented by a foreign dockmaster and a god carved from bronze.

Reverend Jonathan Marsh was a man not yet old but given to long pauses and a robe that hid his thinner figure. He had come to Shie to tend a flock and to teach the catechism; he did his duty on Sundays with a measured voice and prepared homilies. After the Greeks moved the cordon, he began also to hold weekly gatherings after the vespers — or, perhaps more precisely, they began to hold themselves around him. The first nights, the talk was ordinary grief: how a cart had been turned away, how an old coppice had been claimed, how a child had been turned from the priest in the hollow. They brought bread and shared it, which is how many conspiracies begin: sitting close enough to warm one another and to exchange small confidences that cannot be said in market alleys.

"You remember the night of flame," Jonathan said once, cupping a cup of mulled cider in hands that smelled faintly of lemon and ink. The room, a little too warm from the bodies gathered, answered in soft assent. "We did not call for strangers then because we wished to lose our law. We called them because our lives were at stake." He was not angry so much as steady; his steadiness itself had weight. "But a debt exchanged for a berth is not an exchange between equals. It is an exchange that makes men into rent payers and a city into a ledger."

Grace Hale — Margaret Hale's younger sister, who had kept watch over the spice shop when Margaret had been ill — leaned forward. Her voice was quick and small. "What would you have us do?" she asked. "They have oars and they have men. They have laws now sealed in ink and halberds at the gate."

Jonathan folded his hands and answered with a thing he had been taught to say in sermon form, but which here became a stone: "We build a society. A people who hold one another. We will be charitable and vigilant. We will keep the old ways of sharing. We will teach our children to know the river and the wood. We will not give our lives to a foreign purse."

It was not at first a doctrine but a plan of neighborhood: food shared in secret kitchens, a rota of watchmen who would warn of penal patrols, a list of names tucked into the hollow of the church's old altar and passed from hand to hand. Samuel the scribe — who still kept the king's ledgers under duress and whose ink-stained fingers trembled when he wrote the Greeks' decrees — began to keep another book at night. He wrote long lists of names of those who could use a loaf, those whose roofs had leaked after the raid, those who had been fined into ruin. He wrote in a clear hand and left copies under a loose brick at the north side of the market. People who found the lists came away with bread and with a small, fierce shame that someone else had known and had acted.

The society grew because the city had room for one more order: tenderness disguised as doctrine. They called themselves, first in whisper and then in a tone that felt like belonging, the Fellowship of the Pure — not because they fancied themselves holier than others but because they wanted a society that sought to recover what they called a sinless ordinary: the laws of neighborliness, the refusal to sell a child's future for a quay. Their rituals were simple at first. They had nights of confession where one spoke aloud a small failing and others answered not with judgment but with a plan — who would fix the roof, who would watch the baby, who would sit at the bedside. They made oaths not with blood but with bread and salt, and the rite was kept private: a loaf broken in a cellar lit by a single candle, salt pinched and passed between fingers.

"You will come on the eighth night?" Ruth Grayson asked Thomas Whitaker in the grey light before dawn, as he shouldered a basket of loaves. He looked at her as if measuring his life against the proffered warmth. "There will be a place for your hands."

Thomas thought of Mary and of the child they would soon have; he thought of the thin line between feeding a family and keeping the city. He said, quietly, "I will come." He came because the world of ledgers and foreign priests had become thin where his boy's bread should be thick. He came and he saw the city like a loom being rewoven.

The Fellowship carved its rules into memory rather than stone. One of them — the first, the one that sounded truest and most like prayer — was: aid the needy; take only what you need. Another: watch the docks and warn; do not be the hand that betrays a neighbor. These were moralities that fit easily into the church's crouched pews and into the kitchen's small, hot rooms. The people who arrived came with different things in their pockets: Robert Mills brought his ax and his knowledge of trees; Alice Grey brought herbs and needles; Captain Henry's exile friends sent a few notes that were frank and dangerous in equal measure — advice about how to spot a man who had been bought, how to read a ledger for the hidden lines that spelled corruption.

But as the society grew it found in its charity a mirror of the power that had displaced it. The Fellowship used its organization to set standards of conduct. At first this meant protecting the weak and arranging covert delivery of grain to a widow who had been fined out of fuel. Then it meant judging those who seemed too eager to trade with the Greeks: a merchant who had been seen every morning talking with Marcus and who had added a new coil of rope to his lamplight. "He sells more than cloth," a woman said in a meeting, her voice low like cloth dragged over a table. "He sells our silence."

The Fellowship instituted a practice that began as a test and became a law among them: the trial of fidelity. It was a private contrivance, a small bench in the back of the church where a neighbor brought a complaint about a man who had been taking licenses. The accused, if he wished to remain in the Fellowship's care, could come and answer honest questions. If he refused, he was marked as someone who had put profit before people. Marking was not at first violent: it was refusal of aid, a badge of shame, a curt dismissal from a job rota. A potter who had once received work from the Greeks and who refused to account for his hours found his kiln left unhelpful by fellow craftsmen; no one would fill his cart with coal, and his family went hungry until the shame softened.

There were, inevitably, divisions. Grace Hale argued that the Fellowship must never slip into vengeance. "If we begin to punish as they punish," she said one evening, her hands folded over a cup, "we become them." Jonathan listened and said nothing for a long time; then he answered with a patience that carried weight. "It is our sorrow that makes us fierce," he said. "I would have us be fierce for mercy, not for hatred. But mercy must sometimes be the stern hand that keeps a child from danger."

The stern hand had edges. Once a man named Caleb Torrence, a stout cooper who had been seen loading casks for the Greeks at dawn, was brought before the church's back bench. He stood clacking his teeth and said he had good reason—work for his sick father, money promised and counted. The Fellowship's verdict was that Caleb must choose: sign an oath that he would not lend aid to overseers or leave the city for two months, or be shunned. He signed, though later his eyes had the look of someone who understood how easily a man might be caught between hunger and honor. He kept his oath, but his laugh thinned and he walked the market with a small, inward caution.

The society, with its oaths and bread, became a subterranean law. It taught children to hide messages baked into the flatbreads Thomas made; it taught boys to loosen planks at the quay to delay a patrol, and it taught carpenters to fashion small bells that rang warnings when guards came too close. It also taught the art of exclusion. Names were whispered in alleys during curfew: collaborators, collaborators, collaborators. Those names, when spoken softly, carried a weight that could unmake lives. A widow accused of giving Marcus a jar of preserves to help her son was denied a place in the rota and found herself selling the last of her silver to buy a license that would keep her from being removed from her stall. The Fellowship's compassion had, without quite intending, become a moral economy of favors and penalties.

There were scenes of tenderness that brightened the shadow of the city's hardening. Alice Grey would stitch up a hand and then sit by the sick child's bed singing a hymn that had once been sung at weddings. Mary Whitaker, who had sewn a blue stripe to mark her child, stood at the door of the church on mornings to hand out hot porridge to members of the Fellowship who had been on night watch. A helmsman whose face had once been lined by command learned to whistle the old lullaby of Shie's river and soft-chip bread crumbs to a child. Those acts kept the Fellowship humane; they were its saving grace.

But there came a night when the society's reach produced an incident that would not be easily forgiven. A small merchant—Thomas Crane—had been seen taking coin openly from a Greek overseer in exchange for a license to pass the cordon with wood. The Fellowship's bench met as it had met a dozen times and judged that Thomas had breached the oath of mutual aid. They demanded restitution in a public manner that would be a lesson: Thomas must walk the market with a sign on his chest that said he had betrayed his fellows and then hand over a quarter of his stock to the poorest. He refused. The debate stretched long into the night; tempers, fortified by hunger and by righteousness, rose. A small group — men who had seen their own children sleep cold — decided to enact the sentence in the market at dawn.

When the sun came up and Thomas stood shivering beneath the bell, a crowd had gathered — not all from the Fellowship. Some came out of curiosity; some came in hope that the city's own law might speak more gently than the new occupiers' rules. The punishment was administered, and Thomas's cry broke the market's early hush. He would, later, tell of how his stall had been emptied and how neighbors had refused the crumbs he offered, and some would say the sentence had been too harsh. Others would argue that mercy without weight was no mercy at all. The Greeks watched from the quay; Marcus, who had been invited to witness the city's own justice, smiled in a way that looked like satisfaction. He liked to tell merchants later that the city would keep order even when it judged its own; it made his rule look like a mirror of civil law when perhaps it was only a mirror of private fury.

That night, beneath a dark roof patched with new planks, Thomas Whitaker and Mary sat with a silence that tasted of ash. "We made bread for wounds," Mary said at last, "not for tribunals." Thomas cupped his hand around a small roll and looked at the seam where his fingers met the dough. "We wanted a society that would be sinless," he said, the phrase turning in his mouth like a coin whose edge he could not quite see. "But sinlessness is a hard thing to hold. It can harden into a rod."

The Fellowship, in the months that followed, felt both the warmth of purpose and the chill of unintended cruelty. It continued its quiet charity and its night watches; it continued to hide messages in loaves and to teach children to tie slips and holds. It also continued to mark doors and to exclude, and the city's ordinary days carried the new pattern of both care and censure. Reverend Jonathan, who had first spoken of mutual aid, found himself writing names in Samuel's extra ledger and sometimes waking with his hands damp as if from sea-spray. He would pray, and his prayers had the tone of a man who had learned that making a people sinless is not merely a matter of removing wrongs but of choosing what wrongs one will not bear to tolerate.

Outside the church, the river kept moving, and the forest kept its god. Medmica's priests watched the Fellowship's growth with an interest that sometimes read, in their eyes, as threat and sometimes as amusement. Marcus spoke to Nathaniel of the Fellowship as a natural thing — people who close ranks when the taste of foreign salt grows bad on their tongues. Nathaniel nodded and said words about trade and balance; he watched the city's social shifts like a man watching tides and thought, perhaps, of which currents could be guided and which were best left to themselves.

Shie learned then to live with many small laws: the city's rulers, the Greeks', and the Fellowship's. Each law had its own habit of hands and its own penalties. People adapted. Children learned to read the ropes tied at the forest's edge and the knots that meant warning fit for a curfew. Mothers taught songs that contained hiding-places in their verses. Men who had once rowed with

Nathaniel still did so sometimes but kept a careful step on which side of the quay they loitered. The ordinary days preserved their quiet rhythms — bread, clay, barter, lullabies — but they now had a chorus of voices naming what must be done and who must be withheld. In the slow dim of the market, in the hush of the church, in the thud of a hidden bell, Shie stitched itself again: not into the same cloth it had been before, but into one with new threads, some warm, some barbed, all necessary to hold the city together under the weight of an altered world.

The city had known many small violences—fires, fines, a stranger's bell—and each had left its own scar. But nothing scarred as quietly or as steadily as occupation. That slow pressure turned the Fellowship into something else. The soft work of sharing and the hard work of judgement braided together, and from the braid sprung a younger, sharper thing: the Awakened Youth. Where the Fellowship had sheltered and rationed and reproved, the Youth would train and plan; where the older members moved with caution refined by compromise, the young moved with the quickness of hunger and the belief that a single night could reset a ledger.

They did not begin with a banner. They began, as all conspiracies do, with small practice. The first who called themselves Awakened met in a vaulted cellar beneath the church where the stones drank sound. They came with hands that knew craft—Thomas Whitaker with his dough-smoothed palms, Charles Lane with his quick fingers that once reached for purses but now learned to tie secret hooks, Ruth Grayson with a voice that could still rally women on market day. Captain Henry's exile friends sent letters folded into loaves; the letters were brief and precise: come to the quay at moonless dark, bring rope, bring silence. Henry himself did not appear at first. He watched, kept counsel, and taught in secret — not of glory but of steadiness: how to hold a line, how to make a feint, how to read an oar's fatigue.

"Do not think this will be like the stories," Henry told them one night, his breath fogging in the cellar air. "There are no sweeping banners without scoured hands. We will make openings, not miracles. We will use the river the way a tailor uses a seam: gather it, pull tight, then cut. If you expect thunder, you will miss the small, necessary pauses." He looked at Thomas. "Bake, and bring loaves. A warm hand makes a quiet hour easier."

Training was its own pedagogy. Boys and girls who had once learned rope-spirals as tricks for boats now learned to unlace a guard's boot as quietly as the tide takes a pebble; carpenters learned to loosen a plank without breaking its tongue; seamstresses sewed inside-out pockets where scrolls could hide. The older men remembered Henry's lessons from the long night of fighting: that a tide can be turned by a few well-placed ropes and a single raft set against a channel. They practiced quietly on the river under the guise of fishermen learning a new net: small boats threading the reeds, men counting strokes not for speed but for the moment they would be needed.

Recruitment was human and slow. Grace Hale brought children from the market whose lives had no margin for extra hunger and taught them to listen for the rhythm of boots. Alice Grey tended to the hands of those who misstepped and, while she stitched, asked if they had seen the guard's new routes. Samuel the scribe made duplicates of names and hid them under bricks; he also forged, delicately, receipts that would confuse an overseer's ledger for a morning. The Awakened Youth did not hide that it wanted the quay back; they hid only the means so that each small act might ripple into larger leverage.

The first real incident they planned was not a battle but a theft of notice. Nathaniel's men had kept lists and permits; those papers legitimized fines, gate-passes, the sanctum's tolls. If a ship came with a manifest wrongly filled, if a license was missing at a moment's glance, the city could be fined and the cargo detained. The Youth decided to create—carefully, with Samuel's hand—a forger's stack of plausible but blank-stamped forms that would be slipped into the overseers' chests. One night, under a sky that had not decided whether to rain, Charles Lane and two others scaled a storehouse's sill. They were not the sort of men who wanted to be heroes; they wanted slips of paper that could free a cartload of wood from a fine when dawn came.

They succeeded with a tenderness that made them laugh in the dark: a box eased, a chest opened, forms slid out and replaced with blanks. No one hurled a spear; no one murdered a watchman. But in the morning when the overseer discovered the missing forms, a flurry of confusion stretched the Greeks' capacity for order into thinness. It was small victory but instructive: the occupiers could be forced to look inward, and looking inward gave the Youth room.

Resistance widened in quiet ways. A hidden bell was fashioned—thin iron that would ring for warning, not curfew—and children learned its ring as if learning a new hymn. Supply wagons stalled when a plank was loosened; the delay was measured not in hours but in the temper of men whose ledger required timeliness. Aided by those who still sold bread to helmsmen, the Youth intercepted messages between overseers and foreign merchants, and with those messages they mapped habits. Nathaniel watched this new network with the polite interest of a man cataloguing currents. He tightened some routes and loosened others. He was a merchant and therefore a strategist; he tried, by bribery and appointment, to bend the tide back toward commerce. The Youth responded by cutting, small and precise, his options.

There were losses. A boy named Matthew Hargreaves, who volunteered to row in a dark night and whose hands were still callused from stolen work, did not return after a run meant to deliver a note to Henry's men across the river. The group learned his body had been found tangled in the reeds at dawn. The grief then became both a weight and a fuel. Alice Grey stitched more carefully and quietly taught a lesson: that those who risk must be honored, and their families must be held. The Youth fed Matthew's sister with bread and taught her how to carry messages folded like thin leaves. They never forgot his name.

As the months passed, small operations became a map of pressure points. The Awakened Youth realized that the Greeks' strength lay in the quay and the sanctum; these were great places but delicate in their own dependency on provision and public compliance. If the quays were choked, if the priests' bread dwindled, the legitimacy of occupation would erode. They set about making it so with patient cunning: a flood of false complaints to the guard tied up men in courts all day; a run of nocturnal fires—small, placed to blacken but not to burn warehouses—forced Nathaniel's overseers to spend coin and manpower on repairs and watch. Each incident was calibrated to avoid wholesale bloodshed but to make occupation costly.

The turning moment came not as a single battle but as a day of unmoored expectation arranged like a careful prayer. The Youth planned to take the eastern gate during a market day when merchants, overseers, and citizens overlapped. They would not storm the quay at once; they would first cut the bell-rope that summoned the Greek sentries, then fan the market with a simple, human confusion: a staged fight at the fishmongers' that would draw guards, a sudden call that a child had fallen into the river, the clang of the hidden warning bell. While the overseers investigated, teams would slip through the alleyways and wheel into the gatehouse, secure the latch, and let the city's people decide.

Jonathan, who had by then learned the edge required in counsel, argued against haste. "We must not make a coup that replaces one harsh hand with another," he said in the cellar, face lit by a single candle. "Promise me this: when the gate falls, we do not shout vengeance. We call a council and we hold a vote. We show them the choice of living by communal law, not by ledger." He looked at Thomas, at Mary, at Captain Henry's letter-bearers. "If we do not keep our promise to law, we will become another kind of thief."

Thomas touched the bread he had brought and looked at the others. "We will hold our hands," he said slowly. "We will not become what we hate."

Dawn on market day was a thin, pale thing. The Youth moved like a body that had practiced its gait: Ruth Grayson and two cooks created the noisy argument that drew a cluster of guards; Charles and another pair slipped a rope and dampened the bell; boys let a basket of fish tumble in the lane, which sent a merchant into a shout that required overseers' attention. A helmsman distracted at the quay found himself sent away because a "priority" ship needed unloading; his absence meant one fewer arm to raise the gate. And in the gatehouse, hearts beating like small drums, hands worked the latch. The eastern gate opened to a swarm of neighbors—potters with their aprons, bakers with bread, fishermen with hooks sharpened for nets, not for murder.

The moment was messy and human. A guard stumbled, a cart lurched, a widow wept because she had carried flour and now feared it would be taken. But the crowd, for once, chose restraint. They did not lynch overseers. They took the ledgers Nathaniel kept in the market office and locked the warehouse doors. They set simple patrols and posted names of those taken in the night for safe-keeping. Word spread from neighbor to neighbor not by a herald but by hands knocking on doors and the slow thrum of the church bell calling people in—not for a sermon but for an assembly.

Nathaniel convened his captains on the quay with the calm of a man for whom trade had been lost and might be regained. He stood where he could be seen and said, "You have taken a risk." His voice was not only businesslike; it was also a plea. "Return to your boats. Let us talk. There is room for merchants in a city that is free."

But the city had changed. Captain Henry—who had returned at the head of men who had learned the river's courses and the hidden knots—spoke in public for the first time in months. "A city is not a ledger for a man's profit," he said, his voice carrying over the quay like a rope thrown hard. "It is a body. We will not be priced into being."

Negotiations followed, and they were long and raw. The Awakened Youth were not conquerors so much as a populace given the nerve to choose differently. Merchant captains who feared ruin negotiated terms: guaranteed berthing but under city law; dock fees that would go to repair quays and feed the poor rather than to a private ledger; the sanctum's priests allowed to tend the grove so long as the cordon's rules were moderated and licenses priced by labor rather than coin for the destitute. Nathaniel, who had too much sense to fight a city that had risen in his name of debt, bargained. He wanted to keep trading; they wanted a free harbor. The bargaining was bitter and tender: long nights of haggling, of someone crying when the account did not cover a child's fever, of Samuel the scribe writing a charter by candlelight.

In the end they did not restore King Edmund to a throne as some hoped; they restored him to a place of honor with limits. Edmund, who had watched from a room with a guard and had learned the cost of words, walked into the square and, with the hammer of the new assembly, agreed to step down from unilateral rule. The Awakened Youth insisted the city be governed by representatives elected from trade guilds and neighborhoods: bakers, potters, fishermen, weavers, mothers, the midwife, craftsmen who had lent hands in the long nights. It was not romantic; it was pragmatic. They named it the Council of Commons and declared that henceforth major decisions—harbor rules, taxes, the sanctum's oversight—would be taken by vote.

The first election was a chaotic thing. Votes were not high-tech; they were hands raised and names spoken aloud and marked by Samuel's quick pen. There were speeches that tasted of fear and hope: Ruth Grayson spoke of a woman's right to food; Robert Mills spoke, with bark-stained hands, for common access to wood; Grace Hale, steady and unadorned, asked that the council take a pledge never to exile those who could not pay. Nathaniel, surprising many, stood at the quay and promised support for fair trade if the city allowed lines for merchants that did not undercut the poor. He kept his word in part; his men were allowed to operate under new rules, taxed but permitted, because the city chose to make order through law not by force.

The Council of Commons established an electoral rhythm: each quarter the trades would select representatives; neighborhoods would vote a steward who would be the voice of ordinary concerns; the midwife and the church would have a seat to voice social needs.

They wrote small charters that read like prayerful law: no single man could hold dominion over the quay; religious sanctums should be open for aid in sickness unimpeded by coin; fines could be appealed by a council of peers. Samuel's pen made the lines and, later, his shaky hand would sign the first public ledger in the town square.

Change did not wash all wounds away. Some families bore the loss of sons like Matthew forever; some men who had lent ropes to Nathaniel felt betrayed and never forgave the Youth. The Fellowship's old practice of marking was remade into a civic registry rather than a moral blacklist; those who had been ostracized were given paths to reintegration if they performed public service. The Awakened Youth learned humility as a daily practice: they opened meetings to question, they put Jonathan's sermons into law as clauses of mercy, and they built places where the poor could take wood for shelter if they pledged to plant a sapling for every tree taken.

The first sessions of the Council were clumsy and beautiful. Men argued about how to price berthing so that ships could come without splintering the poor; women argued about how to guard the forest's rare roots while allowing enough medicine to pass. Children—who had once hidden messages in bread—now stood at the edges of the council with faces pressed to a rail, learning the sound of debate. One night, in the candle-lit hall, a fisherman named Peter Clarke—who had first seen the dragons' prows and then found his brother drowned in the reeds—rose and spoke simply: "We fought because we could not take being leased. Now we must fight to keep commonness common." The hall answered in a murmur that became applause.

In time the quay hummed differently. Ships came and were counted in a ledger of public use; fees were paid into a chest whose key was kept by a rotating steward chosen by vote. The sanctum still stood in its hollow, but the rope that corded its mouth was loosened where the council decreed; the priests still tended Medmica, but now an elder from the townspeople sat as witness to any decision that barred a healer from gathering herbs. The bell that once tolled curfew now tolled a market hour decided by vote. Thomas Whitaker baked loaves that bore an imprint of the city's seal, and Mary sewed the blue stripe into clothing not as a mark of survival but as a sign of belonging.

The revolution of the Awakened Youth had not given them a perfect world; it had given them, painfully and with many small compromises, a system where law might be remade by a city's voice. They learned to be suspicious of the ease of power and to make law with the clumsiness of people who had been taught to row. The river flowed on, impartial and patient, and the city—now stitched with a different pattern—kept its ordinary days with a new rhythm: public voices, votes called like prayers, and the slow work of mending what power had torn. In the lanes the children still hid notes in bread and freed a plank when needed; in the council the old men and the new youth argued and sometimes made fools of themselves; at night the bell by the quay sometimes tolled not for curfew but for celebration, and those who had borne loss lit a lamp and let it shine. The Awakened Youth had won not by simple violence but by making the city remember how to govern itself: not under a single foreign hand or a sheltered king, but by the small, stubborn choices of people who learned at last to vote for one another.

After the Council had been hammered—awkward, imperfect, human—out of nights of argument and days of knocked-on-doors, a quieter urgency set in: what does a free city make of its freedom? The Awakened Youth answered not with more arms but with an idea whose scale was measured in years rather than hours. One night, in the still-smelling cellar beneath the church where the first plans for resistance had been folded into the bread tins, Thomas Whitaker put down a loaf and, with icing sugar on his fingers, sketched a rectangle on a scrap of Samuel's ledger. "What if," he said, soft as dough under a palm, "we make a place to hold knowing? A place that teaches the river and mends ships and keeps the herbs and the stars in one house?" The words felt oddly sacred in the room's hush.

Jonathan listened and tilted his head, as he did when a sentence might be a sermon. Grace Hale, always quick to see the shape of a practical thing, added, "Not just a school. A workshop and a library and a place for the midwife and for the potter. A place where children learn to read tides and not just oars." Samuel, whose hand had become a kind of public memory, wrote the name they tried on and tried again until it sat even on the paper: Bogston. It was a name like a promise—bog for the land that fed the reeds, ston for the work of human hands.

They moved slowly at first because everything that mattered in Shie had to be coaxed. The Council of Commons convened a committee; Ruth Grayson was named to lead it because she could call more women to a meeting in the market square than most men could gather of soldiers. Nathaniel Rhodes, who had not loved the city's politics but who respected its stubbornness, offered a careful loan from his coffers and a promise of timber at cost. "If what is built is for the common good, then I will help set it in place," he said one dusk on the quay, watching the sun cut like a blade across the water. His voice carried the compromise of a man who had learned both currants and compromise: he would back the school that promised practical returns—better sails, smarter quarriers, healthier workers.

Raising the funds became a choreography of many small measures. Thomas proposed that bakers donate a day's profit each market fortnight; potters put one bowl aside from each kiln; William Brown forged iron hooks and sold them for the chest. There were fairs where children performed the old dances whose steps now had meanings—each coin given for a dance would be marked for Bogston. The Helmsmen's Guild, still adjusting to the Council's laws, sold a crate of fine rope at auction and bade with a blunt propriety. Samuel the scribe took to the square with a ledger that was not for fines but for credit; people signed the pages with hands that trembled because pledges often do.

Designing Bogston occupied entire nights. Samuel's neat hand drew rooms: a low library whose shelves would be open—no small rebellion that—workshops for metal and clay, a wet room for Alice Grey's medicines, a small observatory on the roof with a slit for the stars, and an enclosed garden where healing herbs could be grown under guard for all to use. Jonathan insisted on a public hall where disputation would be not only allowed but prescribed: "Argument is not the enemy of learning," he said, "it is the tool." Grace argued for a seamstress's room and a school for the children; Thomas proposed a kitchen large enough to feed an apprentice corps. They argued gently in the cellar—about drafts, about access, about who might lecture, and about how much of the knowledge would be shared and how much preserved for safety.

Marcus, who still tended Medmica with a guarded grace, came once to the council not as a supplicant but as a man wanting to test what the venture meant for the sanctum. He stood with hands folded and asked, "Will your library hold books about gods other than ours? Will your observatory teach of the heavens without prayer?" His voice had the steady curiosity of one used to making accounts. Jonathan answered in a tone meant to bridge: "We will teach the heavens to anyone who asks. We will not teach to dissolve the faith of men but to enlarge the ways they know God's world." Marcus looked long at the sketch of the observatory and, with the slow thoughtfulness that had become his habit, said at last, "If knowledge can heal and if it keeps our children from dying for want of herbs, then we will not oppose you. But there must be a place in your house for counsel: when a craft is dangerous, you do not hide the danger."

This became an early covenant of Bogston: knowledge would be public, but practice would be careful. The architects of the projects—potters, carpenters, and sailors—insisted on apprenticeship as its moral core. "We teach hands before we teach pride," William Brown told a small crowd of apprentices one afternoon; he held up a small iron ring to show how a flaw in temper could break a man's life at sea. "You will tune an iron until it sings right or we do not let it be used. We will make a manual—the Book of Hands—that is studied as carefully as any sermon." That book—ragged, handwritten, bound in thongs—would become a treasured primer in Bogston's earliest days, full of diagrams of kilns, ways to anneal metal, and the shape of a sail's optimal curve.

Building was work that reshaped people as much as stone. The first foundation stone was laid with a small ceremony that was not ostentatious: a simple hammer strike by King Edmund himself—now a man of honor rather than dominion—followed by Jonathan's prayer and a blessing by Marcus that was given with eyes that did not betray all he had seen. Thomas, with Mary at his side, spread the first mortar. Children watched and left pebbles around the stone like small, impatient offerings—each pebble to be nested into the building's foundation. "We will teach them a different way of reaching the river," Mary whispered to Thomas: "they will know both how to fish and how to measure when the tide will turn." He nodded, thinking of his own child and of a future where that child might read the sky.

Incidents happened as they always do when men build: a crate of iron hooks fell and broke a worker's wrist; a boy slipped on wet mortar and scared an old woman into thinking a curse had been muttered. Each small accident drew the community in—Alice Grey's hands were busy stitching and setting bones those first weeks more than mentors' hands were busy teaching. They set rules for safety: no one worked alone with heat after dusk; apprentices were to be paired with masters; volatile substances were kept in a locked chest with two keys, one kept by Samuel and one by the midwife. The first laboratory they built was modest—a stone-floored room near the garden where experiments on herbal mixtures and dyeing could be done. It smelled of herb and smoke and of careful men learning caution.

Security became a practical conversation, too. After the theft of a single draft—the sketch of an improved sail that Samuel had penned—there was a night the city did not sleep. Someone had come into the workshop and slipped away with a rolled parchment; Nathaniel, who had returned his promise of timber and finance, pressed a hand to his beard and said, "Knowledge will be stolen when it is valuable. That theft means our idea is dangerous to those who profit from ignorance." The Youth did not seek vengeance; they tightened rosters of watchmen and redrafted the plan so that no single patent would be kept secret but rather taught in series so that a thief gained not an easy sale but a crowd of men who could remake what he stole.

Bogston's first classes were humble and overflowing. The observatory's slit became a place of evening gatherings where Reverend Jonathan, Samuel, and a helmsman named Elias—who had once been a guard but now felt a soldier's soul bent toward peace—watched the moon and traced its path across the river with chalk on a board. "Look how the tide follows a line," Elias said one night, mapping a shadow with his finger. "We row on a map we rarely write down." Thomas brought bread and watched as boys who had once stolen purses learned to measure the moon's divergence and to note the wind's subtle change in color. A girl named Anna, whose hands were quick at clay, sat with a copper lens until Samuel realized she had learned, by accident, how to grind it so that it magnified the moon's dark craters. They applauded her discovery as if it were a small miracle: talent found its place.

Medicine began as an urgent matter. Alice Grey's compendium—her decades of remedies gathered from mouth, memory, and experimental tinctures—formed the backbone of Bogston's first codex. She and Mary taught a class on poultices and the proper way to stitch a wound so it would not fester. They invented, in small private experiments, a poultice that would staunch bleeding more effectively, mixing yarrow with an ash from a particular oak that Robert Mills identified. The first woman to pass the course was a fisher's wife who had the steadiness to hold a child while a stitch was placed. She later taught others; the skill spread until the city's mortality from small wounds dropped and people began to believe that knowledge could be as vital as a keel.

There were debates about access. Some argued that Bogston should be administered by the Council, open to any who wished to learn; others—scarred by the occupation—wanted certain crafts to be taught only by master guilds. Grace Hale stood in the middle of a long meeting and said, "We must teach the poor first. They are the backbone of this city; they row and they bake and they mend. If Bogston becomes a house to show off, we have failed." Her words swayed votes; the Council agreed that apprenticeships would be prioritized for those with the least means, and Samuel noted in the ledger that a quarter of Bogston's first bursaries would be allocated to families of lost men like Matthew Hargreaves.

Not everything went smoothly. A jealous baker—whose business had waned because the Council now regulated fees and supported competition—decided to stir trouble and posted a libelous note claiming Bogston hoarded grain for experiments. The rumor took root one cold morning, and a small crowd formed outside the storeroom. Thomas, standing at the door with arms full of loaves, did not shout but invited the crowd into the warm room where the apprentices were kneading. He had Samuel read aloud the ledgers that showed the stores set aside for Bogston's needs and for the poor. He let people see the shelves and the indexed jars. The crowd dispersed with a softer anger; knowledge's transparency had been Bogston's first defense.

Weather itself became a teacher. A spring flood swelled the river and threatened to take the new foundation; the Youth organized a human chain and sandbagged the banks. Nathaniel's helmsmen rowed out in pairs to tie up vulnerable boats and to place anchors where the current might wrench them. The flood would have taken part of Bogston's new wall if it were not for the combined work of many hands. Afterward, they celebrated with a loaf-bake where every hand that had hauled sand was given the first slice; Mary stitched blue ribbons into every apron worn that day as a small, stubborn honor for those who had kept stone and seed safe.

Teaching in Bogston took many forms beyond the formal: a potter's glaze trial led to a stable color that would not flake in salt air; an experiment with kiln airflow reduced fuel consumption and fed more ovens for the town; a navigational adjustment devised by Nathaniel and Henry—based on Samuel's charts—set a new mooring practice that reduced collisions in fog. These small discoveries were celebrated in the market like good fish: practical, delicious, carrying the scent of the town's improvement.

The observatory slowly gained reputation. One autumn night, Jonathan and Elias and a boy named Peter (no relation to the fisherman whose life had been stolen by the river) watched a comet that stretched a pale hair across the sky. Samuel, taking notes, made a careful observation of light and date; a Greek helmsman, who had returned to trade fairly under the new rules, shared a scrap of parchment from a distant harbor that spoke of the comet's appearance across seas. They cross-checked and found their little observatory's record matched those in ports far away. Gratitude and pride flowed: Bogston's small journal would be copied and sent; for the first time, Shie's name sat beside others as a place that measured the heavens.

As Bogston's walls rose, so did the city's sense of possibility. Children apprenticed in its workshops grew confident enough to improvise: a boy who had trimmed sails learned to measure the angle of light upon a new kiln glaze and suggested a tweak that saved hours of firing. A midwife's student devised an improved bandage knot that allowed a wounded torso to breathe more easily. The Council began to convene in Bogston's public hall on many occasions—because the building was neutral space and because knowledge, when present, made dispute less sharp and more honest.

There were also ethical debates that required their own slow counsel. When a craftsman proposed building a device that might pry open a ship's hull with brute leverage—a tool that could be used for salvage or sabotage—the Council paused. Jonathan led a roundtable that included fishermen, potters, the midwife, Nathaniel, and young apprentices. They argued about the potential for harm and for rescue. In the end they wrote a clause in Bogston's charter: inventions that risked harm must be reviewed by a council of peers and tested in safe conditions before distribution. It was a small, early code of ethics, and from its first sentence the tone of

Bogston's work was clear: knowledge without care might be sterile; knowledge framed by community could be a bulwark.

Years passed with the steady, ordinary rhythm that had always made Shie durable. Children who had once hidden messages in bread now carried notebooks and slates. Alice Grey's herbal compendium became a small published tract distributed free to households; the midwives' skills reduced simple mortality. Bogston's library, though small then, gathered hand-copied treatises on boat-building, pottery glazes, the lunar tide, and the mixing of dyes. Nathaniel donated a chest of compasses and a pulley system for teaching, and in return the Council allowed his men to teach navigation classes that were open to all who wished to learn. The helmsmen taught patience and leverage, and the potters taught the patience of kiln while the midwives taught the patience of stitches.

The city's identity shifted slowly: Shie became a place parents considered when they wanted a child to learn a craft that promised more than subsistence. Word traveled beyond the river-mouth—not in the grand way that empires make words travel but in the careful, reputable way of traders who tell one another where bread is good and where a child might learn to read the tides. A travelling weaver came and stayed a season, not because he had to but because his son could apprentice with a potter and learn herb lore in a week that would otherwise have taken years.

Bogston's fame did not arrive as a trumpet but as a string of practical notes: better sails for distant merchants; a manual of kiln safety that saved coal and lives; a compendium of local herbs that helped a fevered child survive when before she might not. Scenes of daily life reflected the new center: men lingered at the library's low window to read while their wives sat at a bench and practiced sutures; apprentices carried tools and books in the same satchel; the Council's votes were sometimes recorded in the margin of Samuel's compendium alongside diagrams of levers and lists of who had pledged wood.

There were, of course, failures—experiments that scorched a kiln, a medicine that proved too strong, a quarrel that left a hand bruised. But the city had learned a different way to respond: to examine, to record, to retry. Bogston became not a single institute but a network: the observatory connected to the shipwrights who changed the keel design; the herb garden worked with the midwives to test poultices; potters learned from navigators how to rate clay's fatness for hull-coating experiments. It was messy and human and therefore real.

In one quiet moment, years after the first stone was laid, Thomas and Mary stood by the garden and watched a young apprentice measure the angle of the slit in the observatory roof. Mary reached for Thomas's hand and, with a laugh that had no bitterness in it, said, "We made a place to learn what the river tells. My child will know the tides before he knows the ledger." Thomas pressed his thumb against the child's small, rough fingers and felt the shape of a future that included both bread and books.

Bogston did not become the world's center of science overnight; it grew into that reputation slowly, carried on the backs of small, repeated discoveries and a stubborn civic ethic that knowledge must be communal. The word spread—first to neighboring ports, then to a network of itinerant craftsmen and curious clerks—and with the spread came new faces at the door: a woman who had been a scholar in a distant city and who wished to teach botany; a mapmaker who wanted to compare coastlines; an old Greek helmsman who brought precise notes on Mediterranean winds and shared them freely with a city that had once feared his name. Each person who came added a stitch.

And so Bogston, begun in a cellar with a loaf and a doodle on a ledger, became the seed of something larger. The Council's elections continued, imperfect and human; the registries Samuel kept were catalogues of both craft and of promise; the river, patient as always, wound its slow way past the observatory and took nothing but gave all the same. Shie had, by hard work and a cautious, communal courage, planted a house of knowledge that would one day be read about in ports farther than any of them could now imagine—built not on the exclusion of a god like Medmica nor on the ledger of a single merchant, but on the stubborn conviction that a people can make their own mind and that the ordinary days—bread, pots, lullabies—deserve the company of learning.

ELEVEN

END OF YOUTHS

Bogston had been built out of bread and candlelight and the patient stubbornness of a city that had learned to govern itself. For a time its name smelled of kiln and ink and soup, and parents spoke it like a benediction: send your child to Bogston and she will learn the tides and the stitch. But every living thing that grows makes its own shade, and what sheltered people one season can, in another, become the place that threatens their light.

The Awakened Youth had been the engine of change: bright, impatient, hungry for a world not brokered by ledgers. They were the ones who thought in small, quick movements and could turn a rumor into a lever. When that energy met the hard work of governing, something brittle entered the edges of their vows. The Fellowship's old language—aid the needy; take only what you need—began to be spoken with a different tone. "Sinless," some began to say, as if the word could be polished until it shone clean enough to cut. "Fit," others said, as if the city were a sail that should be trimmed of any hangers-on.

It started in small rules. The Council of Commons, newly elected and still soft at the joints, listened to petitions and arguments in long sessions that smelled of tallow and ink. At one such session, a young man named Isaac Thorn — who had been a good organizer in the cellar days and who now carried himself with a new forcefulness — rose to speak for a youth deputation.

"We have borne occupation and poor law," Isaac said, voice steady and sharp. His face was clean-shaven and his eyes bright with conviction. "We have endured fines and rationing and excuses. The time has come not only to protect our common goods but to make a city worthy of the children we raise." He looked out at the council: at Jonathan in his robe, at Ruth Grayson with a basket balanced on her knee, at Nathaniel leaning a little back against the rail, and at the small cluster of mothers with knitting on their laps.

"What do you mean by 'worthy'?" Grace asked, quietly. She had learned to watch her words; in the last years such words had been flints.

Isaac's jaw set. "We mean standards. We mean that those who lead must live unspent. We mean that the young should be given precedence in apprenticeship, because the young are the city's strength. We mean that certain behaviors — those that break trust and endanger the fabric of families — must be answered firmly. A sinless society is one that cannot be held ransom by indulgence."

"Indulgence?" Ruth's voice folded around the word like a hand. "You speak as if mercy is a slovenly thing. Our laws are written from reed and bread. We do not want to make a city that eats its own children."

The debate that followed was long and slow, with the City's old rhythms—argument, example, vote—dragging the motion down into something more nuanced. Isaac proposed codes of behavior aimed at curbing what he called "social corrosion" — adultery to be sanctioned, idleness to be curbed, apprenticeship to be strictly merit-based rather than by favor. Some on the Council favored guidelines for curbing corruption; few voted for severity. But the Awakened Youth, organized and impatient, did not wait for unanimous approval. They began to institute practices among their own: application exams that favored the strongest, public shaming rituals for what they named "moral failings," and a vigilante zeal thinly disguised as civic hygiene.

The first terrible rupture came one cold, brittle morning in late autumn, when frost still rimmed the leftover mortar at Bogston's wall. A rumor slipped through the lanes—whispered as if it were a scandal and then as if it were a contagion: a young man, Andrew Marlow, had been found in a tryst with another woman, Esther Pike, both of them married to others. The story threaded quickly through the market and reached the church, as gossip will when it finds a tidy narrative. Andrew was a potter's apprentice, not yet twenty, with freckled hands and a nervous laugh; Esther was a seamstress who had been married but recent grief had left her husband distant and brittle.

At first the tone of outrage was ordinary market anger—the clatter of spoons, the hiss of admonition. Then Isaac Thorn's cohort took note. They called a private meeting in the same vaulted cellar where, years before, the Awakened had planned how to free the quay. The tone there was colder.

"Honour is not a thing that can be sewn back on with pity," Luke Harper, a blunt young man who had once run messages on Henry's behalf, said. He had a soldier's impatience with nuance. "We say the city will be sinless; if we tolerate adultery, what is to stop greater eroding? Children will grow up believing trust is optional."

"We cannot burn a man for love," Ruth whispered, but her voice found little purchase. The Youth were arguing among themselves about the example that would "root" the message. Some wanted public labor; others wanted banishment. A smaller, grimmer faction led by Isaac favoured a punishment meant to fix the eye: a burning.

Jonathan, when he learned of the fevered meeting, went to the cellar. He had always believed that law must be tempered by mercy. He found Isaac pacing.

"You cannot become the judge, jury, and flame," he said softly. "We argued to put law into the open—not to make secret courts."

Isaac's face was lit by a single candle and the lines of conviction were deep. "We make law," he said. "We make order when the Council cannot. If the Council will not act decisively, we must. We owe it to the children who will be apprenticed and to the mothers who have watched their children starve." His words were not shouted; they were practiced. "We will not be lax as our fathers were when the quay burned."

"You will become your fathers' harshness," Jonathan answered. "We replaced tyranny with voice. Do not give us a new tyranny wrapped in the idea of purity."

Jonathan did not stop them. He argued and pleaded; he wrote in his journal in the chapel and prayed into a dawn that would not answer. He thought he might be able to persuade Isaac away from violence. But the Youth had their own calculus: a single, visible deterrent might teach others to keep faith, they thought, by fear if not by conscience.

The trial followed no public process. It was a bench of men in the back of the church by the old vestry, convened with the hush of a house that does not want neighbors' ears. Andrew and Esther were brought before them in ropes that stung their wrists. The accusation was read aloud with a formality that only deepened the horror of the thing: the names, the time, the witnesses who had seen the two and told the youth who had told the youth who had told the wardens. There was no defense counsel. Andrew, bewildered and young, tried to speak. Esther's eyes filled.

"Confess," Isaac said, and his voice had the firmness of scripture. "Name the sin. Name the breach. If you do, you may yet be spared the greater shame."

Andrew's confession was not a robust admission so much as a trembling truth. He owned the act and then, with a boy's defective audacity, begged for mercy. He said he had been lonely in oven-heat, that his master had been cruel and his wages thin, that Esther had come to mend a bowl and they had found each other in a dangerous winter of need.

"It is not for you to judge edges of human need," Jonathan tried to say. "Do not make a law of hunger."

But the Youth wanted a law that would look like sternness. They wanted the sight of consequence. In the end the verdict was given by Isaac with the assent of the dozen men who had sworn to the Youth's code. The punishment declared was cruel and intended to convert fear into obedience: a public burning at a small, ringed space they called the Purging Circle, a place where men had once watched plays.

Thomas Whitaker and Mary heard of the sentence in the market. Their first reaction was disbelief. Thomas closed his hands on a lump of dough and felt the kneading go slack: "We baked to feed, not to provide fuel for a bonfire of boys." Mary's face, always steady, folded with a quiet ferocity. She wanted to go and stop it with hands and a woman's pleading. Jonathan came to their door that night, and for the first time they saw the priest look old.

"Go not to inflame," he told them softly. "But go to bear witness, if you must. Speak for mercy where you can." He wanted them to be a gentle pressure on a thing that had hardened into cruelty.

On the morning appointed, the square filled not just with the Youth but with an uneasy public. Some came because they believed in stern men who would root sin; some because they feared what would follow if they did not appear. Isaac stood at the edge of the Purging Circle with a face composed of ... righteousness; Luke Harper held the rope that tied the scaffold. Andrew stood in the center, hands bound, face pale as the market's flour. Esther, kept away by a cordon of Youth sentries, watched from behind a screen of tradesmen and children.

Thomas shoved through the throng with Mary at his side. He had a small loaf in his apron—the habit of a baker who brings bread for comfort—and he offered it to a woman who had a face like flint. "Do not let fear marry itself to cruelty," he said to the woman who had once fed his children with stew. She did not answer. Some people who had stood in the Council now looked on with blank faces. Ruth Grayson had been there earlier in the night attempting to persuade Isaac by the old uses of speech and memory. She stood now with her hands clenched.

"Please," she said aloud, voice breaking like thin ice, "let the Council try him. Let the law be our instrument, not a hand with a torch."

Isaac looked at Ruth as one looks at a stubborn weed. "We are tired of slow justice," he said. "We will set an example."

There followed the awful choreography of an execution. The flames were kindled from wood gathered from planks that had been set aside for the Bogston scaffolding. The youth who tended the fire had faces that did not look young in the way that matter; instead they were hollowed by belief. When the flames took, the sound was not a single scream but a shriek folded into the morning air, a sound that cut the market like a blade. People turned their faces away; some turned their backs. Mary put her palm to her mouth and the bread she had held dropped to the cobbles, burst thin and black where it hit, and lay like a small accusation. Thomas sank to his knees and could not make prayer.

I will not describe the gore. The scene is seared by its moral consequence rather than by any detail; the body of a young man burned at the command of fellow citizens changed the city's soul. As the fire crept and the guards kept distance, Andrew's voice—where it rose—was small and human. "Forgive me," he said. "Forgive me for flesh that sought warmth." His words lost their reach. Later, people would remember the silence that followed—the market's knives set down, the way the river sounded as if it had been listening and had learned to weep.

After, the circle emptied like a wound that had bled and bled. Some of the Youth stood with satisfaction that the city had been taught. Isaac walked away as if he had executed a necessary surgery. Luke Harper polished his halberd in the sun and called it the day that made discipline. But the square was no longer the same; a smaller, sharp fracture split the city. Children who had watched were marked by the sight; a seamstress's apprentice who had seen Andrew die kept night-sweats for weeks. Thomas and Mary could not sleep for a long while; they baked in a sort of stunned fury, and Thomas's hands trembled with a new care whenever he shaped a loaf.

Within the Council, the reaction was a slow unpeeling of conscience and rage. Jonathan—who had pleaded for law, for procedures, for mercy—called an emergency assembly. His voice, worn by prayer, cut differently that day. "We made law so men would not take flame into their own hands," he said to a hall full of faces that had been children in the rebellion and were now their own judges and sometimes their own executioners. "We will not allow our city to be turned into a tribunal without process."

Ruth Grayson, who had been present at the cellar debates and had seen Isaac transform from eloquent organizer to harsh magistrate, stood up. Her hands were steady. "We must reform the Youth," she said. "We must set statutes that forbid extrajudicial punishment and that require any charge to pass a public court. We must also offer healing to the families harmed by our zeal."

Isaac answered from the back with a hardness that surprised even those who had known him. "We made hard choices to keep a city from being leased," he said. "We will not be weak in the face of relapse." He spoke as if he were making law, not merely argument.

The Council voted to criminalize vigilante punishment, to set up a proper court with defense and appeal, and to call for a public inquiry into Andrew's death. The decision was not universal; many of the Youth abstained or grumbled. Isaac and some of his degree of followers left the hall that night in small groups and began to meet elsewhere—they no longer trusted a Council that would be cautious rather than immediate.

The consequences were slow and corrosive. The Awakened Youth split into factions. A moderate wing—those who had originally wanted the rule of law rather than the rule of flame—stayed within the Council's orbit and worked to strengthen processes. A radical wing—Isaac's—retreated to the corners and began to act in secrecy, interpreting their mission as one of purification rather than governance. They started enforcing dress codes in the alleys, removing apprentices from certain workshops on suspicion alone, and imposing public shames for minor moral slips. In time that radical wing would become less and less a movement for common good and more and more a private police force justified by a doctrine of "fitness."

Bogston suffered as reputation and as conscience. Craftspeople who had once traveled to study glaze now visited with a softer step.

A few master teachers refused to have pupils who were members of Isaac's faction. Nathaniel, who had been a financial partner in Bogston and who still admired the city's ability to learn, spoke privately to the Council one afternoon with frankness that would not flatter them.

"You are forging a republic from ash and bread," he said, sitting by the garden with a mug of ale. "Do not let zeal be your mortar. Buildings ask for patience, not for the quickness of a torch."

"It was a hard choice then," Grace replied, thinking of the men they had lost in defense of the quay. "We are weary of soft measures that cost lives."

"But the cost of harshness is different," Nathaniel answered. "You will trade freedom for order and end with neither."

Reverend Jonathan found his faith tested in a new way. He had preached reconciliation, but the man who now spoke for a communal purity had burned a child for a sin the church would have counselled in private. Jonathan's nights were short with prayer and long with questions. He took to writing letters to distant friends—priests and scholars who had once been his teachers—and asked advice on reconciling justice and mercy. Some replied with patient theology; others wrote cautiously of the need for codes that recognized human frailty.

Alice Grey, who had stitched Andrew's wounds as a small boy and had fed his family in times of lean, never recovered her warmth for years. She would bandage a hand with a fierce tenderness and then, when no one watched, sit by the riverside and cry. She said little in meetings but she carried the grief like someone who had taken a shard from the world and kept it close to the heart.

There were acts of courage that tried to mend the thing. Ruth and Jonathan pushed for a public apology and reparations to Andrew's family. The Council obliged with measures—some coin, a place for Esther to work where she could be sheltered—and an official condemnation of extrajudicial killing. The measures were thin consolation for a death that left both a family and a city different. In the quiet of the market, the potter's wheel turned but with a different cadence; the clay felt less trusting under bare hands.

Worse, the doctrine of "fitness" spread in words and in practices. Isaac and his circle argued in taverns and alleys that the city must favor the young and the strong in apprenticeship because "we cannot afford to train those who will not labor." That language—so easily turned into a kind of social Darwinism—found listeners among those tired of hardship. Small cruelties multiplied: an apprentice with a limp was passed over; a widow's son was told that the bursary would go to a healthier child. The Council tried to codify protections—clauses that forbade discrimination on the basis of infirmity—but enforcement was patchy where ideology had teeth.

Bogston itself, which had stood for communal knowledge, was tarnished by association. Visiting craftsmen watched the city's disputes and sometimes opted to go elsewhere; traders murmured that Shie had become quarrelsome. The observatory continued to chart comets; the herb garden continued to grow yarrow and sage; but the joy that had once greeted discoveries now carried an undertone of carefulness—an awareness that knowledge could be bent to cruel ends.

Over time the city's life continued in a twisted normality. The children learned to read the stars, but some also learned the youth's harsher lessons: that silence could be a survival skill. Thomas, whose hands had once bowed dough into shapes for celebration, found himself baking with a hollow in his step. Mary taught their child to knot two ways—one to bind, one to slip—but the words she used now were also warnings: "Use both well; use neither to burn another."

Not all of Isaac's faction survived the slow politics. Some were absorbed back into the Council's work when the city's merchants and families pushed for gentler governance; others drifted away to ports where harder men found markets for their cruelty. The Awakened Youth retained a shadowed power: their earlier courage had been real, their energy had rebuilt a quay and raised a school. But its darker turn—its attempt to make a sinless society by force—left Shie with a scar that would be noticed for generations. Parents who had once proudly spoken the name Bogston now lowered their eyes when they recalled the Purging Circle.

Jonathan, in the years that followed, read aloud at Bogston's public hall not only scriptures but also the accounts of errors. He set aside hours when the Council would listen to grievances and he insisted on law that offered routes of restitution rather than quick punishments. He organized memorials for those lost to occupation and for Andrew Marlow, whose death became in time a cautionary tale read in the margins of manuals: about how zeal can become cruelty; about how a people must guard not only their common goods but their common mercy.

Slowly, painfully, Shie rebuilt its moral grammar. The Council enacted firm statutes forbidding extrajudicial punishment and offering state-sponsored apprenticeships for those discriminated against. Schools and workshops instituted clauses of equity in their charters. Bogston published a tract on civic ethics that included, along with kiln diagrams and notes on herb lore, essays—short and blunt—about the cost of forgetting mercy. That document was read aloud on market mornings for years; children learned not only how to splice a rope or mend a sail but also how to plead for the life of a neighbor even in the face of anger.

The river kept flowing, reflecting both lamp and flame. The city that had once been saved by alliances and by fire now learned a harsher lesson: revolutions can breed virtue, but when virtue becomes dogma without mercy, it can also make martyrs of the very people it intended to uplift. The ordinary days—bread, pots, lullabies—continued. Men and women went to Bogston to learn and to mend. They carried with them the memory of the Purging Circle like a bruise that would fade but whose outline would remain: a reminder that the courage to change must be paired, always, with the patience to forgive.

Strictness began as small, tidy things that the city at first mistook for discipline. The Awakened Youth took the language of improvement and made it into ordinance. Where once a mother could borrow a kettle from a neighbor and return it warm, now a printed notice ordered such things logged and timed; where a craftsman might spare an apprentice a half-day to help a widow, that mercy would now be recorded and audited. The watchmen who had once been a loose band of neighbors became a rostered force with badges and lists. Their uniforms—plain sashes at first—grew into an array of cords and brass, and those cords came to mean not only service but the right to inspect larders, to demand apprentices' papers, and to arrest for "moral infractions."

Day followed day with small cruelties dressed as care. An apprentice who arrived late because his mother had fallen ill found his name written in the public register as "negligent" and was denied rations for a week. A widow whose stall could not pay the new "sanctity levy" was forced into public labor at the dock to repair a quay plank—ironically the same quay the Youth had once defended—while her flour was measured and parceled out beneath a guard's eye. The Purging Circle, once a one-time horror that the Council had publicly condemned, became a metaphor for discipline; public humiliations—struck on wooden placards, shouted out in market lists—were the first step before any punishment could be escalated.

The Awakened Youth justified everything with rhetoric that sounded good in meetings: "We are making the city fit for the next century," Isaac Thorn would say, voice even and bright as sun on salt. He spoke of "strengthening the loom of society," of "weeding the garden so the best shoots may grow." In private, his tone hardened. At a back-room meeting, Luke Harper said plainly, "A city that tolerates flaccid hearts will sink. We keep only what can haul a rope." Isaac nodded and drew a list: names of those who had been "warned," those who had been fined twice, those now to be suspended from apprenticeship. They made the list with the same care that Samuel had once used in recording births and deaths; ink on paper now became a small instrument of exclusion.

Punishments escalated along a predictable slope. Stocks and public shaming were followed by forced labor, then by expulsions to outlying hamlets during the lean months, and finally by physical punishments carried out beneath the thin pretense of deterrence. The Youth trained squads to carry out sentences quickly and without questioning. Some of the older Council members—people who remembered the night of flame and the chaos that had swallowed the quay—complained at private meetings, arguing for restraint and rule of law. Isaac replied that restraint had been a luxury that had cost the city lives. He spoke of the ocean's hard rules: a keel must be trim or it will capsize. "We will trim the city," he said, "and we will not be softened."

Bogston, once a refuge of communal learning, found its doors narrowing in measure. Entrance exams grew stricter; apprenticeships were awarded only after a public demonstration of "fitness" that now valued brute endurance as much as cleverness. Girls who had once learned midwifery now had to pass a trial of stamina; a young potter with a limp was told to wait a season before applying. Teachers protested and, in whispers that smelled of ash and fear, began to refuse requests to be wage-earners for the Youth's tribunals. Some masters left entirely; others, who stayed, complained about the spirit of inquiry being crushed by the spirit of examination.

Incidents of cruelty accumulated in the ledger of the city. A man named Peter Lowe, old and bent, was accused of hoarding winter wood; with little proof, he was sentenced to a month clearing reeds in the marsh alone, away from the town's help. His daughter walked the lanes in a cloud of shame; she could not bear to meet eyes. A seamstress named Esther Pike—who had been punished with public humiliation after the Purging Circle scandal—lost work when customers feared being associated with "notorious" names. Small children learned to snitch because the Youth offered coin for evidence—their bread a poor substitute for the warmth of a mother's tolerance.

Resistance lurked in ordinary acts. Thomas Whitaker and Mary did what they could: baking late loaves with hidden rations for families who had been docked; Mary sewed secret pouches in aprons to carry spare seed for gardens that were to be taken by "sanctity levies." Alice Grey mended more than hands; she documented injuries inflicted in secret punishments and carried the lists under her shawl to the Council's more moderate members. Reverend Jonathan preached mercy in corners, his sermons threaded with parables that asked the crowd to imagine being the accused. He would tell, quietly, the story of the boy who had hidden in a boat, cold and hungry, and ask if punishment could be the only answer.

Still, the Youth's grip tightened. They spoke of purity as a civic virtue: "A good city must be clean," they said. They organized patrols that sniffed out taverns where older men met to drink and talk. They forced curfews that punished those who worked late by docklight—artists and potters who fired kilns at night—or who studied by lamplight. Bogston's library, once open, put some books behind a two-keyed chest; learning required sponsorship. Isaac's faction argued that knowledge without character could be perilous; they made moral tests a part of admission to higher study. Young men who failed were not merely denied the classroom—they were publicly marked. Their initials, carved into a wooden board kept in the market, were a slow, grinding stain.

Whispers widened beyond the town. Nathaniel Rhodes—who had seen cities rise and fall like tides—watched with an increasing unease. He met discreetly with Captain Henry and with Ruth Grayson and said plainly, "We made this city with our hands. We will not let it be turned into a place where fear does the ruling." Henry, who had learned the river's every mood, knew how control becomes cruelty when those who hold the oars will not let others prove they can row. "If they make laws that kill the heart of the city," Henry said, "they will find the river turns against them."

Those words turned into action. A quiet coalition formed: moderate Council members, tradesmen who had once supported the Youth and now feared their fervor, Nathaniel with a few trusted helmsmen, and a ragged band of men loyal to Captain Henry. They met in the same vaulted cellar that had birthed resistance years before—irony not lost on anyone—and plotted first to curb the Youth's authority through votes and, failing that, to forcibly remove the worst offenders from positions of power. Jonathan advocated for legal process: "If we move against them, let us do so in law and in the light," he said. But as months went by, it became clear that legal process alone would not dislodge men who could command patrols and coin.

Tension escalated into open conflict when the Youth, sensing a threat to their order, tightened their ranks and fortified Bogston itself. They claimed the center of learning as an ideological bastion—"here we train the city's bone," they said—and they posted troops at the gates. Bogston's workshops and gardens were barricaded; ropes were strung across alleys; notices declared that anyone entering without clearance would be treated as an enemy. The Youth refused mediation and denounced the coalition as "arsonists of order." Isaac, standing on Bogston's small parapet and addressing those within, said, "If you would take our work, you must take it by force. We will not be dragged back into ledgered servitude." The phrase "ledgered servitude" struck the crowd like a bell with a sour sound.

War, when it came, was not the glamoured sweep of banners but a civil, grinding thing—skirmishes at dawn, a siege by dusk, and no single day that could be called decisive. Henry's men cut the water lines that fed a portion of Bogston's wells, while Nathaniel's helmsmen blockaded supply barges the Youth relied upon. The council's stewards rallied apprentices and potters who had been overlooked by the Youth's tests; a seamstress who had lost customers taught a knot that unfastened chains without breaking wood. Small raids took storehouses at night; guards answered with flares and ropes. On market mornings the bell tolled for watch, not for trade, and mothers clutched children close.

Inside Bogston the Youth hardened. Isaac led drills, his voice brittle, instructing how to hold spears at close quarters and how to close a door with quick iron. Luke Harper commanded a cohort who patrolled like judges. They spoke openly of purging the city of "weakness," and some among them began to fashion tools not merely for construction but for enforcement: a long-armed pike that could reach a man leaning from a cart, a clamp to fasten a hand to a beam until confession. The city watched, horrified and fascinated, as their defenders became a self-policing militia.

Battle was inevitable when the coalition—backed now by several neighboring hamlets displeased by Bogston's closed doors and the Youth's levies—moved to take the center. The assault began at first light. Men who once sat at benches met at dawn with wood and rope. Henry led a column down the street by the river, his men wearing plain sashes rather than bright cords. Nathaniel's small fleet crept in the river's throat to prevent reinforcements from reaching Bogston by water. The Youth, confident and fierce, repelled the first advance with a hail of stones and quick pikes. The sound of battle was not heroic chanting but the slapping of splintered boards and the pained shout of men who had once been neighbors.

Fighting was personal and in narrow lanes. A potter who had worked in Bogston's kiln now found himself at an alley's corner, confronting a Youth sentry who had once been his apprentice. "Why do you wear that cord?" the potter asked, hands spread as if to show he was unarmed. The sentry, face set, said in a voice stripped of its earlier conviction: "Orders." The potter stepped aside, though rumor later said he had whispered, "Remember clay," as he passed. Skills taught in peace—how to hold a tool, how to bind a wound—became the very things that kept men alive. Alice Grey's apprentices, those who had learned midwifery and sutures, worked in supply tents, stitching the wounded with steady hands while cursing softly under their breath.

After days of fighting the coalition breached Bogston's outer workshops. There was no tumbling the whole complex in a single stroke; rather, sections surrendered as their supplies ran low or as guards were persuaded to lay down arms. Isaac refused to yield. He gathered his followers in the main hall and spoke in a voice that was all iron. "We made a city that would not be cheap," he said. "If you take our work by force, you will not keep it gentle." He vowed to stand, and many of his closest men answered with a nod.

Capture came not in a moment of grand victory but by fracture. Some of Isaac's own men, exhausted and hungry, slipped away when the water went thin. A young guard, seeing his mother among the faces of the besiegers, stepped down and walked to his sister's side—an act that widened the gap between fanaticism and family. After a long night, with smoke and confusion filtering the moon, coalition men found Isaac and his inner circle huddled in Bogston's low library, the books around them like a protective ring. They were taken not in a slaughter but in a clatter of handcuffs and ropes. Isaac's eyes did not plead; they were fixed in the blank way of a man who believes himself persecuted for a higher cause.

The city held a trial—public and deliberately formal after the shame of extrajudicial acts. The Council of Commons convened in the square where the Purging Circle had once stood, because the city wanted to demonstrate that law would now govern the end of fanaticism rather than private vengeance. Charges were read aloud: incitement to violence, extrajudicial killings, unlawful levies, coercion of apprentices, and the abuse of civic power. Witnesses testified: a seamstress recounted her husband's beating by a Youth patrol; an apprentice told of being denied a place at Bogston for failing a "fitness" test that had nothing to do with craft; Jonathan read from his own sermons about mercy, his voice steady though his hands trembled. Isaac and many of his followers were given the chance to speak. Isaac's defense was a brittle philosophy: he had been building a future that required sacrifice. His eyes lit briefly with the old conviction that had once saved the quay; then they dimmed as his words fell on a crowd that had lost patience.

The verdict was not an easy one. Many in the square remembered that the Awakened Youth had once led the city out of flames and had founded Bogston; many had sons and daughters who had been helped by the same people now accused. But the court's duty was clear: a movement that takes the law into its own hands and burns citizens was no safeguard for liberty. The Council declared the leaders guilty and sentenced them to the old, public justice used by the city in former times: a public execution to be carried out by the state, not by mobs—designed as both punishment and a deterrent.

Execution day was planned with a strange mixture of gravity and an attempt at decorum. The square filled early with people who had come not for spectacle but for closure. There were faces split between grief and a weary relief. Thomas and Mary stood among the crowd—Mary with her blue stripe pinned and Thomas with flour still under his nails—because they wanted to witness that civic law would not become the tool of private wrath. Reverend Jonathan prayed aloud for mercy and for truth; he did not plead for clemency so much as for the city to keep its soul. Ruth Grayson moved through the crowd, taking the hands of families she had known since childhood, steadiness in a world still raw.

Isaac and those judged with him were led to a raised scaffold at the quay, not as spectacle but as an instrument of the law's finality. Guards from the reconstituted civic watch—men not of the Youth but chosen by a Council that now strove for fairness—kept the area. The condemned stood in the pale chill, faces composed. Isaac's jaw was set; he had not cried aloud. He looked out over the river, perhaps thinking of the nights when he had watched oars vanish into fog and had sworn the city would be strong.

Before the sentence was carried out, Reverend Jonathan was given a last chance to speak. He stepped forward, his voice raw but clear. "We are men who made law to keep each other alive," he said. "If we make law instruments of revenge, then we are less than what we fought for. Let this day be the closing of a chapter, not the opening of another wound. Remember those we lost by zeal and remember those we lost by neglect. Plant a sapling for each life taken: that is what I ask."

There was a hush, save for the river's steady movement. Then the sentence was enforced—not with raucous joy, but with the sober efficiency of a law that wished to be final and fair. The heads of the condemned were taken in the public square; the city took no pleasure in the act. People who had earlier supported the Youth looked as if they had swallowed iron. Mothers who had lost sons whispered names into sleeves, and men who had led sieges closed their eyes. Thomas, who had once tied a knot to hold a raft, felt his fingers go numb and he pressed his palm into Mary's as if to hold himself to the world. Mary did not cry aloud; she kept silent, her face a map of sorrow and a resolve to rebuild.

I will not linger on detail where gore could be imagined; what mattered to the city was the result and the weight of meaning left behind. The executions did not close the wound neatly. They reopened it in a new way—questions of mercy and of the right limits of state punishment returned like tide. Some people left Shie after the executions, unable to bear the memory of neighbor killing neighbor on public steps. Others stayed to mend. Bogston, its library and observatory and herb garden, bore a different air. The Council took care to purge the building of the paramilitary trappings that had become weapons and to restore its open shelves, but scars remained in both mortar and memory.

In the years that followed the city tried to make amends in living law. The Council enacted strict prohibitions against extrajudicial punishment, clear protections for apprentices and the infirm, and mandatory civic education that included ethics classes drawn from Reverend Jonathan's sermons and Samuel's careful records. They set up a memorial garden where saplings were planted for every person lost to the Purging Circle, to the occupation, and to the fighting—saplings tended by the very children who had watched and learned the cost of zeal without mercy. Bogston refocused on learning and publicly apologized for the way some of its orderings had been used to exclude rather than to include. The Council instituted courts with defense and appeals, and it required that any sanction proposed against a citizen be presented publicly and subject to veto by a citizen jury.

The city's texture changed slowly. Markets reopened with quieter voices; the quay returned to its careful hum rather than the brittle drum of militias. Thomas and Mary continued to bake, kneading their hands into loaves that tasted of memory and patience; Mary taught the child to knot not only for binding but for untying. Reverend Jonathan continued to preach, his sermons tempered by the knowledge that words can both save and slay. Ruth Grayson, who had fought in council and on the ground, turned her energies to rebuilding guilds that actively sought out those who had once been refused. Nathaniel, who had lent timber and money to the city many times, taught navigation classes with an eye to the ethics of command—the lesson that authority requires account.

The executed Awakened Youth left behind complex legacies. Some of their deeds had indeed been necessary—no one denied that the city would have been lost without their courage when the longships had come. But their later descent into zeal created a cautionary tale: energy without checks becomes tyranny. The people of Shie learned to write institutions that tried to prevent such an outcome: regular elections, rotating stewardship, transparent ledgers, and a public memorial meant to keep sorrow from hardening into hatred.

Years later, when children in the market read pamphlets aloud about the city's past, their voices would falter at the line about the Purging Circle. Teachers in Bogston used that chapter as a lesson in civic ethics. "Courage without mercy breeds monsters," they would say, and ask apprentices to debate, to test, and to seek the mean between zeal and sloth. The river flowed on, indifferent and patient, and the city—mended in parts, forever marked in others—kept its ordinary days. People still baked, still potted, still sang lullabies; they did so with an extra care, as if each ordinary act might be the place where the city's future either hardened into cruelty or softened into mercy.

Shie learned, slowly and painfully, that revolutions can save and can wound; that institutions are the scaffolding that must hold the temperatures of human hearts; that knowledge must be paired with law and love; and that in the end the ordinary days—the bread, the pots, the lullabies—are both the prize and the test.

TWELVE

THE GUILT THAT WALKS

Damian opened his eyes to fluorescent light and the sour, antiseptic smell of Bogston Hospital. He lay propped against a cluster of pillows, IV tubing trailing like pale vines, and found he was surrounded—Reed, Kael, Miska, and a half-dozen other faces blurred by fatigue and relief. The machines at his bedside kept a steady, indifferent rhythm. He swallowed once, tasted iron, and let the accusation slide out of him like a blade.

"You've lost my trust," he said, each word careful and cold. "You're with them. You all planned to trap me. As long as I'm alive, you can't touch me."

Reed's expression hardened and softened in the same breath. He stepped forward, palms open as if to soothe a wound he had not caused. "Boss, you're mistaken," he replied. "We didn't—none of us did. We're here because we want you back—back to your life, to yourself."

Damian laughed, a short, bitter sound. "Now you're trying to give me a new identity," he snapped. "Change my name, rewrite my past—think that will fix what you broke? You won't fool me." His eyes searched theirs, daring any one of them to lie. The room seemed to hold its breath, waiting for the truth to land.

Kael's voice cut through the silence, firm but edged with pity. He leaned closer to Damian, his eyes steady, as though speaking to a man caught between worlds.

"You see," Kael said quietly, "you are not a professor. You've been a patient here for a year. The identity you've been clinging to—it's one you built yourself."

Damian's jaw tightened, his breath sharpening into something closer to a growl. Anger rose in him, fierce and unyielding, but Kael pressed on before the outburst could escape.

"First, try to listen," Kael urged. "Listen to what the truth really is. Reed—he isn't your enemy. He's your childhood friend, Choe. And Miska? She's not who you think either. She's Anesthesia—your other friend from those early days. Haven't you noticed the similarities?"

Damian's brow furrowed, confusion flickering across his fury, but Kael didn't falter.

"When you were searching for Reed, remember the man who stood beside you, guiding you? That was Reed too. All along, he's been here. You've stepped so far outside yourself that you don't even recognize him anymore."

The room felt heavier with each word, as if truth itself thickened the air. Kael's tone softened, though his gaze never wavered.

"They tried to bring you back, Damian. To fix you. All of this—your father, the labyrinth, the forest, the brain surgery—every piece of it was your mind's invention. A grand world you built to survive. But it isn't real." He leaned forward, lowering his voice until it was almost a plea.

"Damian... you have to realize it. Try to understand. Come back to us."

ᚦᚦᚦ

REAL STORY

. He wanted the careful, patient work of collecting facts. He wanted a map to the chaos.

"You're too young," his mother said the first time Damian spoke of joining the force. She folded the laundry with a worried, practised economy. "You should finish school. Go to college. There are safer ways."

"It's not about being safe," Damian told her, and the truth of it sat between them like cool glass. "It's about knowing who did it. About not letting the person who hurt others walk away. If I can do that, maybe—" He stopped. The rest of the sentence was private, a knot of unfinished business pointing back to the night he woke to an empty house.

At seventeen he enrolled in the cadet program. The academy was a world of regimentation and ritual, where sleep and food were scheduled, and the clacking of boots became a kind of music. Damian was not the biggest recruit; he wasn't the loudest. He learned to watch—how a man's eyes darted when he lied, the small way a hand flexed when someone spoke of money. Those lessons mattered as much as any textbook.

There were instructors who saw him as brittle and others who thought him impossibly steady. Sergeant Lyle Hale took notice. Hale was broad and unflinching, with a voice that carried the weathered authority of someone who'd seen things and kept them down like a lid on a pot. He pulled Damian aside after a field exercise and said, "You listen more than you speak, kid. That's good. Don't let the world teach you to shout when it needs quiet." The line became a mantra.

Damian's first posting was in a precinct that felt like a cluster of stubborn small towns cramped into one city block. He rode with older officers whose jokes carried the fossilized humor of long-sleeping grief. His first arrest, a man with too many unpaid debts and an afternoon's poor judgment, left Damian surprised by how little his chest tightened when the handcuffs clicked. He felt instead the steady hum of competence. The man in custody muttered about being framed; Damian's notebook filled with observations—scrapes on the knuckles, a smell of oil, the cadence of fear.

Opportunity for real investigation came in the form of a missing person: Elise Martin, a schoolteacher who'd not returned from her evening run. The case came to Damian on an overcast Tuesday, the sort of day where everything seems a shade duller, edges softened.

"You're on surveillance," Sergeant Hale told him. "You and Reed. Watch the park entrances between eight and ten. No heroics, no crosses. Just watch and listen." Reed—an easy-smiling kid Damian had known since childhood—slid into the passenger seat with a thermos and a sardonic grin. Damian felt something like relief. Reed had a way of grounding the room with a single look.

They sat in a police cruiser with the heater ticking, the city breathing outside. Damian kept his eyes on the sidewalks, on the runners who moved like metronomes. Reed spoke softly, as if conserving conversation to keep it useful. "You think she'll come by herself?" he asked.

"I don't know," Damian said. "But someone who disappears doesn't always vanish—they break a habit and fall off a map. We find the habit, we find the map." He thought of his father's notebook and the way small details redrew the shape of a story.

At 9:12 a jogger slowed near the fountain and the radio chirped in the background—a call about a van seen near the river. Reed exchanged a look with Damian, one that asked permission and offered partnership. They moved.

The missing-person case became Damian's education in patient work. He conducted interviews with neighbors who remembered trivial facts—an argument between Elise and a man about a chessboard, the scent of lavender on a balcony—and with the persistent accumulation of those details he rebuilt a timeline. He stood at Elise's kitchen table and fingered the bottom of a mug, noting the direction of dried coffee and a smear on the rim. A smear led to a glove, the glove to prints, and the prints to a man who thought he had been careful.

The arrest was not cinematic. There were no dramatic chases, no last-minute confessions in the drizzle. Instead, there were two quiet knocks at a walk-up's door and a man whose face grew small as the evidence piled up. He tried to lie, then to charm, then to threaten. Each tactic was a different weather; Damian adjusted like a sheltering shape.

After the case closed, Elise's brother found Damian in the hallway, and the man's voice broke in gratitude. "You brought her back," he said simply. The weight of that sentence did not lift immediately. Damian understood then, with a clarity that had the taste of relief and ash, why he'd chosen this life. It was not for revenge. It was not only for justice. It was for the small, exact recoveries—the moments when a life returned to its axis because someone had cared enough to follow the trail.

Years passed like sealed envelopes. Damian learned the law's language and the city's dialects. He made few deep friends—people like Reed who knew how to pull him back from the edge, and Sergeant Hale who kept him honest. He also learned to carry the things the job demanded: witnesses' tremors, the smell of terrified rooms, the ledger of small cruelties. Each case put a new weight on his shoulders, but also sharpened him.

He rose through the ranks not because he sought rank but because the work found him ready. An investigating officer's world is a map of shadows—a place where patience is the compass and memory the key. Damian learned to slow time down inside an interrogation room, to listen for the micro-gestures that betrayed the lie; he learned which condolences to give and when silence would say more.

And through it all, the quiet ache of that thirteenth birthday stayed with him—not as a wound that bled, but as a seam he could follow when everything else unraveled. It reminded him, constantly, of a boy who wanted only to hear one more story. Now, as he translated other people's losses into fact and consequence, he hoped, in the small private corner of himself, that the stories he restored would be enough to fill that boy's nights.

---For months after the Elise Martin case, Damian settled into a rhythm that made the city tolerable: mornings with a black coffee that tasted perpetually of overwork, afternoons spent sifting through reports, evenings where the precinct hummed with low, practical life. But routine is a fragile thing; it can be nicked by a single edge and spill into a new shape. The nick this time came in the form of a woman who kept her hands in her coat pockets and spoke like she had rehearsed apologies.

Her name was Mara Voss, and she arrived at the precinct on a Tuesday thick with rain. She found Damian at his desk—papers arrayed like small islands—and asked if she could speak to him. Reed wasn't on duty; Sergeant Hale was in a meeting. Damian noticed, as he always did, the little betrayals that make a person legible: Mara's nails were bitten to the quick, the collar of her coat had a faint fringe of cigarette ash, and her voice tightened when she said "I think they got to my brother."

"Tell me his name," Damian said, and the simplicity of the request was therapeutic. Names are maps.

"Evan. Evan Voss. He worked nights on the docks. He stopped answering his phone last Friday." She spoke in small measured breaths. "The police said he probably left town. He never left town."

Damian listened and asked the questions that collected facts—when, where, who last saw him—and Mara supplied them like scattered tiles. A security guard at the warehouse, a bartender who had served him a coffee at dawn, a text message cached on a phone that suggested he'd been worried about "shifts in the manifest." The warp and weft of a working life. It gave Damian something steady to hold.

He and Reed went down to the docks that evening. The river smelled of rust and old rain; cranes stood skeletal against sodium light. They found a man who loaded containers with the same careful, habitual movements that make a life legible. He told them about Evan's late nights and his awkward insistence on helping when the tally sheets didn't match the containers. "He'd argue for the manifest to be checked," the man said. "Said if something's off you gotta say so."

That word—manifest—tugged at Damian. He spent the next days building a web: manifests, a company that subcontracted to a shipping firm with a bland, corporate name, a driver who had been paid in cash and left fingerprints on a clipboard. Small details accumulated like sediment until they suggested a seam—an opportunistic theft of small, high-value goods, not a single violent conspiracy. Then an anomaly: one of the manifests listed a cargo that didn't exist in the company's own records.

Damian leaned toward the anomaly the way a miner leans to a glint of ore. He took statements, followed bank records through the quiet, secret alphabet of transfers and small accounts, and met a pattern of men who had been careless with the truth and paid for it in other people's trust. He found Evan's number on a burner phone and tracked the last ping to a stretch of abandoned warehouses by the river—an area where the city stores the things it does not want to remember.

Late on a Sunday, Damian watched the warehouse from the shelter of an idling cruiser with Reed beside him, the two of them quiet in that way police men become when they let observation replace commentary. Reed sipped thermos coffee and said nothing for a long time. "You ever think we'll keep finding the seams?" he asked.

"We have to," Damian answered. "If we don't, the seams unpick the clothes of the city. People walk away without their jackets on."

The raid, when it came, was the kind of tactical exercise that read well on paper: coordinated entries, radios checked, clear lines of support. But even the most careful plan carries human temper and error. In the dark corridors of the warehouse they found the sign of a struggle—overturned crates, a smear of blood on concrete—and a room locked from the inside. They forced the door and found Evan, alive but bruised and watching them with the thin, incredulous expression of someone surprised to be interrupted.

Evan's release was a small victory. There were questions—who had taken him and why—and Evan's answers were knotty with fear and reluctance. He spoke of men who paid off dock foremen, of shipments that were unlisted and vanished into side-channels. He said he had tried to stop small thefts and been told to look the other way. Then, the sentence that lodged in Damian: "I kept notes, sir. I kept a list." He produced, with shaking hands, a paper notebook with entries that looked like legal real estate of daily life—times, names, shorthand.

The notebook did what good evidence does: it changed the shape of the case. What had been a string of petty thefts now suggested a structured scheme—a ring that siphoned goods into a flow tied to other, larger flows. Damian's instinct leaned toward following that flow, and the more he followed, the more the city revealed the edges where small corruption meets organized appetite. That is where choices are sharpened. He had a decision to make: follow the money and risk making enemies in places that wore the city's respectable face, or plate the investigation small and secure and accept the limitation.

He chose the former.

The weeks that followed were a study in patience. Damian made discreet inquiries at the tax office, watched the patterns of small transfers between odd-shell companies, and met a litany of polite denials. A lawyer with a clean name made a polite request for leeway. A foreman with too many stories contradicted himself. The tenor of their denials had a soft arrogance that only increased Damian's resolve.

Not all victories are meant for celebration. One night, as he returned to his flat, he found a pigeon with a clipped wing on his windowsill and a note tucked beneath its feathers—a trivial, childish warning: Mind the seams. It was the sort of threat that reads like an old joke and feels, at the base of the spine, like a bruise. Damian did not tell Reed. He folded the paper and placed it in his pocket like a relic and slept, fitfully.

The pressure mounted. A witness recanted. A camera feed from a side street turned out to have a gap. A man Damian had been sure would talk went missing for a week and then called from a payphone to refuse to answer questions. In those days he learned the solitary skill of persistence: how to return to a cold lead again and again until it told its story. He learned how not to trust the comforting cadence of confirmation and how to accept that sometimes a case invited compromise.

It was in the middle of these frictions that Damian and Reed's friendship showed its private test. Reed, who had been a steady presence since childhood, began to worry that Damian was pushing too far. "You can't take everything on," Reed said one night, his voice raw with fatigue. "You hear the city breathing and you think you can stop its coughing. You can't." He pressed his palms flat on the precinct table as if to anchor himself to reality.

"If I don't," Damian replied, softer than Reed expected, "someone else will be buried under the paperwork. Sometimes it matters who keeps asking."

"And when they aim back?" Reed's question had an edge that cut between them.

Damian could not answer with certainty. He only knew that the direction he had chosen—down into the small dark of middling corruption—was a place that often bled into worse things. He also knew, clearer than almost anything else, that the boy who had once wished for one more story would not rest while other people's stories were stolen.

The case finally cracked not with a confession but with an error: an accountant at a shell company had mis-sent an invoice to a personal email and, in the thread, mentioned a man who liked to meet at a certain café on Wednesday mornings. Damian sat in that café with a cheap cup of coffee and waited. The man arrived—respectable coat, clean hands—and the conversation that followed was a negotiation, not an apology. Damian recorded it, not with a dramatic reveal but with the quiet accumulation of contradiction and evidentiary weight. When the arrest was made, a knot of men were taken in separate locations, picked from the city's respectable light like moths.

The press called it a tidy case. The paperwork was satisfying, but Damian felt none of the triumph reporters like to stamp across headlines. He felt, instead, a small numbness, as if the city's skin had been scraped and the sensation that followed was slow to return. The pigeon's note, Reed's worry, the nights of fraying patience—those did not evaporate with arrests and indictments. Instead they turned inward, catalogued in the private ledger Damian kept for thoughts that could not be spoken aloud.

In the quiet after the arrests, he returned home to his mother, who had grown thinner with years but steadier in a way that comforted him like an old coat. They ate stew warmed by the oven and spoke of the ordinary things—groceries, a cracked tile in the sink. But in the night, he woke with the memory of the pigeon and the sense that the city had only shifted its weight. The seams had been found and stitched in one place; they would tear somewhere else.

He had learned to accept a certain loneliness as part of the job: the knowledge that truth often arrives costumed in alien forms and that the cost of following it sometimes includes losing easy comforts. It was a price he believed the boy from his thirteenth birthday would have accepted. But he also felt an unease that was not merely professional. He was learning, layer by layer, how far his own patience could be trimmed before the shape of him changed.

And that change, as quiet as rain, pushed against the fragile peace he had managed to build with those around him.

Would you like me to continue with a scene where Damian's choices begin to have personal consequences—threats to his mother, pressure on Reed, or an incident that leads to the hospital event we previously wrote about? Or shall I keep exploring cases and procedural details in the same slow, deep style?

The warning in the pigeon's note did not read as a threat so much as a conversation starter—childish, almost polite. That was what made it worse: it presumed a language between men who had nothing to do with each other, and yet it landed in Damian's pocket like a stone whose weight he could not ignore.

For a week he treated it as he treated other small anomalies: he catalogued it. He photographed the paper, logged the incident with internal affairs as a "harassment note," and kept the pigeon's feather in an evidence envelope he tucked into a drawer. He told himself that the police work would absorb the discomfort. It usually did.

But threats have a way of rearranging the furniture of people's lives. The first real sign of intrusion came on a rain-soft night when his mother phoned in a voice he could not immediately place—thin, tight as a wire.

"Damian?" she said. "Someone's been at the back door. I think they tried the lock."

He left his flat without coffee, without the ritual of smoking the edge off sleep. Rain stitched his jacket to his shoulders as he ran. The lock on his mother's back door was indeed tampered with: vise marks, a shallow groove as if someone had forced a tool and then stopped. Inside, the kitchen drawers were slightly out of place, a recipe card missing, a chair nudged toward the sink as if someone had searched and then decided the search was wasteful.

"They didn't take anything," his mother said, ladling tea with the steadiness of habit. "They looked, Damian. They wanted me to know they could." Her hands trembled; she made the motion into the tea like a practiced gesture of denial.

"Did you touch anything?" Damian asked, surveying the small, intimate geography of the house—the photograph of his father on the mantel, the chessboard in the corner with pieces mid-game, a childhood drawing pinned to the fridge. He crouched, not to search but to be nearer the floor on which so many small truths gathered.

"No, I didn't want to disturb—" she began, but stopped when she noticed him studying the photograph. "You should sit down, Damian. Take a breath."

He sat at the kitchen table and felt the grain of the wood like a map under his fingertips. The house had always been a repository for ordinary things that make up a life: unpaid bills, a box of winter scarves, a tin of snaps. Someone else had trespassed into that ordinariness and returned it to him altered. It was an intimate affront; it was a message.

Word of the break-in spread slowly among the precinct. Sergeant Hale arrived with the efficient gravity of someone who wears worry like a second coat. He moved through the house with the ease of a man who had sat in more kitchens than most people had sat at tables.

"Any sign of forced entry elsewhere?" he asked.

"Only the back door," Damian replied. "No windows. Whoever it was, they wanted it quiet."

Hale's gaze landed on Damian with an expression that mixed paternal concern and professional calculation. "Consider this escalated," he said. "Increase patrols near your mother's street. Reed will ride point with you tonight."

Reed arrived that evening with a worn thermos and a look that had lost some of its sardonic edge. He had the look of a man who'd been asked to carry the results of someone else's gravity and found the load heavier than expected.

"You sure you want to go alone with this?" Reed asked as they walked the block in the thin rain. "These aren't small-time kids looking for loot. They're precise."

"They left the recipe card," Damian said quietly. "It wasn't about stealing. It was about being seen."

"Being seen is the point of some people," Reed said. "But being seen like that—it's personal."

Damian had always regarded Reed as a lodestar, someone who could measure his own drift and call him back. That night, Reed tried another tack.

"You need to let this one rotate into someone else's docket, D. You can't be the one who has to follow every seam to the end. It changes you." He chose his words slow, as if each had a delicate balance to maintain. "Hale can reassign it. Take a step back."

Damian felt the old seam—his thirteenth birthday—pull taut in his chest. "If I step back, who asks the questions?" he said. "Who keeps watching the seam?"

"Us," Reed answered. "Sometimes that's enough."

They did not have the luxury of stepping back. Two nights later, a man Damian had been tracking—one of the accountants who had misdirected an invoice—turned up dead in an alley, a neat, clinical end that smelled faintly of administration and cleaned things. The autopsy would later describe the wounds as purposeful; the coroner's notes would call the manner of death homicide with a signature of silence.

It was a message, the precinct decided. The death tightened the air. Damian's mother began sleeping with the kettle on, a small noise to puncture the silence. Reed's smile thinned to something fragile.

The pressure changed the texture of small decisions. Damian stopped eating lunch sometimes; he took to working late and leaving the lights on in his mother's house with the stubbornness of someone trying to keep a vigil. He found himself watching faces not only for lies but for the distance between something said and something meant. He logged calls and names in a private notebook, the way his father had. He started arriving home to the sound of his mother's radio, a slow, familiar hum that soothed the edges of fear.

Then came the confrontation. It was the sort of confrontation that began as a sentence and became a weather system.

Damian had trailed one of the men to a café on the river—an unremarkable place where the window gazed down on water that reflected sodium light in angry little glints. He had no warrant and no backup beyond Reed, who had agreed to sit in the car and watch. Damian moved like a shadow between tables until he sat opposite the man whose pleasant face now looked brittle with the knowledge of being watched.

"You keep your books odd for a reason," Damian said, keeping his voice low. He slid a photograph across the table: the accounting thread that had been mis-sent, the email header circled. "Why protect the shipments?"

The man's hands flexed on his coffee cup. "You don't understand how things work," he said. "You don't understand the practicalities of moving product in a city."

"I understand people who get hurt when things get moved in the dark," Damian said.

The man smiled, a small, dangerous thing. "You think you're a boy who can fix wrongs by being neat, Damian. You think counting receipts will save people. Sometimes the city makes choices for you."

"Not for my mother," Damian said.

When the exchange ended, Damian left with more questions than answers. As he crossed the street a van rolled up, windows black, and men with faces like folded paper stepped out as if from an instruction manual. He felt the world tilt. There was a punch—a hard, disorienting instrument of force—and then another. The air tasted of iron. A fist connected with his temple and sent him into a place without edges.

He woke to light that did not have the city's sodium warmth, light that was clinical and precise. Machines made small, steady noises. There was a bandage across his head and a cotton taste in his mouth. Reed hovered at the periphery like a constellation—eyes rimmed in exhaustion, jaw set.

"You gave us a scare," Reed said when Damian could manage a whisper. "You were found in an alley. They say you were beaten pretty badly. You had a piece of rebar—had it with you."

Damian tried to remember the van, the faces, the coffee. The memory was a smear, like grease across a photograph. He felt a hollowness where a sequence should be—a missed stitch in a story he had been telling himself ever since the thirteenth birthday.

Surgeons later described a bleed that had to be controlled; an operation that stitched the city's violence to his skull. He had bits of his memory quarantined by trauma; the doctors used words—concussion, amnesia—that read like technical furniture and left the room hollow. He was told later that he would have lapses, gaps the size of wells.

When he woke again days later, the edges around faces thinned and sometimes blurred; names slid like pebbles under a current. He knew he had been an investigating officer. He knew his mother's name. But sequences—a line of events that led to a choice, a confrontation—fell away when he tried to grasp them. It was an insistent void.

Reed sat with him for hours and told stories he believed would anchor Damian back to himself: the petty theft case, the way Damian had taught him to steady a witness's hands, the little jokes that had kept them young when the city tried to make them old. Reed's voice was patient, and sometimes it stitched small truths back together.

But the hole that had opened in Damian's continuity would not be closed quickly. Memory, the doctors warned, is a fragile ledger; pieces can be recovered, some never will. Damian felt the seam of his life more keenly now: the boy who wanted one more story had been given maw after which stories might slide away.

He lay in the hospital with the slow machinery of recovery and the slower arithmetic of fear. Outside, the city moved in its indifferent orbit, and somewhere in its skin other seams would be found and tested. Inside, speech and recognition worked like careful locksmiths; each conversation with Reed, each cautious visit from his mother, was a tool.

He promised himself—quietly, in the hours when morphine thinned his edges—that he would reclaim the story. That he would count the seams until he could map the whole cloth. What he did not know then, in the white rooms and under the steady beeps, was how much the cost of that counting would be asked of him.

The transfer request arrived as a sealed envelope in the morning mail—bureaucracy's polite knock: formal language, a case number, a stamped urgency. "Shie," Damian read, the name of the city tasting like a challenge. The department wanted him there for a high-profile investigation: a series of deaths across the region, each classified at first as suicide until small, deliberate details suggested otherwise. The victims were men between seventeen and thirty, ordinary enough in their professions—students, a clerk, a mechanic—but connected by a single, impossible thing: a small labyrinth pendant hung about their necks after their deaths, always centered, always gleaming like a punctuation point at the base of the throat.

Damian packed slowly, as if moving through his life required ceremony. He folded shirts the way one folds maps, neat and economical, and tucked his father's battered notebook into the front pocket of the suitcase. Reed met him at the station with that thermos and a look that had been too familiar over the past months—an expression that combined loyalty and warning.

"Shie is a different animal," Reed said as the train slid out from the city. The countryside scrolled by in a watercolor blur. "They've got the press here and politicians who want the streets back for Sunday markets. They'll want quick answers."

"They'll want comfort more than answers," Damian said. "Comfort comes cheaper than truth most days."

The city of Shie met him in slate and glass, a place where municipal banners insisted on normalcy and a river cut the center into a clean, official looking curve. The case office had been set up in a precinct annex near the riverwalk; reporters clustered in the square like gulls, but once inside the room with its corkboards and printed maps, the noise condensed into useful information.

Chief Inspector Miren Kosta ran the task force. She was all compact motion, hands that spoke as quickly as her mouth, the kind of leader who rewired a room with directives. She greeted Damian with an efficiency that did not hide a careful appraisal. "We need someone who can see the seam other people miss," she said. "We've had public pressure, and we have bodies that look tidy on paper. We need tidy undone."

The first scene Damian walked through was a boy's bedroom lit by the thin, honest light of a late morning. The detective who briefed him—Officer Lian—moved around the room with a practiced intimacy.

"Seventeen, college first year," Lian said. "Found by his roommate. No forced entry. No sign of a struggle. The ligature suggested suicide at first sight. But the pendant—look." He held out a small evidence bag with the labyrinth locket sitting at its center. It was old-fashioned in its design: an unremarkable metal disc with an etched spiral that wound in toward a tiny, perfect center.

Damian handled it like one handles an accusation. The pendant was light between his fingers and braided to a slender chain that bore the faint scent of the skin where it had rested. He turned it, watching the spiral catch the light like a finger tracing a map.

"Staged," he said. "Not everyone who chooses death takes the trouble to dress the corpse afterward."

"Exactly," Lian answered. "Whoever did this wanted the message to be seen."

The autopsy reports across the cases repeated a pattern of clinical restraint: no signs of prolonged trauma, ligatures applied with knowledge of anatomy, toxicology clean of major sedatives, a throat treated with antiseptic as if by someone who expected scrutiny. Coroner Dr. Sera Hollis had the cool, slightly amused manner of someone who has seen the public's appetite for explanation and learned how to keep it honest.

"It's tidy," she said, handing Damian a chart. "They stage the scene to minimize panic. The deaths read as suicide to casual glance. What worries us are the hands—no tremor smear, no clumsy adjustments. Whoever applied the ligature knew what they were doing." She tapped the report. "And every pendant was added post-mortem, neatly arranged." Her eyes lingered on Damian with a clinical curiosity. "Why a labyrinth?"

The symbol lodged in Damian's mind like a foreign coin. A labyrinth is not a maze, he told himself—its single path to the center is a journey inward, a design with intention and history. He thought of myths: journeys that sought truth through controlled confusion. He thought of the way people use symbols to speak without speaking. He felt, with the small, honest chill of a man who has read the margins of human behavior for years, that this symbol was a communication.

As the team mapped wounds and watched the city's reactions, the media framed the story with easy narratives: a cult preying on young men, a copycat phenomenon, a grim new trend. Politicians leaned into rhetoric about public safety and curfews; a municipal subcommittee demanded a visible police presence and a quick arrest. The pressure to produce a face for the city's fear was immediate and stifling.

Damian's instincts, tempered by years of following threads, pushed him in a direction the headlines could not care for: motive. The question was not only who could kill skillfully or why they chose those particular victims; it was who would gain from sewing a pattern in the city's seams. He began to build profiles not just from the victims' lives but from their absences—the internships that led nowhere, the unpaid bills that whispered compromise, the friends who vanished from lists and left only anechoic silence.

He spent long, slow hours in interrogation rooms where sound became a thing to measure. He asked questions that looked like friendship: Did you ever feel afraid? Who'd he been talking to? What did he talk about when he drank too much? People answered in fragments; the truth filled itself in the blank places like a developing photograph.

Late one evening, as rain skated across the river, Damian sat with a survivor's notebook—a habit Reed had helped him maintain after the hospital. He copied names and times and the small things that later become keystones: a bar where two victims had both bought last calls, a tutor who had been paid cash, an online forum where a discrete group discussed "finding center." He read and reread posts that sounded like homework assigned by a charismatic teacher.

He did not yet have a suspect. What he had was shape: a choreography of care, a message made of ritual. The labyrinth was both the signature and the riddle. Whoever placed it wanted to compel someone—perhaps the living, perhaps the authorities—to follow its line and find the center.

Reed's visits were short and weighted. "You don't have to be the man who untangles everything," he said one night, shelving compassion in the way he folded his sentence. "You have to be the man who keeps people safe while we ask the hard questions." He did not tell Damian his own nights were full of worrying about the men whose names lined the notebook.

There were moments when the task felt like knifing through fog. One afternoon, a lead brought them to an old men's support group that met in a church basement. They had been open, polite, and, on the surface, harmless. Yet one member's manner suggested a person who kept too much neat—neat notes, neat thoughts, a habit of offering advice that fit into a tidy metaphor. He had once been seen speaking to one of the victims about "finding the center," and his name flickered on Damian's list like a candle's hesitant flame.

But accusation without proof is a careless thing. Damian's work, slow and hammer-quiet, bent toward evidence. He watched the man, traced his purchases, spoke to acquaintances who said the man had once been a teacher of sorts—philosophy, mythology—someone who loved symbols. The man was polite when confronted, his answers the shade of plausible; he would not yield easily to the web Damian tried to throw.

Shie's mayor demanded swift closure and the media wanted a villain they could photograph. Damian moved between those urgencies and the tact of truth, feeling the strain like a stone pressing into his palm. He had come to understand, again and again, that the city prefers tidy endings, but the world he mapped rarely agreed. The labyrinth on those young throats would not be untangled with slogans or press conferences. It would need patience, quiet accumulation, and a willingness to follow the line to its center—even if that center was not one he liked.

Night after night, in a rented room near the river, Damian dreamed of spirals. The dreams were not frightening so much as insistently curious; a small voice in them kept urging him to follow the path until the heart revealed itself. He woke with the taste of metal and the compass of the city's demands heavy on his chest. The case had become a test—not only of skill but of the small moral choices that decide who one becomes when one follows a line of doubt all the way in.

THIRTEEN

THE FATHER IN THE SPIRAL

The case had become a test—not only of skill but of the small moral choices that decide who one becomes when one follows a line of doubt all the way in.

Damian's days began to thin, little by little, at the edges. He woke before dawn most mornings, laced into his boots in the dim of the rented room, and walked the river as if movement could press the fog from his head. The river carried the city away as it always had—paper wrappers, the tang of iron, the occasional gull that had misaccustomed itself to urban tides—and he would stand and watch reflections make the buildings into crooked scripture until the light felt honest enough to begin the work again.

One morning he carried the pendant to the coroner's lab himself. Under Dr. Sera Hollis's lamp the metal became a planet: minute pockmarks, hairline scratches, the way the spiral's grooves had been burnished in one place as if someone had rubbed them often with a thumb. Sera's fingers were steady and precise; she passed him a jeweler's loupe and a thin, square of gauze.

"Not just staged," she said, voice low in the hum of refrigeration units. "Ceremony. The way this is handled—no frantic fingerprints, no roughness—Someone took their time after death. Look here." She pointed to a microscopic crescent of residue lodged in the pendant's seam. "This is not just sweat. It's surgical antiseptic. I can test it, but it's the smell—chlorhexidine, iodine derivatives, the kind used in minor operating rooms or emergency kits. Whoever did the final dressing had access to supplies and knew how to use them."

Damian turned the pendant again, the spiral catching the fluorescent light differently each time. "Medical training," he said. "Or someone who mimics it well."

Sera shrugged, half-smile brittle. "Mimicry leaves a different signature. This is practiced. Whoever touches these bodies after death treats them like living tissue."

From the lab he went to the first victim's building, to the thin hallway where Mrs. Arun—a woman whose kitchen smelled of lemon oil and laundry starch—remembered her son with a tenderness and an economy that made the facts heavier. She showed him the scarf he used to leave on the hall peg, the stack of overdue notices folded into a neat rectangle. She moved her hands exactly as people do when they are mapping grief into work.

"He always said he was looking for something," she told Damian in the cramped light of her kitchen. "Not that 'found the center' phrase you boys said, but—he would doodle circles at the bottom of his notebooks. He loved puzzles. He never liked crossings out." Her voice held at the last syllable, waiting. "Did they at least—did they do it quickly?"

Damian tasted the question in his mouth. The family wanted answers that soothed motion into grief: who, why, how fast. He told her the truth he had—no easy answers, only slow ones. "They made it look tidy," he said. "That was on purpose."

At a bar called the Low Lantern, which smelled of spilled stout and old citrus peels, he talked to the bartender, Tanya, who kept the tab ledger in her head and never trusted a story that presented itself without edges.

"He came in two nights before," Tanya said, wiping a glass with a rag as if she could polish memory into clarity. "Ordered the same thing every time—black coffee, no sugar. Would sit at table three, stare at the window. Once he said to me, louder than necessary, 'I think I'm getting closer.' Some things he said were not jokes." She tapped the tabletop with a nail. "He was reading a book on myths. He left his phone once. I looked at it—texts from a user called 'CenterFind'—just short things. 'Turn toward the heart.' 'Don't be afraid of the loop.'"

"Can you remember any of the messages?" Damian asked.

"Only one. 'The center is not what you fear; it's what you avoid.' He read it like a translation."

Back at the precinct Damian sat with Lian and Miren and the corkboard that had become a map of absence. Pins and red string gathered like constellations. Miren's patience, which had the texture of a tight-held purse, rattled against the mayor's request for a public statement.

"We need to show action," Miren said, tapping the board so the pins clicked. "Curfews, more patrols. People need to feel safe."

"Action is not the same as answers," Damian replied. "Put more officers in the street and the pattern continues. Whoever's doing this wants the plain view. They want the city to call the center by name."

Miren's hands stilled. "So what do you propose, detective? Sit back and let bodies tell the story in their own time?"

He explained the thread he was following—small things, not press-friendly: antiseptic brands traced to certain clinics, overlapping visits to a free community health clinic on the east side, a tutor who taught classical literature on Tuesday nights and whose receipts matched cash withdrawals from two victims. Miren absorbed each detail like a surgeon assessing an organ. Then she leaned back, hand on her chin.

"Then find the proof," she said. "Make it court-ready. I will shield you here. But I need progress. The mayor already has a talking point written."

Progress came as increments. Damian sat in front of a clinic's receptionist who chewed the inside of her mouth and recited names with the mechanical precision of someone who had been asked to remember a parade. The clinic had been set up to serve night-shift workers and students—discounted services, volunteer staff. Records were paper-heavy and imperfect, which was both a curse and a door. He pulled shifts and sign-in sheets and found a familiar handwriting: short, careful, the same stroke on intake forms signed by several of the victims. The signature matched the name of a volunteer, Jonas Hale, who taught a mythology class on the outskirts of town.

Jonas was forty, with the kind of tidy hair that had learned to resist wind. He lived above a small shop that sold used books and prints of constellations. Damian went late, under the excuse of asking about class times; Jonas opened the door in a cardigan that still smelled faintly of pipe tobacco.

"I run a small group," Jonas said without invitation. "We talk about myth as metaphor. We talk about journeys. It's not a club. People come, they speak, and they leave better or worse." He smiled a smile that did not reach his eyes. "You are not the first inspector to come knocking."

"Did you speak with any of the victims about 'finding center'?" Damian asked. He watched Jonas's hands—long, careful, capable.

"Words like that are easy to borrow," Jonas said. "I said 'center' once in a class. It's a poetic word. I push people. Sometimes they take the push the wrong way. That is their choice, and it is not mine."

Damian pressed. "You volunteer at the clinic."

"Occasionally. I help with intake, yes. There's a lot of loneliness in Shie. People want a map." His voice had the soft precision of a teacher reciting a lesson.

At night, the spirals visited Damian in sleep again. This time they unrolled in a room that smelled of antiseptic and lemon oil, and at the heart of the spiral sat a small, impossible light. He woke with the taste of metal and the quiet knowledge that someone was trying to make him follow it.

Two nights later, he found a small folded envelope tucked under his door. The brass of the lock left a crescent shadow when he picked it up. Inside was a single necklace, exactly like the others, its chain coiled on a square of tissue paper, and beneath it a strip of paper with inked handwriting: Follow the line.

He did not show it to anyone at first. He carried it instead like a hot coal, weighing whether he should drop it into evidence or read it like a plea. Reed saw the shade behind his eyes and sat across from him at the small kitchen table Miren had insisted he use in the precinct annex.

"You took it?" Reed asked quietly. He did not reach for the pendant; he knew Damian would not hand it over. "Why take a bait like that?"

"Because it's part of the language," Damian said. "Either it's a threat or an invitation. Either way it speaks."

"Then don't answer it from your chest." Reed leaned forward. "Answer it from your head. Turn it into data. Whoever left that wants a conversation. They also want you to feel like you're being led."

Damian uncoiled the chain with slow, deliberate fingers and laid the pendant on the table. It gleamed under the strip of fluorescent light like a tiny moon. He turned it so that the grooves lined up with the grain of the wood and thought of all the tiny decisions that form a line—one witness who remembers a phrase, a clerk who misfiled a note, a volunteer who wears neat cardigans and teaches about journeys.

Outside, the city continued to look like a place that refused to unravel in public: bakers setting croissants in neat rows, a child carrying a plastic sword, commuters folding umbrellas into polite packages. Inside the precinct a map of absences waited for him. He traced a pin with his thumb and felt, for the first time in weeks, that he was not merely following a line but beginning to make one. The spiral, he realized, did not always point inward to a single darkness; sometimes it pointed outward, toward everyone who had ever suggested to a vulnerable man that not finding the center was a failure.

He slept less. He listened more. He began to haunt the edges of Jonah's classes, the clinic's waiting room, the Low Lantern after midnight. He read forum posts as if they were Scripture, following the usernames like the footsteps of faint, private processions. Each new detail stuck to the fabric of the case like rain to thread, small and persistent and not yet decisive.

Somewhere in the city, someone had placed a symbol on a throat and expected an audience to understand. Damian had promised himself he would not give them that comfort. He would not hand them a photograph and a verdict that smoothed things into neatness. He had begun to learn patience the way a man learns to breathe through cold: slowly, with the awareness that every inhale was part of keeping the world intact.

When he finally turned the pendant over to Sera for a deeper chemical read, he did so in the light of a man who had decided to follow the line not because he wanted to be right, but because he owed the dead something more than tidy closure. The spiral hummed in his pocket like a small, insistent answer. He clung to it as if it were a compass—knowing, foolishly perhaps, that compasses show direction not destiny.

Sera's call came at an hour that should have belonged to sleep. The lab's voice on the other end was a practiced thing—practical, careful—but when she said, "You'll want to see this," there was a tilt that made Damian sit up straight in the dark.

The lab smelled of cold metal and coffee. Sera met him at the bench, hair pinned back, gloves still on, and pushed over a tray holding the pendant in a small dish and a second dish with a smear of material magnified into a map.

"It's not just antiseptic," she said, tapping the slide so the light snagged on a tiny pattern. "There are traces of a lanolin-based softener and an organic compound they use in handmade soaps and therapeutic balms. It's the kind of thing you wouldn't expect in a hospital scrub room. It suggests someone who handles both medical supplies and—hobbies. Or crafts."

She handed him a printout with microscopic photos and a note he didn't need read: a brand name she'd seen before in a receipt she couldn't account for. "Also," she added, softer, "there's a partial fingerprint on the inside curve of the pendant. Too smudged for direct ID, but it's there. And someone took extraordinary care not to leave anything else."

Damian stared at the photos until the edges softened. A lanolin signature—softener used in ointments, soap bars—paired with antiseptic suggested a person who moved between two worlds: clinical competence and intimate craft. It fit the quiet profile he'd sketched of Jonas Hale: volunteer at a clinic, seller of small curios in a bookshop, a man who patched people and read them myths at the same time.

"Run the brand against local suppliers," Damian said, already thinking of routes, receipts, what could be matched. "And check the clinic's volunteers for purchases."

Sera nodded. "I'll run chromatography tomorrow. You should eat something." Her voice was a gentle, professional reprimand. He left with the pendant in an evidence envelope, feeling as if he'd carried a small moon in his palm.

For the next week Damian became a fixture at the edges of Jonas's life. He watched the Tuesday class through the shop window one rainy evening—Jonas standing in a half-circle of folding chairs with a whiteboard behind him, the room lit like a stage. The people who came were ordinary: a nurse with tired hands, a student with a satchel, a factory line-worker who kept checking the time. They spoke in small, careful phrases about myth and meaning; Jonas folded their words into lectures like a seamstress folding a hem.

After class, people trailed toward the counter where Jonas sold battered copies of primary texts and wrapped bars of soap in plain brown paper. He handled each purchase like a benediction, tying string around the paper with long, precise fingers.

Damian entered once under the pretense of buying a book. The bell above the door had a low, melancholy note that made the shop feel older than it was. Books leaned in small, intimate towers; the air smelled faintly of pipe tobacco, beeswax, and citrus—the same lanolin-sweet warmth Sera had mentioned.

Jonas looked up and smiled in the way a man who has taught people to find comfort in language smiles: slow, practiced, disarming. "You like older runs," he said, glancing at the book in Damian's hand. "Good choice. Labyrinths are a classroom, in their own way."

"I wanted to ask about your class," Damian said. "You encourage metaphor. How far do you push people?"

Jonas's fingers paused on the corner of a book as if feeling its grain. "Not far. People push themselves. I simply offer a shape. Some of my students take what I say and warm it up in their lives. Others set it down." He folded his hands on the counter and watched Damian. "What is the line between help and harm when you teach someone to look inward? It's a question I'm fond of asking."

Damian let the question hang. Jonas's face gave away nothing—only the slow brightness of someone used to inhabiting rhetorical space. "Do you visit the clinic often?" he asked, easing the conversation where he needed it.

"Sometimes," Jonas said. "Mostly for intake days. It's a place for people who fall through the gaps. I do what I can." He wrapped a bar of soap and tied it with string, then added a small slip of paper with neat handwriting: a quote from a poem about journeys. "For comfort," he said. "Not instruction."

Damian left unsettled and more convinced. Language was Jonas's instrument. So was ritual—the careful wrapping, the string, the scent. It made the line between comfort and command thin.

Reed helped him stitch surveillance together. They used unmarked cars and quiet shifts, trading the brunt of public expectation for long waits in rain and the unsettling intimacy of watching a man from the shadow of a lamppost. Reed smoked cigarettes with one hand and held the thermos with the other, a small domestic ritual that kept his patience steady.

"You can't arrest a metaphor," Reed said one night as they watched Jonas lock the shop and speak with a young man in a coat who had lingered to ask a question about a book. The man looked nervous; his fingers fumbled at the coin in his pocket. Jonas's voice lowered, his posture changed to the ease of someone who meets confessions daily.

"Watch," Reed said. "See the little slackening. He takes people who have tautness and gives them a place to loosen."

Damian watched Jonas draw the young man in the shop's doorway like a tide. He saw the exchange of a small object—Jonas pressing what looked like a folded paper into the boy's hands. The boy's shoulders dropped as if a weight had been taken away. They left together toward the clinic's direction.

Damian wanted to follow. He also wanted—not for the first time—to be sure he wasn't converting curiosity into accusation. He followed them at a distance, keeping to the pools of streetlight, watching as Jonas slipped into the clinic's back entrance while the boy waited at the curb. Jonas moved with the furtive ease of someone used to keeping certain acts private.

They trailed Jonas to a rear room in the clinic, a cramped intake area with a poster about wound care on the wall. From the alley Damian could see through a smeared window: Jonas kneeling in front of the boy, removing his coat, speaking in low, measured phrases. The boy's face was a map of confusion and relief; he let Jonas examine his sleeve, his throat. Jonas took a small bottle from his cardigan and dabbed something near the boy's collarbone—nothing violent, nothing overtly sinister—but the motion was intimate, practiced, the kind of touch that might be comfort or might be compulsion.

Damian stepped back and felt the old moral muscles tightening: when to act; when to observe. If Jonas was a predator, an intervention might save one life and ruin a dozen evidentiary threads. If Jonas was a healer, watching and doing nothing would be a coward's sin.

He called Miren from the alley. Her voice over the phone was a thin knife between public pressure and private procedure. "If you intervene, you make it an arrestable incident," she said. "If you wait, you risk another death. What's your read?"

Damian listened to the boy's laugh drifting through the window, Jonass's low voice folding around him. "Not an attack," he said finally. "Not tonight."

Reed's cigarette burned down in his fingers. "Then we gather," he said. "We watch who sees what, who buys what. If this is a man who knows how to make ritual into compulsion, he leaves traces. We don't pounce—yet."

They did not pounce. They gathered: a ledger from the clinic, receipts for soap and lanolin from a small cooperative that sold to craftspeople, a bus pass stub, a late-night purchase at a pharmacy. Each small piece was slow work but it began to look like a line rather than an accident. Each detail was a little stitch.

Back at the precinct, Damian sat under a lamp with the notebook his father had once used. He wrote names and times and the consistencies that now mapped themselves into a faint, slow outline: Jonas's classes, the clinic visits, the soap. He thought of the boy's face in the window and the private ritual they'd witnessed. Was the soap a comfort or a token? Was the antiseptic a medical habit or a practiced deception?

When the mayor lectured again about speed and visible action, Damian read the press releases with a polite, worn patience. He had learned that the city needed comfort. He had also learned that comfort could be manufactured and sold as truth.

The next morning the ledger they'd obtained from the clinic had an entry that matched a recent cash withdrawal and the handwriting of a volunteer who had signed in under a thin, careful scrawl. Sera's chromatography had come back: the lanolin signature matched soap sold at a cooperative that listed a small wholesale buyer—Jonas Hale.

It was not a smoking gun. It was the next step.

Damian folded the paper and slid it into his notebook, like an arrow placed into a quiver. Outside, rain began again, thin and steady, pulling the city into the same soft washing that had become the backdrop for so much of his work. He thought of spirals—how a line can lead inward or outward—and of the small ethical pressures that shaped each move the way water shapes stone.

He stood, put on his coat, and went to find Jonas. Not to accuse, not yet. To see a man up close, to hear the shape of his language in full. To decide, with sticky, patient hands, whether Jonas was a guide offering maps or a cartographer drawing traps. The line had a center; he did not yet know what waited there. But he would follow it. Slowly, piece by piece, he would unroll the spiral until it named itself.

Damian found Jonas at the back of the shop, bent over a tray of soaps as if he were arranging minnows. The bell chimed when Damian entered; Jonas looked up with that same practiced calm, then blinked as the detective crossed the floor and set his coat on a chair.

"You returned," Jonas said without surprise. He dried his hands on a cloth that smelled faintly of citrus and cedar. "I hope the book was satisfactory."

"It was," Damian said, and did not sit. He watched the way Jonas moved around the counter—the small, precise choreography of a man who has turned care into habit. The shop was quieter in daylight: fewer customers, the rain seeping clothily against the window. Sunlight made the soap bars look like warm stones.

"I need to ask you more about the clinic," Damian said. "About what you do there."

Jonas folded his hands, a teacher at the front of class. "I help with intake. I patch bruises, literally and figuratively. People come in with holes and leaves and I help them sew it up. Or I show them a way to sew it themselves."

"Do you ever give them a course of treatment?" Damian asked. "Anything you would describe as a ritual? An at-home practice?"

Jonas's smile thinned. "I sometimes suggest small practices—breaths, tactile reminders. A sensory anchor can be helpful for someone with panic or despair." He picked up a bar of soap and turned it in his palms. "We all use objects to remind ourselves we can hold on."

"Have you ever instructed someone to take a step that could harm them? Told them the center requires suffering?"

"Never." Jonas's voice had the brittle firmness of someone defending a principle. "People take what I say and make what they will of it. I teach metaphor. I do not prescribe fate."

Damian let the words sit. He had watched the clinic window from the alley; he'd seen the boy loosen his shoulders when Jonas dabbed something near his collarbone. He had the chromatography results; the lanolin compound traced to Jonas's cooperative. He had the ledger entry. None of those were a verdict—but they were the shape of one.

"Would you let me look around?" Damian asked. "For inventory records. For receipts. For—" He gestured to the piles of wrapped soap. "—anything that might connect the things Sera found to what you sell."

Jonas hesitated for only a breath. "You can look," he said. "You may take what you will." He stepped aside with the faint courtesy of someone offering the threshold to his privacy.

Damian walked the shop like a careful thief, not touching what he did not need to. He opened a drawer behind the counter and found bundles of receipts tied with twine, small notebooks with lists in Jonas's careful hand, and a battered wooden box with small vials of oils. One notebook fell open to a page with dates and initials—enough to make a pattern if someone threaded time through it. Beside the cash ledger was a folded piece of paper that made his breath slow: a list of names, neatly written, with dates and a single word after each—"intake," "soap," "follow-up." The handwriting matched the scrawl on the clinic forms.

Damian straightened the paper and asked, "What is this?"

Jonas's hands folded on the counter. "Notes," he said. "A teacher keeps notes. I track people who want follow-ups, who need soap for skin irritations, who ask for additional reading. Because resources are thin, I prioritize."

"How do you decide who to prioritize?"

Jonas's eyes flicked up and held Damian's. "Who asks. Who answers. Who returns."

There was a small pause, full of the quiet things that are not confessions and not denials. Damian wanted a crack—something that would let the truth in like light—but Jonas offered only the slow, patient dignity of a man who knows how to wait.

Two hours later, outside in the rain, Damian called Reed. The ledger, the soap, the vials—the accumulation felt like a slow tightening rather than a slam; it was the kind of evidence prosecutors would chew on until it yielded a core or until the case dissolved into questions of intent.

"We have a map," Damian said. "Not a gun. A map."

Reed took a drag of his cigarette and let the smoke stain the rain. "Maps can be deadly," he said. "But maps can also be maps. We need someone who can tell the difference."

They did not have to wait long for a new voice to provide direction. Late that evening a woman came to the precinct clutching a grocery bag as if it held a prayer. She introduced herself as Mara—twenty-one, student, a face with small, stubborn bruises from sleeplessness.

"I went to Jonas's class for three weeks," she said once she'd been taken to an interview room. "I thought it would help me get through the job. My shift at the bakery was killing me. He gave everyone these things—soap, a little balm. He told us to rub it when the spiral rose. He told us the spiral is a way to find the center. He said, 'You must make room for the spiral.'"

"Did anyone tell you to harm yourself?" Damian asked. He kept his voice low, as if speaking softly could coax memory rather than force it.

Mara's fingers twisted the plastic handle of the bag. "Not straight out. But he said the center is a cost. He told us you can't find the center if you don't let go of something. He said, 'Letting go is the way the center finds you.'" Her eyes were carefully open, measuring the room with the vigilance of someone who had learned to see threats in small gestures. "One night he told a boy to 'finish' what he started to find the center. He said it like it was an exercise."

Damian felt the floor shift. Mara's testimony was not a smoking gun either—language is slippery, and intent can hide behind metaphor. But the way she framed Jonas's words—less lecture than instruction—pulled at a seam.

"Did you ever feel pressured to hurt yourself?" he asked.

She shook her head. "No. But I saw it once. There was a kid—Micah. He came to class thin and quiet. Jonas gave him a bar of soap and told him to rub until he felt the spiral. Micah smiled like it was a joke. The next week I saw him with a new pendant around his neck. He looked...different. He wouldn't talk about it. Two weeks later the papers said suicide."

Damian sat very still. The name lit a pale match—Micah had been one of the victims. Mara's story connected two otherwise disparate marks. It gave a motion to the ledger and a voice to the soap.

He asked more questions. Mara described the small performances Jonas used: a low voice, a ritual of wrapping the soap in brown paper, a slip of paper with a line of verse tucked inside. "He told people to keep the paper close to their skin," she said. "He said it warmed intention."

Mara's testimony fit with the physical traces Sera had found; it also introduced a new dimension—language made into instruction, objects given ritual weight. Damian felt the case pivot. He had a line that might be followed through words as well as through receipts.

He took Mara's statement and added it to the ledger stack in his notebook. He phoned Miren, who came down to the precinct and read Mara's words with an expression that folded into something harder.

"Enough to warrant an interview," Miren said. "We bring him in on the soap, on the ledger, and we read him his rights. We see how he answers to that."

Damian hesitated. He had wanted more than interviews; he wanted the kind of evidence that would stand up to a defense of metaphor. But prosecution sometimes begins at interrogation. "If we arrest him now, we might make enemies of people who describe him as a comfort. We'll tip the whole town into a massacre of reputations if we're wrong."

Miren's face was a geometry of lines. "We weigh the risk of being wrong against the risk of being too slow. Which would you rather be?"

He knew which answer Miren expected. He also knew how the city would react to a rushed arrest: triumph for the mayor, a dangerous neatness that left open the possibility of another body. He breathed and let the slow work guide him.

"We interview," he said. "We bring him in and we watch him answer. We look for inconsistency. We put a senior officer in on the questions. We don't shout guilt in public."

They prepared an interview room like a stage set: neutral chairs, a recording device, Miren present, Reed observing from the glass. They asked Sera to re-verify the lab results. She came into the room in the afternoon, white coat in hand, and described the compounds in plain language that left no room for metaphor.

Jonas walked into the room with his cardigan buttoned and his hands folded like a man who expected to be heard. He listened as Damian read out the ledger entries, the cooperative receipts, Mara's statement.

"You understand how this must look," Damian said. "Soap, antiseptic, an instruction to use a ritual—people have died who had your objects on them after death."

Jonas's face did not collapse. He tilted his head the way a teacher asks a student to rethink a problem. "I am sorry for the families," he said. "But I have never told anyone to die. I suggest practices to help anchor people. I teach metaphor. If my language is misread, I am responsible to explain it better. Not to be blamed for the misreading."

"Do you ever tell people they must let go of something to find the center?" Miren asked. "Do you ever say 'finish' something to complete the spiral?"

"They asked me to push them," Jonas said. "Young people want permission to be tougher, to feel they have done something heroic. I give them challenges—reading assignments, journaling. Never self-harm. I would never—" He stopped, and for a fraction of a breath something unsteady creaked in him. "I would never ask anyone to die."

Damian watched the small motions—the throat working, the fingers flexing—searching a face for the absence of lies. Jonas's words were careful; his composure was the product of practice. He had a plausible defense rooted in the slipperiness of metaphor. Protestations alone would not be enough.

After Jonas left the room, Miren turned to Damian. "We have a case to build," she said. "Not just about soaps and lectures—but about causation. If people hear 'finish' and then kill themselves, and that pattern matches your objects and your presence—that's our lever. We will need corroboration. More witnesses like Mara. Medical notes linking the balms to direct contact. Something that connects sermon to act."

Damian thought of Micah and the boy in the clinic doorway and the pendant in his palm. The spiral was folding in and laying its path across lives. He felt both nearer and more distant from its center—their evidence a lattice, not a blade.

He left the precinct that night into rain that had a clean, new smell, as if the city itself were trying to wash away its complicity. He had a direction now: gather more voices, find more receipts, and watch Jonas until the pattern either resolved into culpability or unraveled into metaphor. He had to be careful; he had to be exact. The city wanted a villain. He wanted truth.

As he walked, he imagined the spiral again, not as a trap or a target but as a way of motion—people circling some interior grief and sometimes finding the rim too thin. His work, he understood, would be to follow that motion without mistaking the map for the heart. He would follow, slowly, and listen for the moment where words were not words anymore but commands that guided a hand to an unfathomable center.

Damian kept the spiral in his pocket the way some people keep a talisman: heavy with questions. After Mara's statement, after Jonas's ledger and Sera's chromatography, the case felt like a wound that could either scar slowly or fester forever. He slept in the precinct some nights, let the lamp in the interview room be his moon, and read the names he'd written until their meaning rearranged.

One night, flipping through an old microfiche file in the municipal records room—a habit from an earlier life when he chased political corruption more than ritual—he found a margin note that slapped the edge of his patience awake. It was a small, yellowed article from twenty-three years prior: a city council hearing about a youth movement called the Awakened Youth. The piece was a perfunctory thing—flinty, a record of panic more than of fact. The council had banned the group after accusations of intimidation and strange rites; a handful of their leaders had been fined and ostracized. The explicit charge had been vague: "purity demonstrations." The symbol in the margin—an etched spiral—was the same as the pendant.

He carried the microfiche home like contraband. The article was thin on details, but the name stuck: Awakened Youth. He ran the term through old forum posts he'd salvaged from the victims' phones and found usernames that used variants—AwakeAgain, CenterFound, YouthAwake. The forums had gone quiet after one particular thread: a string of messages in which users joked about "purifications" and then the thread had been deleted in a flood of new accounts. Someone on those posts had once linked to an old manifesto—an angular PDF that spoke of "removing rot to restore a sinless society" and used the labyrinth as a symbol of both testing and purification.

The more Damian pulled at threads, the more connections warmed into outline. The cooperative that sold lanolin to artisans had invoices shipped to a postbox rented under a different name, one that traced back to an address in an old textile mill on the river's north bend—an abandoned place with broken windows and a smell of long-dried oil. The mill's ledger, when they got it with a subpoena, showed small purchases of antiseptic, cloth, and soap ingredients—orders placed in the middle of the night. The handwriting on the ledger matched Jonas's careful scrawl.

"It's like somebody opened a book of the city and wrote themselves into the margins," Damian said to Reed in the car as rain scored the windshield. "Only these marginalia keep bleeding."

Reed's jaw worked. "So the old Awakened Youth got back together, though in smaller, meaner clothes."

"Or someone used the myth of them," Damian said. "Either way, that spiral means something—an initiation, or a brand."

They began to watch the mill. They posted a camera in the alley across from a boarded doorway and sat in a van under the cold light of a dome lamp, trading cigarettes and notes. For three nights, nothing but wind and rats moved in and out of the mill. On the fourth night, figures came: small at first, a single bike light bobbing, then more; they walked with the studied hush of people who had rehearsed secrecy. Someone hung a lantern, and a pale light pooled in a back room. A figure moved in the doorway who carried a presence like a held breath—smooth, sure. The watchers in the van watched the shapes rearrange into a cluster the way constellations yield patterns only when you know where to look.

"I think that's him," Reed whispered. "The speaker."

They took his picture. They recorded voices with a parabolic mic. The audio came back hours later—distant, with the rattle of rain caught in the microphone, but the words were clear enough in the room's center: "...we do what is necessary so the city may be made sinless again. The center demands a cost. We remove the rot... so the rest can breathe." The speaker's voice was neither young nor old; it had been trained.

They had, in the hour after they played the recording back, a tighter map. The mill meetings had structure: lessons, readings, a small ritual in which a bar of soap was wrapped in brown paper and tied with string, a slip of verse inserted, a short phrase intoned—"find the center"—and, in the dark, a selection process. Names were called. A few left in tears; some left resolved. The circles were designed to affirm and then to bind.

Damian called Miren. "We have a meeting place and a voice. We have ritual and recruits. We have the spiral's choreography. We need to move."

Miren's voice was economy. "We need evidence, not theater. We need to know who commits the killings, and how the society's structure works. If the Awakened Youth are behind this, they're not just a singular killer—they're a machine."

The machine had a motor. They found it in pieces and in whispers. A member arrested for petty theft in the old neighborhood volunteered details in exchange for leniency: the group had a hierarchy of elders and speakers, they curated a "purity list," and they believed that some youths—those who committed "sins" against the idea of a perfect city—had to be asked to leave the world. The ritual was more than ideology; it was instruction in method. The antiseptic and lanolin were practical—used, they said, to make the death look clinical and to remove evidence of panic. The pendent, the spiral, was a finishing touch: the "seal."

Jonas's name recurred in the machine's upholstery. He had not been the executing hand, the petty thief said, but he was a "binder"—someone who supplied the materials and the language. He taught the mythic frames that made killing feel like obedience. He wrapped soaps and tied strings and taught the line between metaphor and directive until it blurred for some. The binder, the machine said, made the ritual plausible.

Damian sat in on an interview with the petty thief, a kid with a jaw like a hinge who spoke rapidly as if to outrun a memory. "We thought we were saving them," he said. "You don't get into a group like that if you haven't been told the city's broken. They told us about contagion—the rot of small sins that metastasized. They showed us a list of people—those who 'didn't fit'—and told us to ask them to step into the center. If they refused, we'd help them find peace. I didn't do the helping. I just watched."

"Who helps?" Damian asked.

"The elders," the kid said. "They decide." He rubbed his hands. "Cassian Voss—he's the one everyone listens to now. He was in the old movement. He came back and said we'd been right all along—about the rot, about sacrifice."

Cassian Voss. The name felt like a bell. Damian pulled older files, found an old photograph of a young Cassian with a shaved head and an arm raised at a rally, his face full of furnace-intent. He had been indicted once, then quietly rebuffed by an injunction and had faded into the city's underbelly—until now, when he had re-stitched himself into a new pattern and people had followed.

The investigators moved with the slow precision of people folding together threads. Undercover operatives, careful subpoenas, a list of names that had grown in the margins of the ledger. The more Damian pried, the more uncomfortable names surfaced: a minor council aide, an owner of a small security firm, a volunteer nurse who'd been seen at two of the victims' last check-ins. These were not caricatures of evil—many were people who had tasted some kind of moral certainty and had let it harden.

Damian watched one evening as Sera interviewed a clinic volunteer who admitted she had been asked by "friends from the Awakened Youth" to hand out bars of soap and to use certain phrases in intake. "It sounded harmless," she said, and then: "They called it a cleansing." Her voice broke less for the danger to herself than for what it meant to have helped unwittingly.

The night they finally moved—Miren orchestrating a quiet, all-night sweep—Damian felt the old familiar spike of adrenaline, but it was tethered now to something more complicated: pity, anger, and an ache for what had been allowed to grow. They breached the textile mill at dawn. The light came in long and certain; the men and women inside were not monsters in the theatrical sense but people who had constructed a theology out of grievance. Cassian stood at the center of the largest room like a man who had arranged his life as a pulpit. He did not run. He watched the officers with an expression that could have been exhaustion or contempt.

"You will not stop us," he said when Miren read the warrants. His voice had a preacher's cadence. "You will not halt the necessity of our work."

"We're stopping the murders," Miren said. "You're under arrest for conspiracy, for aiding and abetting, for the murders themselves."

Her badge shone in the sallow light.

Cassian laughed once, a sound like spare metal. "You call them murders. I call them purifications." He paused, and his face smoothed into something resembling sorrow. "You will not quiet the rot. That is on you—on your laws."

They found, in the milling room's back shelves, rows of wrapped soaps, tagged slips of verse, scrapbooks where new recruits' notes were kept, and a ledger of "targets"—lists scrawled with names, observations, and a chilling notation on the date column that matched the times of several deaths. They found the antiseptics and vials, the postbox registrations, and a ledger connecting purchases to names that corresponded to known volunteers. A dozen people were taken into custody that day, from low-level binders who assembled kits to elders who had given "advice" about methods. Jonas was not in the mill; he had apparently fled.

They traced Jonas through the bus stubs in his notebooks and found him at a small waystation on the city's edge, hiding in the dim of a coffeehouse. When Damian found him, Jonas's face had the look of a man who had forgotten how to be surprised by consequence.

"You ran," Damian said without preamble, the tiredness in his voice not a question.

Jonas folded his hands on the table and looked at Damian with something like repentance. "I didn't run because I wanted to," he said. "I left because I woke at night and couldn't breathe. I thought if I removed myself, maybe no one I cared about would follow me. I thought that would be enough."

"You handed people the ropes," Damian said. "You taught them a grammar that could be read as instruction. You wrapped the soap and tied the paper. You wrote names in a ledger."

Jonas's fingers trembled. "I gave them tools to soothe. I did not realize that the metaphor would be used as a weapon. I see now that words can be sharp enough to bleed."

"Did you know about the 'purifications'?" Damian asked, pressing for the line between ignorance and complicity.

Jonas's voice was small. "I knew of a doctrine, abstract. I believed in the possibility of change—of people who wanted to be better. Cassian—he convinced us it was about the city's health. He told us the center required refusal of the unclean. He said we were guardians. I thought we were giving people a chance to choose. I did not know they would turn that choice into coercion."

Jonas cried then, quietly, like a man who had finally been allowed to reach a grief he had denied seeing. "If I could pull back every bar, every word, I would. I thought I was teaching people to find solace, not to die for it."

Damian's mouth was dry. Stories like these bent the world into questions that had no easy margins. He thought of Micah, whose smile had been a pale thing in Mara's memory. He thought of the carefulness in Sera's lab, of the antiseptic smell in the evidence bag, of the pendant's spiral catching light in his palm. He felt the justice of the law's weight and the strange human failure behind these actions.

The arrests were public and messy. Cassian and half a dozen elders were charged with conspiracy to commit murder and multiple counts of manslaughter; several ranks of the society were arraigned for aiding and abetting. The press called it a cult resurgence; politicians leaned into the narrative of moral panic and pledged further funding for youth services. Some members of the community called for harsh sentences. Others, oddly, offered defenses in hushed church basements: "They believed they were saving us." The city that wanted tidy endings got none that felt clean.

At the trials that followed, the prosecution wove the ledger, the receipts, the audio recordings from the mill, and the forensic matches into a case that painted the Awakened Youth not as an abstraction but as a deliberate apparatus. The defense argued about metaphor and intention. Cassidy — a witness who had moved from being a binder to a cooperator—testified, voice shaking, about the exact moment language hardened into command. "We began with poetry," she said. "We ended with instruction. We told people to let go, and then we—" She broke down, unable to finish the sentence. The jury saw more than words; they saw patterns.

Jonas pleaded guilty to providing materials and for reckless endangerment; he received a sentence that balanced punishment and recognition of his partial culpability—community service, mandatory counseling, and a term of supervised probation that would keep him in the city's vigilance. Cassian and several elders received longer sentences. Some members cooperated and had reduced sentences; others fled and were arrested on warrants later.

After the convictions, Damian sat at the river, the city's banners flapping like a memory. People resumed markets and Sunday walks. The mayor gave a speech about safety. But when the cameras left, the gutters still had that latent shine that comes after a rain—clean but not cured.

Mira Kosta came to him once, after the court had adjourned and the press had thinned. They leaned against the precinct's back wall, the same wall he'd leaned against in the early days. "You did the slow work," she said. "You didn't give them what they wanted."

He looked at her. "We caught a machine that turned grief into doctrine," he said. "But the machine used tools most people use—language, care, community. The danger is not always obvious."

They talked then about the victims—about Micah, about the others who had been named in the ledger—and about what the city would need if it wanted to heal. The list was long: more outreach, tighter oversight of volunteer groups, public education about coercive language, resources for youth who drift toward belief systems promising clean answers.

Damian found Mara again, months later, in a small bakery where she'd started a morning shift. She had gone back to study, cautiously, like someone who had dipped a toe in open water and was testing the current. She passed him a paper bag with a plain bun and said, "We keep threads from being pulled, sometimes—one small thing at a time."

He held the bun and felt the small, domestic weight of it. "You did good," he said.

"So did you," she answered. "You let us tell it. You didn't make us silent."

On his last night in Shie—because a quiet other city was waiting for him elsewhere—Damian sat at the river and pulled the spiral pendant from his pocket. It had been sent to evidence, then returned to him for safekeeping with a small, official note. He turned it between his fingers. It was only a small disc of metal, scratched and burnished by many hands. It whispered nothing.

He thought of the Awakened Youth and of Cassian's sermonizing voice, of Jonas's tears and Mara's small courage. He thought of the blade-edge where metaphor becomes order and of how easily meaning can be used to make people act. He thought, not for the first time, of the moral praxes of policing: to be exact, to be merciful, to be relentless when the cost was human life.

The city slept in a way that made no promises. Damian placed the pendant on the lip of the river and watched the current take it, just a little, spinning slowly like a boat losing its mooring. It floated a while, the spiral catching light, then turned and drifted away into the river's long sentence.

He did not feel triumphant. He felt, as he had felt from the first night he opened Jonas's ledger, the steady weight of the work: to follow the line, to name the center without pretending the world could be made sinless, and to keep walking when the spiral did not promise an end but rather demanded attention.

Later something strange happened .There was a head who made this Awakened Youth Society again alive.They finally had him in motion because the case had taught them where the machine liked to move—along old rails, in the spaces city planners forgot. A tip from an informant had named a safe house in a narrow row of warehouses near the old ferry slips. Damian drove the van into the fog before dawn, the city reduced to muffled shapes and the dull orange of streetlamps. Miren, Reed, two uniformed officers and a pair of plainclothes moved with the practiced silence of people who have rehearsed entry until it became a ritual.

There were voices—low, tidy—behind a corrugated door. The team stacked, Miren whispered coordinates, and then the door was down and light spilled into the room like a question. Men and women froze among their scrapbooks and boxes of wrapped soap; the elders' faces were set into the old certainty that had built their theology. They yelled commands and read rights. People were cuffed. Cassian Voss sat very still on a crate as officers photographed the ledger and bundles of ritual paraphernalia.

One figure broke toward a fire exit while the rest were taking stock—slipped past a line, a human shadow folding into the alley. Damian saw the movement and went after him without waiting for the official order; his feet found rhythm the way they had at other chases. The back alleys of Shie are a patchwork of refuse and memory—old millstones, slick stairwells, a metal gangway that led toward the river's shoulder. The man ran lean and fast, a silhouette with practiced escape.

Damian kept him in sight until the alley tightened and the fugitive moved to the gangway that cut between the mill's dark flank and a stack of disused pallets. The man didn't turn. He moved like someone certain of his path. Damian called his name—once, twice. The man did not look back. In the hush of anticipation Damian fired a single round; it hit the man in the back. He pitched forward and hit the metal with a soft, awful sound.

There is a moment immediately after violence—less a sound than the sudden rearrangement of the world's furniture. Time thinned. Men in uniforms became actors in slow motion: hands came for medical kits, someone shouted for an ambulance, an officer slammed a fist to find a pulse. Damian found himself kneeling, heart an instrument of someone else's unspooling.

The man moaned and then was still. In the minutes before the ambulance, in the shallow theater of hot breath and rain, Damian's fingers slipped into the jacket pocket of the fallen figure because the instinct to see who a person is can be a way to make the act mean something. He found a wallet and, without thinking, opened it.

There was no photograph. No little boy with a crooked smile. There was, instead, a name—unfamiliar—and a clumsy card for a community center, a folded piece of paper with an address. The man had no ID that shouted the kind of truth that unstitched the night's tension. A badge finally confirmed what the scene had not—an officer called out the name they'd received from a witness: a local organizer they'd wanted to question, a name that did not match anything Damian had kept in his memory.

They moved the body. They booked it. They processed the scene with the cold, efficient routine of people who use gloves the way priests use ritual. Damian felt the world go hard at the edges; his hands trembled with adrenaline that stayed even as the officers moved on to check boxes and tally events. He did not sleep for the next stretch; he watched the hospital staff, he sat through the preliminary autopsy report delivered in clipped sentences by a coroner on call. For all the efficiency, there was nothing in those reports that named him—only a trajectory of death.

It was not until Sera called him in the gray hour of the second morning that the world folded in on itself. She was quiet on the phone in a way that made him listen for more than words. "We have a positive identification," she said. "You should come to the lab."

He drove there as if moving through someone else's weather. The lab smelled like bleach and paper. Sera had the fallen man's printout on the bench and, when she slid it toward him, he tried to read it as if the letters were someone else's script. They were not.

"Match came in through the missing persons database," Sera said. "We cross-checked dental records and a partial DNA from the wound area. It's precise. It's... Damian." Her voice carried like a small bell dropped in a deep room.

He stared until the letters blurred. The name on the printout was his father's.

When the word landed, it did not arrive as an event with a beginning and an end. It uncoiled as a series of old things—one memory folding into another until they became a map: the smell of engine grease and lemon oil in a kitchen where a man hummed and stitched; a small boy climbing into a lap to read a book about sailors; the afternoon his mother had answered the phone with a voice that folded away and then left the house quiet like it had been showered. He had been thirteen the last time he'd seen a full face of his father. Then the house had other rhythms—his mother who stopped humming, a police report that read like a bureaucrat's lullaby. Damian had grown into a man knowing the fact of absence, not the manner of it.

He sat down. Around him, Sera and Miren and Reed moved with corroboration: the dental matches, the partial DNA on file, cross-references with the old missing person's case. They brought him photographs and an old police report, yellow at the edges. The man on the slab in the photo, in the new printout, had his father's jawline, the same way his father's mouth had once turned on a joke.

"How—" Damian's voice broke. "How could he be involved in this?"

"No one knows why people rejoin the wrong parts of themselves," Miren said softly. She looked older in that moment, as if sympathy had been folded into her face. "People change. People come back. Or maybe he never left what he believed."

Sera's hands were steady as she pushed the identification card across the bench. "We can show you the techniques," she said. "The prints, the DNA. It's him."

Damian took the card and looked at the photograph as if the face could refuse the accusation. He remembered a small crescent scar behind his father's ear from a machine at the mill—he remembered pressing his fingertip there once when he was little, feeling the roughness beneath skin. The same thin ridge was visible on the dead man's neck.

He vomited later, alone in the corridor, the sterile smell a betrayal. The lab went on being procedural. But for Damian the machinery of evidence had become a private crucible. He had pulled a trigger and hit a man who, by all forensic accounts, was his father.

The days that followed fractured. The city treated the revelation like a new headline: the detective who shot his own father. Reporters leaned into it with the taste of narrative: tragedy folded into justice. Colleagues who had spoken his name as Damian now had their voices leavened with awkward sympathy. Miren stood by him in public statements—"protocol followed," she said in press rooms—and privately she kept a watch that was less managerial than maternal. Reed smoked more and watched him like a man who waits to see when a friend will stop weathering a storm and start drowning.

Damian could not breathe in the shape of his life. Sleep retreated into a place of hot, looping dreams. He dreamed in spirals—his father at the center of a dark labyrinth, hands measured, smiling the precise smile of a man who had once told stories. He woke from those dreams with fingers curled around the pendant that had been in evidence, the spiral imprinted like a compass needle in his skin. He tried to read the ledger again and the names shifted.

Guilt is a slow animal. It does not announce itself as guilt immediately but settles like an ache in the jaw, the back, a conscience made somatic. Damian's days narrowed to ritual acts that had about them the steadiness of penance. He took to walking the river at night again, but now the motion was not clearing as much as wearing. He pulled the pendant from his pocket and turned it until the grooves were bright. He talked to the pendant once, under his breath, saying his father's name as if naming could locate.

People tried to reach him. Reed brought sandwiches that went untouched. Miren pressed for him to take leave, to enter counseling. "This is more than a badge can hold," she said. "We will support you—get you help." He nodded and then declined. He could hear their good intentions echoing, like furniture moved by polite hands.

He began to do strange things, the kind of small myth-making that transforms grief into a scaffolding. He spent hours at the municipal archives, tracing the Awakened Youth's ban and the names associated with its early days. He mapped out every abandoned building, every underground room where rituals could have been rehearsed. He took the same notebook his father had once used—worn at the corners—and filled it with labyrinths drawn to scale, small concentric circles inked in until they blurred into one another. Each drawing had annotations: dates, names, a notation of how one could move from entrance to center. He lined his apartment walls with maps the way a sailor plots a course by remembered stars.

Friends noticed the change. Mara found him in a bakery one morning and watched as he traced the crumb pattern of a bun with a finger. "You look like someone holding a bruise too close to a lamp," she said, because she had seen men wear pain like clothing and she knew the language of it. He smiled at her like a man only half present. "He's gone," he said to her once—simple, true—and then the sentence bent around itself. "But not gone. He is at the center. He needs me to find him."

The case had become a test—not only of skill but of the small moral choices that decide who one becomes when one follows a line of doubt all the way in.

Damian's days began to thin, little by little, at the edges. He woke before dawn most mornings, laced into his boots in the dim of the rented room, and walked the river as if movement could press the fog from his head. The river carried the city away as it always had—paper wrappers, the tang of iron, the occasional gull that had misaccustomed itself to urban tides—and he would stand and watch reflections make the buildings into crooked scripture until the light felt honest enough to begin the work again.

One morning he carried the pendant to the coroner's lab himself. Under Dr. Sera Hollis's lamp the metal became a planet: minute pockmarks, hairline scratches, the way the spiral's grooves had been burnished in one place as if someone had rubbed them often with a thumb. Sera's fingers were steady and precise; she passed him a jeweler's loupe and a thin, square of gauze.

"Not just staged," she said, voice low in the hum of refrigeration units. "Ceremony. The way this is handled—no frantic fingerprints, no roughness—Someone took their time after death. Look here." She pointed to a microscopic crescent of residue lodged in the pendant's seam. "This is not just sweat. It's surgical antiseptic. I can test it, but it's the smell—chlorhexidine, iodine derivatives, the kind used in minor operating rooms or emergency kits. Whoever did the final dressing had access to supplies and knew how to use them."

Damian turned the pendant again, the spiral catching the fluorescent light differently each time. "Medical training," he said. "Or someone who mimics it well."

Sera shrugged, half-smile brittle. "Mimicry leaves a different signature. This is practiced. Whoever touches these bodies after death treats them like living tissue."

From the lab he went to the first victim's building, to the thin hallway where Mrs. Arun—a woman whose kitchen smelled of lemon oil and laundry starch—remembered her son with a tenderness and an economy that made the facts heavier. She showed him the scarf he used to leave on the hall peg, the stack of overdue notices folded into a neat rectangle. She moved her hands exactly as people do when they are mapping grief into work.

"He always said he was looking for something," she told Damian in the cramped light of her kitchen. "Not that 'found the center' phrase you boys said, but—he would doodle circles at the bottom of his notebooks. He loved puzzles. He never liked crossings out." Her voice held at the last syllable, waiting. "Did they at least—did they do it quickly?"

Damian tasted the question in his mouth. The family wanted answers that soothed motion into grief: who, why, how fast. He told her the truth he had—no easy answers, only slow ones. "They made it look tidy," he said. "That was on purpose."

At a bar called the Low Lantern, which smelled of spilled stout and old citrus peels, he talked to the bartender, Tanya, who kept the tab ledger in her head and never trusted a story that presented itself without edges.

"He came in two nights before," Tanya said, wiping a glass with a rag as if she could polish memory into clarity. "Ordered the same thing every time—black coffee, no sugar. Would sit at table three, stare at the window. Once he said to me, louder than necessary, 'I think I'm getting closer.' Some things he said were not jokes." She tapped the tabletop with a nail. "He was reading a book on myths. He left his phone once. I looked at it—texts from a user called 'CenterFind'—just short things. 'Turn toward the heart.' 'Don't be afraid of the loop.'"

"Can you remember any of the messages?" Damian asked.

"Only one. 'The center is not what you fear; it's what you avoid.' He read it like a translation."

Back at the precinct Damian sat with Lian and Miren and the corkboard that had become a map of absence. Pins and red string gathered like constellations. Miren's patience, which had the texture of a tight-held purse, rattled against the mayor's request for a public statement.

"We need to show action," Miren said, tapping the board so the pins clicked. "Curfews, more patrols. People need to feel safe."

"Action is not the same as answers," Damian replied. "Put more officers in the street and the pattern continues. Whoever's doing this wants the plain view. They want the city to call the center by name."

Miren's hands stilled. "So what do you propose, detective? Sit back and let bodies tell the story in their own time?"

He explained the thread he was following—small things, not press-friendly: antiseptic brands traced to certain clinics, overlapping visits to a free community health clinic on the east side, a tutor who taught classical literature on Tuesday nights and whose receipts matched cash withdrawals from two victims. Miren absorbed each detail like a surgeon assessing an organ. Then she leaned back, hand on her chin.

"Then find the proof," she said. "Make it court-ready. I will shield you here. But I need progress. The mayor already has a talking point written."

Progress came as increments. Damian sat in front of a clinic's receptionist who chewed the inside of her mouth and recited names with the mechanical precision of someone who had been asked to remember a parade. The clinic had been set up to serve night-shift workers and students—discounted services, volunteer staff.

Records were paper-heavy and imperfect, which was both a curse and a door. He pulled shifts and sign-in sheets and found a familiar handwriting: short, careful, the same stroke on intake forms signed by several of the victims. The signature matched the name of a volunteer, Jonas Hale, who taught a mythology class on the outskirts of town.

Jonas was forty, with the kind of tidy hair that had learned to resist wind. He lived above a small shop that sold used books and prints of constellations. Damian went late, under the excuse of asking about class times; Jonas opened the door in a cardigan that still smelled faintly of pipe tobacco.

"I run a small group," Jonas said without invitation. "We talk about myth as metaphor. We talk about journeys. It's not a club. People come, they speak, and they leave better or worse." He smiled a smile that did not reach his eyes. "You are not the first inspector to come knocking."

"Did you speak with any of the victims about 'finding center'?" Damian asked. He watched Jonas's hands—long, careful, capable.

"Words like that are easy to borrow," Jonas said. "I said 'center' once in a class. It's a poetic word. I push people. Sometimes they take the push the wrong way. That is their choice, and it is not mine."

Damian pressed. "You volunteer at the clinic."

"Occasionally. I help with intake, yes. There's a lot of loneliness in Shie. People want a map." His voice had the soft precision of a teacher reciting a lesson.

At night, the spirals visited Damian in sleep again. This time they unrolled in a room that smelled of antiseptic and lemon oil, and at the heart of the spiral sat a small, impossible light. He woke with the taste of metal and the quiet knowledge that someone was trying to make him follow it.

Two nights later, he found a small folded envelope tucked under his door. The brass of the lock left a crescent shadow when he picked it up. Inside was a single necklace, exactly like the others, its chain coiled on a square of tissue paper, and beneath it a strip of paper with inked handwriting: Follow the line.

He did not show it to anyone at first. He carried it instead like a hot coal, weighing whether he should drop it into evidence or read it like a plea. Reed saw the shade behind his eyes and sat across from him at the small kitchen table Miren had insisted he use in the precinct annex.

"You took it?" Reed asked quietly. He did not reach for the pendant; he knew Damian would not hand it over. "Why take a bait like that?"

"Because it's part of the language," Damian said. "Either it's a threat or an invitation. Either way it speaks."

"Then don't answer it from your chest." Reed leaned forward. "Answer it from your head. Turn it into data. Whoever left that wants a conversation. They also want you to feel like you're being led."

Damian uncoiled the chain with slow, deliberate fingers and laid the pendant on the table. It gleamed under the strip of fluorescent light like a tiny moon. He turned it so that the grooves lined up with the grain of the wood and thought of all the tiny decisions that form a line—one witness who remembers a phrase, a clerk who misfiled a note, a volunteer who wears neat cardigans and teaches about journeys.

Outside, the city continued to look like a place that refused to unravel in public: bakers setting croissants in neat rows, a child carrying a plastic sword, commuters folding umbrellas into polite packages. Inside the precinct a map of absences waited for him. He traced a pin with his thumb and felt, for the first time in weeks, that he was not merely following a line but beginning to make one. The spiral, he realized, did not always point inward to a single darkness; sometimes it pointed outward, toward everyone who had ever suggested to a vulnerable man that not finding the center was a failure.

He slept less. He listened more. He began to haunt the edges of Jonah's classes, the clinic's waiting room, the Low Lantern after midnight. He read forum posts as if they were Scripture, following the usernames like the footsteps of faint, private processions. Each new detail stuck to the fabric of the case like rain to thread, small and persistent and not yet decisive.

Somewhere in the city, someone had placed a symbol on a throat and expected an audience to understand. Damian had promised himself he would not give them that comfort. He would not hand them a photograph and a verdict that smoothed things into neatness. He had begun to learn patience the way a man learns to breathe through cold: slowly, with the awareness that every inhale was part of keeping the world intact.

When he finally turned the pendant over to Sera for a deeper chemical read, he did so in the light of a man who had decided to follow the line not because he wanted to be right, but because he owed the dead something more than tidy closure. The spiral hummed in his pocket like a small, insistent answer. He clung to it as if it were a compass—knowing, foolishly perhaps, that compasses show direction not destiny.

Sera's call came at an hour that should have belonged to sleep. The lab's voice on the other end was a practiced thing—practical, careful—but when she said, "You'll want to see this," there was a tilt that made Damian sit up straight in the dark.

The lab smelled of cold metal and coffee. Sera met him at the bench, hair pinned back, gloves still on, and pushed over a tray holding the pendant in a small dish and a second dish with a smear of material magnified into a map.

"It's not just antiseptic," she said, tapping the slide so the light snagged on a tiny pattern. "There are traces of a lanolin-based softener and an organic compound they use in handmade soaps and therapeutic balms. It's the kind of thing you wouldn't expect in a hospital scrub room. It suggests someone who handles both medical supplies and—hobbies. Or crafts."

She handed him a printout with microscopic photos and a note he didn't need read: a brand name she'd seen before in a receipt she couldn't account for. "Also," she added, softer, "there's a partial fingerprint on the inside curve of the pendant. Too smudged for direct ID, but it's there. And someone took extraordinary care not to leave anything else."

Damian stared at the photos until the edges softened. A lanolin signature—softener used in ointments, soap bars—paired with antiseptic suggested a person who moved between two worlds: clinical competence and intimate craft. It fit the quiet profile he'd sketched of Jonas Hale: volunteer at a clinic, seller of small curios in a bookshop, a man who patched people and read them myths at the same time.

"Run the brand against local suppliers," Damian said, already thinking of routes, receipts, what could be matched. "And check the clinic's volunteers for purchases."

Sera nodded. "I'll run chromatography tomorrow. You should eat something." Her voice was a gentle, professional reprimand. He left with the pendant in an evidence envelope, feeling as if he'd carried a small moon in his palm.

For the next week Damian became a fixture at the edges of Jonas's life. He watched the Tuesday class through the shop window one rainy evening—Jonas standing in a half-circle of folding chairs with a whiteboard behind him, the room lit like a stage. The people who came were ordinary: a nurse with tired hands, a student with a satchel, a factory line-worker who kept checking the time. They spoke in small, careful phrases about myth and meaning; Jonas folded their words into lectures like a seamstress folding a hem.

After class, people trailed toward the counter where Jonas sold battered copies of primary texts and wrapped bars of soap in plain brown paper. He handled each purchase like a benediction, tying string around the paper with long, precise fingers.

Damian entered once under the pretense of buying a book. The bell above the door had a low, melancholy note that made the shop feel older than it was. Books leaned in small, intimate towers; the air smelled faintly of pipe tobacco, beeswax, and citrus—the same lanolin-sweet warmth Sera had mentioned.

Jonas looked up and smiled in the way a man who has taught people to find comfort in language smiles: slow, practiced, disarming. "You like older runs," he said, glancing at the book in

Damian's hand. "Good choice. Labyrinths are a classroom, in their own way."

"I wanted to ask about your class," Damian said. "You encourage metaphor. How far do you push people?"

Jonas's fingers paused on the corner of a book as if feeling its grain. "Not far. People push themselves. I simply offer a shape. Some of my students take what I say and warm it up in their lives. Others set it down." He folded his hands on the counter and watched Damian. "What is the line between help and harm when you teach someone to look inward? It's a question I'm fond of asking."

Damian let the question hang. Jonas's face gave away nothing—only the slow brightness of someone used to inhabiting rhetorical space. "Do you visit the clinic often?" he asked, easing the conversation where he needed it.

"Sometimes," Jonas said. "Mostly for intake days. It's a place for people who fall through the gaps. I do what I can." He wrapped a bar of soap and tied it with string, then added a small slip of paper with neat handwriting: a quote from a poem about journeys. "For comfort," he said. "Not instruction."

Damian left unsettled and more convinced. Language was Jonas's instrument. So was ritual—the careful wrapping, the string, the scent. It made the line between comfort and command thin.

Reed helped him stitch surveillance together. They used unmarked cars and quiet shifts, trading the brunt of public expectation for long waits in rain and the unsettling intimacy of watching a man from the shadow of a lamppost. Reed smoked cigarettes with one hand and held the thermos with the other, a small domestic ritual that kept his patience steady.

"You can't arrest a metaphor," Reed said one night as they watched Jonas lock the shop and speak with a young man in a coat who had lingered to ask a question about a book. The man looked nervous; his fingers fumbled at the coin in his pocket. Jonas's voice lowered, his posture changed to the ease of someone who meets confessions daily.

"Watch," Reed said. "See the little slackening. He takes people who have tautness and gives them a place to loosen."

Damian watched Jonas draw the young man in the shop's doorway like a tide. He saw the exchange of a small object—Jonas pressing what looked like a folded paper into the boy's hands. The boy's shoulders dropped as if a weight had been taken away. They left together toward the clinic's direction.

Damian wanted to follow. He also wanted—not for the first time—to be sure he wasn't converting curiosity into accusation. He followed them at a distance, keeping to the pools of streetlight, watching as Jonas slipped into the clinic's back entrance while the boy waited at the curb. Jonas moved with the furtive ease of someone used to keeping certain acts private.

They trailed Jonas to a rear room in the clinic, a cramped intake area with a poster about wound care on the wall. From the alley Damian could see through a smeared window: Jonas kneeling in front of the boy, removing his coat, speaking in low, measured phrases. The boy's face was a map of confusion and relief; he let Jonas examine his sleeve, his throat. Jonas took a small bottle from his cardigan and dabbed something near the boy's collarbone—nothing violent, nothing overtly sinister—but the motion was intimate, practiced, the kind of touch that might be comfort or might be compulsion.

Damian stepped back and felt the old moral muscles tightening: when to act; when to observe. If Jonas was a predator, an intervention might save one life and ruin a dozen evidentiary threads. If Jonas was a healer, watching and doing nothing would be a coward's sin.

He called Miren from the alley. Her voice over the phone was a thin knife between public pressure and private procedure. "If you intervene, you make it an arrestable incident," she said. "If you wait, you risk another death. What's your read?"

Damian listened to the boy's laugh drifting through the window, Jonass's low voice folding around him. "Not an attack," he said finally. "Not tonight."

Reed's cigarette burned down in his fingers. "Then we gather," he said. "We watch who sees what, who buys what. If this is a man who knows how to make ritual into compulsion, he leaves traces. We don't pounce—yet."

They did not pounce. They gathered: a ledger from the clinic, receipts for soap and lanolin from a small cooperative that sold to craftspeople, a bus pass stub, a late-night purchase at a pharmacy. Each small piece was slow work but it began to look like a line rather than an accident. Each detail was a little stitch.

Back at the precinct, Damian sat under a lamp with the notebook his father had once used. He wrote names and times and the consistencies that now mapped themselves into a faint, slow outline: Jonas's classes, the clinic visits, the soap. He thought of the boy's face in the window and the private ritual they'd witnessed. Was the soap a comfort or a token? Was the antiseptic a medical habit or a practiced deception?

When the mayor lectured again about speed and visible action, Damian read the press releases with a polite, worn patience. He had learned that the city needed comfort. He had also learned that comfort could be manufactured and sold as truth.

The next morning the ledger they'd obtained from the clinic had an entry that matched a recent cash withdrawal and the handwriting of a volunteer who had signed in under a thin, careful scrawl. Sera's chromatography had come back: the lanolin signature matched soap sold at a cooperative that listed a small wholesale buyer—Jonas Hale.

It was not a smoking gun. It was the next step.

Damian folded the paper and slid it into his notebook, like an arrow placed into a quiver. Outside, rain began again, thin and steady, pulling the city into the same soft washing that had become the backdrop for so much of his work. He thought of spirals—how a line can lead inward or outward—and of the small ethical pressures that shaped each move the way water shapes stone.

He stood, put on his coat, and went to find Jonas. Not to accuse, not yet. To see a man up close, to hear the shape of his language in full. To decide, with sticky, patient hands, whether Jonas was a guide offering maps or a cartographer drawing traps. The line had a center; he did not yet know what waited there. But he would follow it. Slowly, piece by piece, he would unroll the spiral until it named itself.

Damian found Jonas at the back of the shop, bent over a tray of soaps as if he were arranging minnows. The bell chimed when Damian entered; Jonas looked up with that same practiced calm, then blinked as the detective crossed the floor and set his coat on a chair.

"You returned," Jonas said without surprise. He dried his hands on a cloth that smelled faintly of citrus and cedar. "I hope the book was satisfactory."

"It was," Damian said, and did not sit. He watched the way Jonas moved around the counter—the small, precise choreography of a man who has turned care into habit. The shop was quieter in daylight: fewer customers, the rain seeping clothily against the window. Sunlight made the soap bars look like warm stones.

"I need to ask you more about the clinic," Damian said. "About what you do there."

Jonas folded his hands, a teacher at the front of class. "I help with intake. I patch bruises, literally and figuratively. People come in with holes and leaves and I help them sew it up. Or I show them a way to sew it themselves."

"Do you ever give them a course of treatment?" Damian asked. "Anything you would describe as a ritual? An at-home practice?"

Jonas's smile thinned. "I sometimes suggest small practices—breaths, tactile reminders. A sensory anchor can be helpful for someone with panic or despair." He picked up a bar of soap and turned it in his palms. "We all use objects to remind ourselves we can hold on."

"Have you ever instructed someone to take a step that could harm them? Told them the center requires suffering?"

"Never." Jonas's voice had the brittle firmness of someone defending a principle. "People take what I say and make what they will of it. I teach metaphor. I do not prescribe fate."

Damian let the words sit. He had watched the clinic window from the alley; he'd seen the boy loosen his shoulders when Jonas dabbed something near his collarbone. He had the chromatography results; the lanolin compound traced to Jonas's cooperative. He had the ledger entry. None of those were a verdict—but they were the shape of one.

"Would you let me look around?" Damian asked. "For inventory records. For receipts. For—" He gestured to the piles of wrapped soap. "—anything that might connect the things Sera found to what you sell."

Jonas hesitated for only a breath. "You can look," he said. "You may take what you will." He stepped aside with the faint courtesy of someone offering the threshold to his privacy.

Damian walked the shop like a careful thief, not touching what he did not need to. He opened a drawer behind the counter and found bundles of receipts tied with twine, small notebooks with lists in Jonas's careful hand, and a battered wooden box with small vials of oils. One notebook fell open to a page with dates and initials—enough to make a pattern if someone threaded time through it. Beside the cash ledger was a folded piece of paper that made his breath slow: a list of names, neatly written, with dates and a single word after each—"intake," "soap," "follow-up." The handwriting matched the scrawl on the clinic forms.

Damian straightened the paper and asked, "What is this?"

Jonas's hands folded on the counter. "Notes," he said. "A teacher keeps notes. I track people who want follow-ups, who need soap for skin irritations, who ask for additional reading. Because resources are thin, I prioritize."

"How do you decide who to prioritize?"

Jonas's eyes flicked up and held Damian's. "Who asks. Who answers. Who returns."

There was a small pause, full of the quiet things that are not confessions and not denials. Damian wanted a crack—something that would let the truth in like light—but Jonas offered only the slow, patient dignity of a man who knows how to wait.

Two hours later, outside in the rain, Damian called Reed. The ledger, the soap, the vials—the accumulation felt like a slow tightening rather than a slam; it was the kind of evidence prosecutors would chew on until it yielded a core or until the case dissolved into questions of intent.

"We have a map," Damian said. "Not a gun. A map."

Reed took a drag of his cigarette and let the smoke stain the rain. "Maps can be deadly," he said. "But maps can also be maps. We need someone who can tell the difference."

They did not have to wait long for a new voice to provide direction. Late that evening a woman came to the precinct clutching a grocery bag as if it held a prayer. She introduced herself as Mara—twenty-one, student, a face with small, stubborn bruises from sleeplessness.

"I went to Jonas's class for three weeks," she said once she'd been taken to an interview room. "I thought it would help me get through the job. My shift at the bakery was killing me. He gave everyone these things—soap, a little balm. He told us to rub it when the spiral rose. He told us the spiral is a way to find the center. He said, 'You must make room for the spiral.'"

"Did anyone tell you to harm yourself?" Damian asked. He kept his voice low, as if speaking softly could coax memory rather than force it.

Mara's fingers twisted the plastic handle of the bag. "Not straight out. But he said the center is a cost. He told us you can't find the center if you don't let go of something. He said, 'Letting go is the way the center finds you.'" Her eyes were carefully open, measuring the room with the vigilance of someone who had learned to see threats in small gestures. "One night he told a boy to 'finish' what he started to find the center. He said it like it was an exercise."

Damian felt the floor shift. Mara's testimony was not a smoking gun either—language is slippery, and intent can hide behind metaphor. But the way she framed Jonas's words—less lecture than instruction—pulled at a seam.

"Did you ever feel pressured to hurt yourself?" he asked.

She shook her head. "No. But I saw it once. There was a kid—Micah. He came to class thin and quiet. Jonas gave him a bar of soap and told him to rub until he felt the spiral. Micah smiled like it was a joke. The next week I saw him with a new pendant around his neck. He looked...different. He wouldn't talk about it. Two weeks later the papers said suicide."

Damian sat very still. The name lit a pale match—Micah had been one of the victims. Mara's story connected two otherwise disparate marks. It gave a motion to the ledger and a voice to the soap.

He asked more questions. Mara described the small performances Jonas used: a low voice, a ritual of wrapping the soap in brown paper, a slip of paper with a line of verse tucked inside. "He told people to keep the paper close to their skin," she said. "He said it warmed intention."

Mara's testimony fit with the physical traces Sera had found; it also introduced a new dimension—language made into instruction, objects given ritual weight. Damian felt the case pivot. He had a line that might be followed through words as well as through receipts.

He took Mara's statement and added it to the ledger stack in his notebook. He phoned Miren, who came down to the precinct and read Mara's words with an expression that folded into something harder.

"Enough to warrant an interview," Miren said. "We bring him in on the soap, on the ledger, and we read him his rights. We see how he answers to that."

Damian hesitated. He had wanted more than interviews; he wanted the kind of evidence that would stand up to a defense of metaphor. But prosecution sometimes begins at interrogation. "If we arrest him now, we might make enemies of people who describe him as a comfort. We'll tip the whole town into a massacre of reputations if we're wrong."

Miren's face was a geometry of lines. "We weigh the risk of being wrong against the risk of being too slow. Which would you rather be?"

He knew which answer Miren expected. He also knew how the city would react to a rushed arrest: triumph for the mayor, a dangerous neatness that left open the possibility of another body. He breathed and let the slow work guide him.

"We interview," he said. "We bring him in and we watch him answer. We look for inconsistency. We put a senior officer in on the questions. We don't shout guilt in public."

They prepared an interview room like a stage set: neutral chairs, a recording device, Miren present, Reed observing from the glass. They asked Sera to re-verify the lab results. She came into the room in the afternoon, white coat in hand, and described the compounds in plain language that left no room for metaphor.

Jonas walked into the room with his cardigan buttoned and his hands folded like a man who expected to be heard. He listened as Damian read out the ledger entries, the cooperative receipts, Mara's statement.

"You understand how this must look," Damian said. "Soap, antiseptic, an instruction to use a ritual—people have died who had your objects on them after death."

Jonas's face did not collapse. He tilted his head the way a teacher asks a student to rethink a problem. "I am sorry for the families," he said. "But I have never told anyone to die. I suggest practices to help anchor people. I teach metaphor. If my language is misread, I am responsible to explain it better. Not to be blamed for the misreading."

"Do you ever tell people they must let go of something to find the center?" Miren asked. "Do you ever say 'finish' something to complete the spiral?"

"They asked me to push them," Jonas said. "Young people want permission to be tougher, to feel they have done something heroic. I give them challenges—reading assignments, journaling. Never self-harm. I would never—" He stopped, and for a fraction of a breath something unsteady creaked in him. "I would never ask anyone to die."

Damian watched the small motions—the throat working, the fingers flexing—searching a face for the absence of lies. Jonas's words were careful; his composure was the product of practice. He had a plausible defense rooted in the slipperiness of metaphor. Protestations alone would not be enough.

After Jonas left the room, Miren turned to Damian. "We have a case to build," she said. "Not just about soaps and lectures—but about causation. If people hear 'finish' and then kill themselves, and that pattern matches your objects and your presence—that's our lever. We will need corroboration. More witnesses like Mara. Medical notes linking the balms to direct contact. Something that connects sermon to act."

Damian thought of Micah and the boy in the clinic doorway and the pendant in his palm. The spiral was folding in and laying its path across lives. He felt both nearer and more distant from its center—their evidence a lattice, not a blade.

He left the precinct that night into rain that had a clean, new smell, as if the city itself were trying to wash away its complicity. He had a direction now: gather more voices, find more receipts, and watch Jonas until the pattern either resolved into culpability or unraveled into metaphor. He had to be careful; he had to be exact. The city wanted a villain. He wanted truth.

As he walked, he imagined the spiral again, not as a trap or a target but as a way of motion—people circling some interior grief and sometimes finding the rim too thin. His work, he understood, would be to follow that motion without mistaking the map for the heart. He would follow, slowly, and listen for the moment where words were not words anymore but commands that guided a hand to an unfathomable center.

Damian kept the spiral in his pocket the way some people keep a talisman: heavy with questions. After Mara's statement, after Jonas's ledger and Sera's chromatography, the case felt like a wound that could either scar slowly or fester forever. He slept in the precinct some nights, let the lamp in the interview room be his moon, and read the names he'd written until their meaning rearranged.

One night, flipping through an old microfiche file in the municipal records room—a habit from an earlier life when he chased political corruption more than ritual—he found a margin note that slapped the edge of his patience awake. It was a small, yellowed article from twenty-three years prior: a city council hearing about a youth movement called the Awakened Youth. The piece was a perfunctory thing—flinty, a record of panic more than of fact. The council had banned the group after accusations of intimidation and strange rites; a handful of their leaders had been fined and ostracized. The explicit charge had been vague: "purity demonstrations." The symbol in the margin—an etched spiral—was the same as the pendant.

He carried the microfiche home like contraband. The article was thin on details, but the name stuck: Awakened Youth. He ran the term through old forum posts he'd salvaged from the victims' phones and found usernames that used variants—AwakeAgain, CenterFound, YouthAwake. The forums had gone quiet after one particular thread: a string of messages in which users joked about "purifications" and then the thread had been deleted in a flood of new accounts. Someone on those posts had once linked to an old manifesto—an angular PDF that spoke of "removing rot to restore a sinless society" and used the labyrinth as a symbol of both testing and purification.

The more Damian pulled at threads, the more connections warmed into outline. The cooperative that sold lanolin to artisans had invoices shipped to a postbox rented under a different name, one that traced back to an address in an old textile mill on the river's north bend—an abandoned place with broken windows and a smell of long-dried oil. The mill's ledger, when they got it with a subpoena, showed small purchases of antiseptic, cloth, and soap ingredients—orders placed in the middle of the night. The handwriting on the ledger matched Jonas's careful scrawl.

"It's like somebody opened a book of the city and wrote themselves into the margins," Damian said to Reed in the car as rain scored the windshield. "Only these marginalia keep bleeding."

Reed's jaw worked. "So the old Awakened Youth got back together, though in smaller, meaner clothes."

"Or someone used the myth of them," Damian said. "Either way, that spiral means something—an initiation, or a brand."

They began to watch the mill. They posted a camera in the alley across from a boarded doorway and sat in a van under the cold light of a dome lamp, trading cigarettes and notes. For three nights, nothing but wind and rats moved in and out of the mill. On the fourth night, figures came: small at first, a single bike light bobbing, then more; they walked with the studied hush of people who had rehearsed secrecy. Someone hung a lantern, and a pale light pooled in a back room. A figure moved in the doorway who carried a presence like a held breath—smooth, sure. The watchers in the van watched the shapes rearrange into a cluster the way constellations yield patterns only when you know where to look.

"I think that's him," Reed whispered. "The speaker."

They took his picture. They recorded voices with a parabolic mic. The audio came back hours later—distant, with the rattle of rain caught in the microphone, but the words were clear enough in the room's center: "...we do what is necessary so the city may be made sinless again. The center demands a cost. We remove the rot... so the rest can breathe." The speaker's voice was neither young nor old; it had been trained.

They had, in the hour after they played the recording back, a tighter map. The mill meetings had structure: lessons, readings, a small ritual in which a bar of soap was wrapped in brown paper and tied with string, a slip of verse inserted, a short phrase intoned—"find the center"—and, in the dark, a selection process. Names were called. A few left in tears; some left resolved. The circles were designed to affirm and then to bind.

Damian called Miren. "We have a meeting place and a voice. We have ritual and recruits. We have the spiral's choreography. We need to move."

Miren's voice was economy. "We need evidence, not theater. We need to know who commits the killings, and how the society's structure works. If the Awakened Youth are behind this, they're not just a singular killer—they're a machine."

The machine had a motor. They found it in pieces and in whispers. A member arrested for petty theft in the old neighborhood volunteered details in exchange for leniency: the group had a hierarchy of elders and speakers, they curated a "purity list," and they believed that some youths—those who committed "sins" against the idea of a perfect city—had to be asked to leave the world. The ritual was more than ideology; it was instruction in method. The antiseptic and lanolin were practical—used, they said, to make the death look clinical and to remove evidence of panic. The pendent, the spiral, was a finishing touch: the "seal."

Jonas's name recurred in the machine's upholstery. He had not been the executing hand, the petty thief said, but he was a "binder"—someone who supplied the materials and the language. He taught the mythic frames that made killing feel like obedience. He wrapped soaps and tied strings and taught the line between metaphor and directive until it blurred for some. The binder, the machine said, made the ritual plausible.

Damian sat in on an interview with the petty thief, a kid with a jaw like a hinge who spoke rapidly as if to outrun a memory. "We thought we were saving them," he said. "You don't get into a group like that if you haven't been told the city's broken. They told us about contagion—the rot of small sins that metastasized. They showed us a list of people—those who 'didn't fit'—and told us to ask them to step into the center. If they refused, we'd help them find peace. I didn't do the helping. I just watched."

"Who helps?" Damian asked.

"The elders," the kid said. "They decide." He rubbed his hands. "Cassian Voss—he's the one everyone listens to now. He was in the old movement. He came back and said we'd been right all along—about the rot, about sacrifice."

Cassian Voss. The name felt like a bell. Damian pulled older files, found an old photograph of a young Cassian with a shaved head and an arm raised at a rally, his face full of furnace-intent. He had been indicted once, then quietly rebuffed by an injunction and had faded into the city's underbelly—until now, when he had re-stitched himself into a new pattern and people had followed.

The investigators moved with the slow precision of people folding together threads. Undercover operatives, careful subpoenas, a list of names that had grown in the margins of the ledger. The more Damian pried, the more uncomfortable names surfaced: a minor council aide, an owner of a small security firm, a volunteer nurse who'd been seen at two of the victims' last check-ins. These were not caricatures of evil—many were people who had tasted some kind of moral certainty and had let it harden.

Damian watched one evening as Sera interviewed a clinic volunteer who admitted she had been asked by "friends from the Awakened Youth" to hand out bars of soap and to use certain phrases in intake. "It sounded harmless," she said, and then: "They called it a cleansing." Her voice broke less for the danger to herself than for what it meant to have helped unwittingly.

The night they finally moved—Miren orchestrating a quiet, all-night sweep—Damian felt the old familiar spike of adrenaline, but it was tethered now to something more complicated: pity, anger, and an ache for what had been allowed to grow. They breached the textile mill at dawn. The light came in long and certain; the men and women inside were not monsters in the theatrical sense but people who had constructed a theology out of grievance. Cassian stood at the center of the largest room like a man who had arranged his life as a pulpit. He did not run. He watched the officers with an expression that could have been exhaustion or contempt.

"You will not stop us," he said when Miren read the warrants. His voice had a preacher's cadence. "You will not halt the necessity of our work."

"We're stopping the murders," Miren said. "You're under arrest for conspiracy, for aiding and abetting, for the murders themselves."

Her badge shone in the sallow light.

Cassian laughed once, a sound like spare metal. "You call them murders. I call them purifications." He paused, and his face smoothed into something resembling sorrow. "You will not quiet the rot. That is on you—on your laws."

They found, in the milling room's back shelves, rows of wrapped soaps, tagged slips of verse, scrapbooks where new recruits' notes were kept, and a ledger of "targets"—lists scrawled with names, observations, and a chilling notation on the date column that matched the times of several deaths. They found the antiseptics and vials, the postbox registrations, and a ledger connecting purchases to names that corresponded to known volunteers. A dozen people were taken into custody that day, from low-level binders who assembled kits to elders who had given "advice" about methods. Jonas was not in the mill; he had apparently fled.

They traced Jonas through the bus stubs in his notebooks and found him at a small waystation on the city's edge, hiding in the dim of a coffeehouse. When Damian found him, Jonas's face had the look of a man who had forgotten how to be surprised by consequence.

"You ran," Damian said without preamble, the tiredness in his voice not a question.

Jonas folded his hands on the table and looked at Damian with something like repentance. "I didn't run because I wanted to," he said. "I left because I woke at night and couldn't breathe. I thought if I removed myself, maybe no one I cared about would follow me. I thought that would be enough."

"You handed people the ropes," Damian said. "You taught them a grammar that could be read as instruction. You wrapped the soap and tied the paper. You wrote names in a ledger."

Jonas's fingers trembled. "I gave them tools to soothe. I did not realize that the metaphor would be used as a weapon. I see now that words can be sharp enough to bleed."

"Did you know about the 'purifications'?" Damian asked, pressing for the line between ignorance and complicity.

Jonas's voice was small. "I knew of a doctrine, abstract. I believed in the possibility of change—of people who wanted to be better. Cassian—he convinced us it was about the city's health. He told us the center required refusal of the unclean. He said we were guardians. I thought we were giving people a chance to choose. I did not know they would turn that choice into coercion."

Jonas cried then, quietly, like a man who had finally been allowed to reach a grief he had denied seeing. "If I could pull back every bar, every word, I would. I thought I was teaching people to find solace, not to die for it."

Damian's mouth was dry. Stories like these bent the world into questions that had no easy margins. He thought of Micah, whose smile had been a pale thing in Mara's memory. He thought of the carefulness in Sera's lab, of the antiseptic smell in the evidence bag, of the pendant's spiral catching light in his palm. He felt the justice of the law's weight and the strange human failure behind these actions.

The arrests were public and messy. Cassian and half a dozen elders were charged with conspiracy to commit murder and multiple counts of manslaughter; several ranks of the society were arraigned for aiding and abetting. The press called it a cult resurgence; politicians leaned into the narrative of moral panic and pledged further funding for youth services. Some members of the community called for harsh sentences. Others, oddly, offered defenses in hushed church basements: "They believed they were saving us." The city that wanted tidy endings got none that felt clean.

At the trials that followed, the prosecution wove the ledger, the receipts, the audio recordings from the mill, and the forensic matches into a case that painted the Awakened Youth not as an abstraction but as a deliberate apparatus. The defense argued about metaphor and intention. Cassidy — a witness who had moved from being a binder to a cooperator—testified, voice shaking, about the exact moment language hardened into command. "We began with poetry," she said. "We ended with instruction. We told people to let go, and then we—" She broke down, unable to finish the sentence. The jury saw more than words; they saw patterns.

Jonas pleaded guilty to providing materials and for reckless endangerment; he received a sentence that balanced punishment and recognition of his partial culpability—community service, mandatory counseling, and a term of supervised probation that would keep him in the city's vigilance. Cassian and several elders received longer sentences. Some members cooperated and had reduced sentences; others fled and were arrested on warrants later.

After the convictions, Damian sat at the river, the city's banners flapping like a memory. People resumed markets and Sunday walks. The mayor gave a speech about safety. But when the cameras left, the gutters still had that latent shine that comes after a rain—clean but not cured.

Mira Kosta came to him once, after the court had adjourned and the press had thinned. They leaned against the precinct's back wall, the same wall he'd leaned against in the early days. "You did the slow work," she said. "You didn't give them what they wanted."

He looked at her. "We caught a machine that turned grief into doctrine," he said. "But the machine used tools most people use—language, care, community. The danger is not always obvious."

They talked then about the victims—about Micah, about the others who had been named in the ledger—and about what the city would need if it wanted to heal. The list was long: more outreach, tighter oversight of volunteer groups, public education about coercive language, resources for youth who drift toward belief systems promising clean answers.

Damian found Mara again, months later, in a small bakery where she'd started a morning shift. She had gone back to study, cautiously, like someone who had dipped a toe in open water and was testing the current. She passed him a paper bag with a plain bun and said, "We keep threads from being pulled, sometimes—one small thing at a time."

He held the bun and felt the small, domestic weight of it. "You did good," he said.

"So did you," she answered. "You let us tell it. You didn't make us silent."

On his last night in Shie—because a quiet other city was waiting for him elsewhere—Damian sat at the river and pulled the spiral pendant from his pocket. It had been sent to evidence, then returned to him for safekeeping with a small, official note. He turned it between his fingers. It was only a small disc of metal, scratched and burnished by many hands. It whispered nothing.

He thought of the Awakened Youth and of Cassian's sermonizing voice, of Jonas's tears and Mara's small courage. He thought of the blade-edge where metaphor becomes order and of how easily meaning can be used to make people act. He thought, not for the first time, of the moral praxes of policing: to be exact, to be merciful, to be relentless when the cost was human life.

The city slept in a way that made no promises. Damian placed the pendant on the lip of the river and watched the current take it, just a little, spinning slowly like a boat losing its mooring. It floated a while, the spiral catching light, then turned and drifted away into the river's long sentence.

He did not feel triumphant. He felt, as he had felt from the first night he opened Jonas's ledger, the steady weight of the work: to follow the line, to name the center without pretending the world could be made sinless, and to keep walking when the spiral did not promise an end but rather demanded attention.

Later something strange happened .There was a head who made this Awakened Youth Society again alive.They finally had him in motion because the case had taught them where the machine liked to move—along old rails, in the spaces city planners forgot. A tip from an informant had named a safe house in a narrow row of warehouses near the old ferry slips. Damian drove the van into the fog before dawn, the city reduced to muffled shapes and the dull orange of streetlamps. Miren, Reed, two uniformed officers and a pair of plainclothes moved with the practiced silence of people who have rehearsed entry until it became a ritual.

There were voices—low, tidy—behind a corrugated door. The team stacked, Miren whispered coordinates, and then the door was down and light spilled into the room like a question. Men and women froze among their scrapbooks and boxes of wrapped soap; the elders' faces were set into the old certainty that had built their theology. They yelled commands and read rights. People were cuffed. Cassian Voss sat very still on a crate as officers photographed the ledger and bundles of ritual paraphernalia.

One figure broke toward a fire exit while the rest were taking stock—slipped past a line, a human shadow folding into the alley. Damian saw the movement and went after him without waiting for the official order; his feet found rhythm the way they had at other chases. The back alleys of Shie are a patchwork of refuse and memory—old millstones, slick stairwells, a metal gangway that led toward the river's shoulder. The man ran lean and fast, a silhouette with practiced escape.

Damian kept him in sight until the alley tightened and the fugitive moved to the gangway that cut between the mill's dark flank and a stack of disused pallets. The man didn't turn. He moved like someone certain of his path. Damian called his name—once, twice. The man did not look back. In the hush of anticipation Damian fired a single round; it hit the man in the back. He pitched forward and hit the metal with a soft, awful sound.

There is a moment immediately after violence—less a sound than the sudden rearrangement of the world's furniture. Time thinned. Men in uniforms became actors in slow motion: hands came for medical kits, someone shouted for an ambulance, an officer slammed a fist to find a pulse. Damian found himself kneeling, heart an instrument of someone else's unspooling.

The man moaned and then was still. In the minutes before the ambulance, in the shallow theater of hot breath and rain, Damian's fingers slipped into the jacket pocket of the fallen figure because the instinct to see who a person is can be a way to make the act mean something. He found a wallet and, without thinking, opened it.

There was no photograph. No little boy with a crooked smile. There was, instead, a name—unfamiliar—and a clumsy card for a community center, a folded piece of paper with an address. The man had no ID that shouted the kind of truth that unstitched the night's tension. A badge finally confirmed what the scene had not—an officer called out the name they'd received from a witness: a local organizer they'd wanted to question, a name that did not match anything Damian had kept in his memory.

They moved the body. They booked it. They processed the scene with the cold, efficient routine of people who use gloves the way priests use ritual. Damian felt the world go hard at the edges; his hands trembled with adrenaline that stayed even as the officers moved on to check boxes and tally events. He did not sleep for the next stretch; he watched the hospital staff, he sat through the preliminary autopsy report delivered in clipped sentences by a coroner on call. For all the efficiency, there was nothing in those reports that named him—only a trajectory of death.

It was not until Sera called him in the gray hour of the second morning that the world folded in on itself. She was quiet on the phone in a way that made him listen for more than words. "We have a positive identification," she said. "You should come to the lab."

He drove there as if moving through someone else's weather. The lab smelled like bleach and paper. Sera had the fallen man's printout on the bench and, when she slid it toward him, he tried to read it as if the letters were someone else's script. They were not.

"Match came in through the missing persons database," Sera said. "We cross-checked dental records and a partial DNA from the wound area. It's precise. It's... Damian." Her voice carried like a small bell dropped in a deep room.

He stared until the letters blurred. The name on the printout was his father's.

When the word landed, it did not arrive as an event with a beginning and an end. It uncoiled as a series of old things—one memory folding into another until they became a map: the smell of engine grease and lemon oil in a kitchen where a man hummed and stitched; a small boy climbing into a lap to read a book about sailors; the afternoon his mother had answered the phone with a voice that folded away and then left the house quiet like it had been showered. He had been thirteen the last time he'd seen a full face of his father. Then the house had other rhythms—his mother who stopped humming, a police report that read like a bureaucrat's lullaby. Damian had grown into a man knowing the fact of absence, not the manner of it.

He sat down. Around him, Sera and Miren and Reed moved with corroboration: the dental matches, the partial DNA on file, cross-references with the old missing person's case. They brought him photographs and an old police report, yellow at the edges. The man on the slab in the photo, in the new printout, had his father's jawline, the same way his father's mouth had once turned on a joke.

"How—" Damian's voice broke. "How could he be involved in this?"

"No one knows why people rejoin the wrong parts of themselves," Miren said softly. She looked older in that moment, as if sympathy had been folded into her face. "People change. People come back. Or maybe he never left what he believed."

Sera's hands were steady as she pushed the identification card across the bench. "We can show you the techniques," she said. "The prints, the DNA. It's him."

Damian took the card and looked at the photograph as if the face could refuse the accusation. He remembered a small crescent scar behind his father's ear from a machine at the mill—he remembered pressing his fingertip there once when he was little, feeling the roughness beneath skin. The same thin ridge was visible on the dead man's neck.

He vomited later, alone in the corridor, the sterile smell a betrayal. The lab went on being procedural. But for Damian the machinery of evidence had become a private crucible. He had pulled a trigger and hit a man who, by all forensic accounts, was his father.

The days that followed fractured. The city treated the revelation like a new headline: the detective who shot his own father. Reporters leaned into it with the taste of narrative: tragedy folded into justice. Colleagues who had spoken his name as Damian now had their voices leavened with awkward sympathy. Miren stood by him in public statements—"protocol followed," she said in press rooms—and privately she kept a watch that was less managerial than maternal. Reed smoked more and watched him like a man who waits to see when a friend will stop weathering a storm and start drowning.

Damian could not breathe in the shape of his life. Sleep retreated into a place of hot, looping dreams. He dreamed in spirals—his father at the center of a dark labyrinth, hands measured, smiling the precise smile of a man who had once told stories. He woke from those dreams with fingers curled around the pendant that had been in evidence, the spiral imprinted like a compass needle in his skin. He tried to read the ledger again and the names shifted.

Guilt is a slow animal. It does not announce itself as guilt immediately but settles like an ache in the jaw, the back, a conscience made somatic. Damian's days narrowed to ritual acts that had about them the steadiness of penance. He took to walking the river at night again, but now the motion was not clearing as much as wearing. He pulled the pendant from his pocket and turned it until the grooves were bright. He talked to the pendant once, under his breath, saying his father's name as if naming could locate.

People tried to reach him. Reed brought sandwiches that went untouched. Miren pressed for him to take leave, to enter counseling. "This is more than a badge can hold," she said. "We will support you—get you help." He nodded and then declined. He could hear their good intentions echoing, like furniture moved by polite hands.

He began to do strange things, the kind of small myth-making that transforms grief into a scaffolding. He spent hours at the municipal archives, tracing the Awakened Youth's ban and the names associated with its early days. He mapped out every abandoned building, every underground room where rituals could have been rehearsed. He took the same notebook his father had once used—worn at the corners—and filled it with labyrinths drawn to scale, small concentric circles inked in until they blurred into one another. Each drawing had annotations: dates, names, a notation of how one could move from entrance to center. He lined his apartment walls with maps the way a sailor plots a course by remembered stars.

Friends noticed the change. Mara found him in a bakery one morning and watched as he traced the crumb pattern of a bun with a finger. "You look like someone holding a bruise too close to a lamp," she said, because she had seen men wear pain like clothing and she knew the language of it. He smiled at her like a man only half present. "He's gone," he said to her once—simple, true—and then the sentence bent around itself. "But not gone. He is at the center. He needs me to find him."

FOURTEEN

CONFESSION

Damian kept repeating it, as if saying it enough would make it true. "I understand. I understand," he murmured.

Reed stared at him, tired amusement and accusation in his voice. "You said that six months ago," he snapped. "And yet again—you forget who you are."

"Don't worry, brother," Damian replied, gentle and earnest. "In my story you were Choe, Reed, a police colleague, Belen. You did so much for me."

Reed shook his head. "Not just me," he said. "Ani as well — she was the anesthesia, Miska for you."

Damian's face warmed. "You are real friends," he said.

Kael, who had been watching from the doorway, pushed forward. "What about us, sir? We supported you in your play. We became villains."

Damian laughed softly. "Nice, Kael," he said, and the sound eased the tension for a handful of moments.

Many days later, a different morning arrived.

Damian woke with a single, terrible urgency. He crossed the room and crouched by Reed's side, calling his name. "Did they harm you?" he asked, voice tight. "Ani and I searched for you everywhere. If anything's happened to Kael, I will kill them."

Reed's eyes met him, a haunted, weary light there. "You will not let me live," he whispered.

JONAS REED
LADY MISKA
DR DAMIAN DEY
PROFESSOR KAEL
AWAKENED YOUTH

With lotz of love
-----Mahammed Zahid.